GRAPES
INTO
WINE

GRAPES

A Guide to Winemaking

INTO

in America

WINE

Philip M. Wagner

Alfred A. Knopf · New York · 1976

THIS IS A BORZOI BOOK
PUBLISHED BY ALFRED A. KNOPF, INC.

ACKNOWLEDGMENTS. I thank the Editor of *Scientific American* for permission to use material from an article of mine entitled "Wines, Grape Vines and Climate" that appeared in the June 1974 issue. Illustrations were kindly provided by Prof. Maynard A. Amerine, the Wine Institute, the Comité Interprofessionel du Vin de Champagne, Dr. Willard Robinson and his colleagues of the Geneva, New York, Experiment Station, Mr. Albert Koyama of the Davis, California, Experiment Station, and Mr. Seaton Mendall. Others are credited on pages ix–xii. Most of the photographs taken in and about the premises of Boordy Vineyards are the work of Mr. Steve Kraft, to whom my gratitude for his patience and competence.

P. M. W.

Library of Congress Cataloging in Publication Data

Wagner, Philip Marshall, [Date]
Grapes into wine.

Bibliography: p.
Includes index.
1. Wine and wine making—Amateurs' manuals. I. Title.
TP548.2.W33   1976   633'.22   75–36814
ISBN 0–394–49919–0
ISBN 0–394–73172–7   [Paperback]

Manufactured in the United States of America
First Edition

FOR JOCELYN

Contents

Illustrations

Foreword

TOWARD THE END of that strange episode in our national history called prohibition, I wrote a brief book on winemaking. Something of the sort was badly needed, since in those days much wine was being made on a do-it-yourself basis yet there existed no contemporary work in English treating the subject. The book found a place for itself that it has held up to the present in spite of immense changes that have taken place since.

The most obvious changes have been the rebirth of commercial winegrowing and the acceptance of wine as a normal thing in American life. As well, there have been less obvious but equally important changes, such as the spectacular increase in the knowledge of what wine is and how it comes into being, the revolution in winemaking techniques, the emergence of enology as a profession. As a result, now that wine is so much more freely used, a body of amateurs has emerged who treat winemaking as a serious and absorbing avocation or who wish simply as wine drinkers to know more about the nature of wine and the why of its infinite variations.

All of these factors demanded that numerous revisions

be made in the text of my book over the years; at one point I even changed the title. But by the time the book had reached its fortieth birthday in 1973 (coinciding with the seventh printing of the fifth edition), it became obvious that patchwork revisions would no longer do. Too much had happened. And so, on the invitation of my publisher, I put a clean sheet of paper in my typewriter and began all over again. Only in this way, by writing a new book, could justice be done to the altered scene.

And yet the word "new" requires qualification. The origin and use of wine are lost in prehistory. Our knowledge of wine has grown by accretion. In writing about it, one starts with whatever is already known and on record, including what one has written oneself. Moreover, in a practical but not too technical treatise of this sort, the subject and the purpose dictate the structure. In any book on the art-science of winemaking, whatever the language, much of what is set forth has been written many times before in other ways, and aspects of the subject are bound to follow much the same sequence. Such originality as this book has lies in the treatment rather than the structure: what I have included and what I have left out, how I have explained things, the gleanings of years of personal observation and experience. That is the extent of this book's newness, and to claim more would be presumptuous.

As I think back over the decades of work and pleasure that lie behind this book, I find endless obligations. I find myself thinking of that entire generation of wine people whose careers have paralleled the wine renaissance that began with repeal, and who admitted J. & P. Wagner into their company. They were young at the dawn of it. Retirement and death now begin to reduce their numbers: the men of science, the teachers, the growers and producers, the merchants. What they have had in common, those I have known, has been amateurism: an absorption in what they were doing that goes beyond livelihood. There is something about winegrowing in all its aspects which brings this out. With due thanks to all the others, I will name only a few: Maynard Amerine, the late

Frank Schoonmaker, the late Adhemar de Chaunac, Charles Fournier, Leon Adams, Robert Dunstan.

I also think of those abroad, especially in France, who have welcomed us into their vineyards and *caves* and homes, and taught us so much, and shown by their example that the wine world is one even though the political world is not. I will name only one of them: the late Gérard Marot of Poitiers, who labored so long and valiantly for the future of *les hybrides*, the grapes that are now building a new viticulture in many parts of this country.

I think of Boordy Vineyards as an enterprise now less mortal than we are thanks to the intervention of Arthur S. Wolcott.

I think of the books on our shelves and the names on their spines, ranging as far back as Cato and Columella and as far forward as the day before yesterday: those are building blocks, and a selection of them constitutes my bibliography.

And I think most of all of my wife, Jocelyn, partner in everything we have done with grapes and wine. Perhaps this book will bring other such partnerships into being: the grape and its blood make a good bond.

PHILIP M. WAGNER

Boordy Vineyards
Riderwood, Maryland
January, 1976

Part I

WINES
AND
VINES

CHAPTER 1

What Wine Is, and Isn't

 THERE ARE two ways of approaching a bottle of wine: from the outside in and from the inside out. Each has its advantages.

The first leans heavily on externals, including what we already know about wines: the literature of them, the history, the lore, advertising, the word of friends, which wines have appealed to us and which haven't, the bottle itself and the way it is got up, and so on. All in all, these factors are powerful persuaders.

And then there is what the label actually says. Much of the information is mandatory, and one soon learns to distinguish between such facts and puffery. When the label says *Pommard* or *Napa Valley Zinfandel* and also says *appellation contrôlée* or its equivalent, the wine drinker can make a reasonable assumption that the wine inside the bottle is representative of what the label says. Back labels sometimes help too. And so he learns to find his way around among wines, to discover how different they can be, to distinguish between the fine and the not-so-fine—all without having to know what wine really is.

He does not have to know anything about the biochemistry of fermentation, any more than he needs to know the difference between an ohm and a watt in order to turn on a light.

Going at it the other way, from the inside out, judgment is suspended until the wine is in the glass. This is the way of the everyday user, who takes wine as regularly as any other food. It is also the way of the expert wine man, or woman,* who often prefers to taste a wine before seeing what the label says. He is wary of the power of suggestion. He is interested in substance first, externals second. Using his senses as tools, he examines the intrinsic nature of the stuff in his glass. Knowing what wine consists of and how it becomes what it is, he looks first for what he calls good balance, then for distinguishing characteristics, and in the course of this he notes defects or virtues familiar enough to any winemaker but easily passed over by others. Only then does he compare his impressions with what the label says and settle down to enjoy his glass, whether it is something special or just wine.

There is much to be said for both ways of approaching a wine, though I think the second is more rewarding than the first. The satisfaction to be had from wine increases greatly if one knows what it is, how and why one wine differs from another, the sequence of changes that take place as grapes become wine.

So let us be clear at the outset what this book is concerned with, and what it is not. By a definition accepted with only slight variations in every winegrowing country, wine is "the product of the normal fermentation of sound, ripe grapes, without addition or abstraction, except such as may occur in the usual cellar treatment." The operative word in the definition is "grapes." A fermented beverage of a sort may be made out of almost anything that contains sugar or starch—beer, for example, or cider. Such oddities as dandelion wine, parsnip

---

* Many of the world's memorable winemakers and tasters and proprietors are and have been women. La Veuve Clicquot had her California counterpart in A. Finke's widow. Madame Bollinger is only one of many contemporaries. So when I write "man" or "he," I also usually mean "woman" or "she."

wine, or rose hip wine have their admirers, although these are considered wine only by courtesy and always require appropriate qualification. It was settled long ago, as the Bible will confirm, that wine is made only from grapes. Nothing else will do. This book is about nothing else.

The other thing to be noticed in the definition is the phrase "usual cellar treatment." What may be usual cellar treatment in one region or country may not be usual in another because in the fermenting and finishing of wines tradition varies a good deal. Treatment also depends on the sort of wine being made, for though fermentation is common to them all, the steps that lead ultimately to sherry are not those that lead to champagne or red table wine. And besides, we keep learning more about what goes on as wine evolves. The way wine is escorted to maturity is therefore not the same in a peasant's cellar as it is in the great wine tank farms of California's Central Valley. Winemaking can be as simple or as highly controlled as you want it to be and still conform to the definition. There will be a much more detailed discussion of variations in "cellar treatment" as we go along.

With those two points cleared up, let it be said immediately that the definition, narrow as it seems, takes in a great deal. Some wines are sweet but more are dry (which is to say non-sweet). There are sparkling wines and there are still (or non-sparkling) wines. There are natural wines of moderate alcoholic content and wines fortified by the addition of spirit. There are red wines and white. There are fine wines and ordinary. There are wines best drunk when young and others that gain by aging. All come within the definition.

RED WINES. For reasons that will become clear it seems probable that the first wine, undoubtedly made by accident, was red; and to this day most of the world's wines are red. These run the gamut from the great masterpieces of Bordeaux and Burgundy down through a host of worthy challengers (including the best reds of California's coastal counties, of the Rhône and Beaujolais and Loire regions of France, of the Spanish Rioja, of the Italian Piedmont and Chianti districts, of Chile, of the Swiss and Italian Alps, perhaps of South Australia), to the solid and unpretentious stuff which constitutes the bulk of all wine, which the French call *pinard* or *ordinaire* or *gros rouge*, the British call *plonk*, and Americans call jug wine. The color may range from darkest purple to the faded amber-rose of a tired but distinguished old claret.

The color derives from the pigment of the grapes, which is lodged almost entirely in the skins and is extracted during fermentation. The intensity of color is determined mainly by the nature of the grapes, some varieties being much richer in pigment than others. Color is modified by the length of time the fermenting juice, or must, is left "on the skins" while fermenting, and often by blending with lighter or darker wines to achieve a predetermined hue.

But the term "red wine" signifies more than color, since there is much else that may be extracted from the skins besides pigment, notably the substances which give body, firmness, and astringency and also contribute to a wine's aroma and ultimately its bouquet. Thus white grapes fermented on the skins red-wine fashion will yield a wine that is more akin to red than to white in terms of body and aroma though there may be no red in its color. If sampled by a critical taster blindfolded, it will seem more like a red than a white.

WHITE WINES. Again, the range is extraordinary: the big full-bodied white Burgundies like Montrachet or Meursault; the lighter and more flowery wines of Germany, Alsace, Austria, and Slovenia; such wines as Muscadet from the Loire Valley which are never better than when very young; the heavier, less fruity, and more "wooden" wines so characteristic of the Mediterranean and other hot regions.

None of these is actually white, and for that matter extreme pallor is a symptom of excessive manipulation more often than not. Their color ranges from pale yellow with a greenish nuance, as found in some Moselles, on through every degree of gold and amber and brown, again depending on the grape and the age and the style sought.

But to the winemaker what distinguishes white wine from red is the method of fermentation. Unlike the procedure for red wines, the juice of the fresh grapes is separated from the skins immedately or soon after crushing, by pressing, and so leaves behind the pigment and other materials to be found in the skins, and is fermented simply as juice. Lacking these ingredients, white wine is a quite different thing from red both chemically and sensually. It is less "solid," less "complete," more "fragile"; and in particular it lacks the normal astringency of red wine. Comparing a Moselle with a big Bordeaux claret is as futile as comparing a Dufy watercolor with a Holbein.

ROSÉ WINES. This is an ambiguous category, because there is no common denominator. The ordinary rosés are often no more than a cheap white wine blended to a standard with the help of a little red. But the classic rosés are something else again. These are of two sorts. The first is made by crushing grapes as though to make red wine, then drawing off the must in a matter of hours, when only a modest proportion of pigment has been extracted, and from then on fermenting white-wine fashion. The other sort is made by crushing certain deeply pigmented red-wine grapes and then pressing immediately as though to make white wine, depending for color entirely on some leaching of pigment during this brief period. The first method yields a rosé more closely approaching a red wine than a white, the second, a much paler rosé which otherwise has the character of a white. The palest of these, with barely a hint of grayish pink, are known in France as *vins gris* and are also to be found in many parts of central Europe. Both sorts, when well made from superior grapes, can be a delight, as anyone knows who has tasted a Pinot Grigio from the Italian finger lakes, a well-made Tavel, or one of the Pinot rosés from the Burgundian Côte Chalonnaise. It is not generally understood, but the wines that first gave Burgundy its reputation were rosés, not reds: only centuries later was the fame transferred to the true red Burgundies.*

NATURAL SWEET WINES. We have been concerned so far with wines that are dry, meaning that all the sugar has been used up by the yeasts during fermentation. Other natural wines show varying degrees of sweetness, particularly when the grapes are so rich in sugar that the yeasts cannot stay the course and give up trying while some of the sugar still remains: the classical examples are the French Sauternes, the German Trockenbeeren Auslese, and the Hungarian Tokay. Such wines are real *tours de force*, difficult to make and almost overpoweringly rich and luscious.

Others, more suitable to be drunk for casual consumption, have a modest but still perceptible sweetness, either because the grapes were less sweet in the beginning, or the fermentation was stopped deliberately before it was completed. The French Graves and many German wines have this nature, and the best of them are elegant and beautifully balanced. But if there is too much striving for the effect, the effort shows through and the wine is nondescript.

SPARKLING WINES. The model for all of these is real champagne, grown and made on the chalky slopes between Épernay and Reims in northeastern France, accounted a great luxury by most of us, and often associated with high living and low thinking. It is an effervescent wine produced from a few specified grape varieties that must struggle to maturity, made by a highly sophisticated process, and matured in the vast chalk cellars that lie beneath Épernay and Reims. The *grandes marques* of Champagne have no serious competi-

---

* This is confirmed by the famous and very beautiful tapestry in the Cluny Museum of Paris, which depicts the winegrowing calendar all the year round. Cluny is Burgundian. People have often been puzzled because nowhere in the sequence is a *cuve*, or red-wine fermenting vat, depicted. Grapes are shown being trampled in tubs, and the flow of juice is then transferred directly to barrels for fermentation. Prolonged trampling together with the first onset of fermentation did extract some of the color and the resulting wine, fermented out of contact with the skins, was a pale red or deep rosé— what the French today call a *clairet*.

tors, the proof being that sparkling wines, wherever they are made, go by the name of champagne if the law will allow them to. The French dislike this, and in some jurisdictions, notably Great Britain, have made their objection stick. Actually it is a harmless deception because no one is fooled. Many other sparkling wines are excellent in their own right—the German Sekt, many of the *mousseux* from other parts of France, and the best of those from New York State and California. But the resemblance to real champagne generally begins with the pop and ends with the bubbles.

Sparkling wines with the full pressure of champagne (and sometimes more) are produced by several different processes, which will be described in due course. In addition there are many wines that do not pop but only sparkle gently, showing hardly more than a few vagrant bubbles that trickle up in the glass; examples are the red Lambrusco from Italy and the *vins pétillants* and spritzer wines from many parts of France and central Europe. They have a liveliness and freshness that grows on one; the natural source of these qualities is a bit of residual fermentation gas.

FORTIFIED WINES. As is true of champagne, the best of the fortified wines, the sherries of Spain and the ports of the Douro Valley in Portugal, are everywhere flattered by imitation of both name and style. Since they are essentially fabricated wines, and the methods of fabrication can be duplicated elsewhere, some of the sherries and ports from other parts of the world compare favorably with the originals. The best *flor* sherries from California are worth anyone's attention. Fortified wines are made by the addition of brandy, sometimes during fermentation and sometimes after. The alcoholic content is thus much higher than that of the natural wines discussed up to now, and this ordinarily excludes them from use as table wines. They are often called apéritif or dessert wines, depending on which end of the meal they are intended for: the dry sherries are served beforehand as a rule and the rich, sweet ports afterward.

Many other fortified wines have earned reputations of

their own, such as the Madeiras, the Marsala from Sicily, and the Muscats from parts of southern France, Samos, and other Mediterranean islands. All are typically produced in hot countries where the desired grapes develop extreme sweetness and low acidity. The hot Central Valley of California is very well adapted to the making of wines of this sort.

Unfortunately, the cheaper grades of fortified wines are a mixed blessing. Being the cheapest legal form of drinkable alcohol in many jurisdictions, they are ordinarily used strictly for the alcohol, which is to say, the shortest way to oblivion. They are what the wino lives, or perhaps dies, for.

But I'm not writing a treatise on the misuse of wine, or rather of those wines that lend themselves most easily to misuse. All good things are harmful in excess, and this is as true of wine as of anything else.

And so we come back to the main subject of this book, which is the natural dry wines. Some few of them are entitled to be called "great": they are the supreme achievements of the winegrowing art. These are the wines we are most likely to hear about and read about, and it is not an exaggeration to say that a valid aesthetic can be built upon them. The qualities which have gained them their reputations will be lost on those who come to them without preparation, as is equally true of a great painting, a musical masterpiece, or the best literature. There has to be a basis of appreciation. The subtle perfection of a great wine escapes those who are unaware of the unique conjunction of the right climate, the right grapes, and the human knowledge and skill that brought the wine into being.

But this is lofty stuff. Most of the world's wine is not great and doesn't pretend to be. In wine-using cultures it is as familiar as bread and is an essential part of the daily fare. Some bread is better than other bread. But no one has built an aesthetic around bread, and so it is with the world's ordinary wines, the making of which can be as much a part of the ménage as bread baking. In the winegrowing parts of Europe most farmers have their little block of vineyard, and the annual vintage is as important in family and neighborhood life as the Thanksgiving feast is here; and it is carried out with a special lift of the spirit that sets the vintage apart from the harvesting of any other crop.

The next step beyond family winemaking is communal winemaking, families banding together and designating the most competent neighbor as supervisor. Communal ventures were quite common in this country during prohibition, especially in Italian-American neighborhoods, when many families would combine assets to bring a shipment of wine grapes east from California. Though customary in many parts of the world, such communal winemaking was not legal in the United States then and isn't now.

Nevertheless, the planting of a domestic vineyard for a family's own use is a growing practice in this country now that better and more adaptable grape varieties are available, and this, of course, is entirely legal. There is much trading around of equipment among amateur winemakers, and people help each other in the same spirit as the barn raisings of an earlier day. Thanks to the availability of concentrated grape juice especially put up for the purpose, even city cliff dwellers can try their hand—and do in large numbers.

In most wine-producing countries, the individual wine-grower who produces wine for sale tends to be superseded by small cooperatives, and the small cooperatives by larger ones —each grower later drawing his share of the proceeds (and of wine for his own use where the law allows) from the total production. What is lost in individuality is usually made up for by more consistent quality. Of course it is a logical step from such arrangements to large-scale industrial winemaking, still often a cooperative but often too a private commercial enterprise that buys its grapes under contract from surrounding growers. The immense consumption of a city like Paris is taken care of by these large operations, the wine being made and assembled in the Midi of France, shipped north in tank trucks, and then blended and bottled in Bercy, a city within a city which exists only for that purpose. In the United States most large enterprises given over primarily to everyday wine are in California's Central Valley around the towns of Lodi, Modesto, Fresno, Delano, and Bakersfield. Such concentration of production is congenial to America's big-scale way of doing things.

These everyday wines, whether from small growers or giant enterprises, are familiar rather than great. They nourish. They taste good and make other foods taste better. The list of elements they contribute to the diet is almost as formidable as those lists of "minimum daily requirements" on boxes of breakfast food. Better than any pill they ease tension and replace it with a sense of relaxed well-being. They bring good cheer and merriment, yielding that special satisfaction which is only possible when the digestive system is at ease and functioning well. Their therapeutic properties are well established, not least for the elderly. Such wine is the stuff that the elder Pliny had in mind when he wrote, two thousand years ago, that wine "refreshes the stomach, sharpens the appetite, blunts care and sadness, and conduces to slumber."

Let us enjoy the ordinary wines. The production of the truly great or fine wines is infinitesimal as compared with the bulk of the world's wine. But then, life does not consist solely of great occasions. For ordinary occasions ordinary wines are best.

CHAPTER 2

The Vine Comes First

 VISITORS TO our vineyard in Maryland often ask whether the soil of this part of the country is especially suitable for winegrowing, so expressing a common misconception. The nature of the soil matters, but it does not have top priority. The order of priorities runs this way: first, grapes that are suitable for winemaking, since many are not; second, a climate in which the grapevines will survive and ripen their crop; third, the art of the winemaker; and a poor fourth, the soil, as evidenced by the fact that many a famous vineyard contains a half-dozen different soil types.

The vine comes first. The history of wine is the history of the vine. For the most part, it has been the history of a single species of the genus *Vitis*. The family of grapevines actually embraces many species which are spread throughout the temperate parts of the world (although there are no indigenous species in the southern hemisphere). But it is the Eurasian species *Vitis vinifera* that gave wine to man in the beginning and today still predominates in the vineyards of the world, though during the past century certain other species have been found useful in hybridizing.

So far as the archaeologists and the paleo-botanists have been able to determine (and they are pretty sure of their ground), the center of diffusion of cultivated grapes and of wine was the Middle East, in the general area of the Black and the Caspian seas. If you want to consider mythology, the legend of Noah supports this theory too. Wine was already being dealt in as a commodity probably a millennium before Christ, and the Russians have excavated and studied prehistoric towns in the Black Sea area which had winegrowing as their chief occupation.

From this area the making and use of wine diffused in two directions. One was by way of Palestine, as everyone who is familar with the Old Testament knows, and from there by degrees into Egypt and along the North African coast and eventually to the Iberian Peninsula. The other was toward Greece and its islands and westward into other lands bordering the Mediterranean on the north. The diffusion was by sea as well as by land, and a penetration into central Europe by way of the valley of the Danube.

Thus, the cultivated vine spread and wine impregnated the very fabric of Mediterranean life, having its own gods and goddesses and folklore, its ceremonial uses, its eventual symbolism in the rites of Christianity, its use as an article of luxury and also as an essential ingredient of daily living. One can hardly exaggerate the importance of wine, then and now, in Mediterranean life. And the continuity between past and present is striking. The famous book on farming by Cato the Elder, who was born in 234 B.C., deals with winegrowing in full practical detail. It is worthwhile reading today for anyone interested in the art, not so much for the differences in technique that have come about during the subsequent two thousand years as for the substantial identity between winegrowing practice as Cato knew it and as we know it still. His specifications for the layout of a winery are not greatly different from what follows in this book. His descriptions of a wine press and the other essential tools and equipment are instantly recognizable, as are his descriptions of grape varieties still largely used in Mediterranean viticulture. His outline of vine-yard practice still makes sense. It is at once disconcerting and reassuring to go back to the ancient text: disconcerting to realize how little of novelty there really is in winegrowing, reassuring to find oneself so closely involved in a continuing tradition.

From its Mediterranean base the cultivated vine, always *Vitis vinifera*, continued to spread north into the temperate regions of Europe. In what was then Gaul, the wines eventually became competitors of those of Imperial Rome; in fact, they were of such high quality that efforts were made to suppress their production. By the second century A.D. the outlines of viticulture in France and the Rhineland were already established, and there were flourishing vineyards along the Danube and in many other parts of temperate central Europe. The late Middle Ages saw vineyards being developed beyond Europe on the Canary Islands and Madeira. And from then until now the cultivation of this species has continued to spread wherever the climate is congenial.

The term *Vitis vinifera* is a sort of grab bag. In the course of its evolution the vine has thrown off innumerable varieties and subvarieties, many of them so different from each other that the question is sometimes asked how "pure" the species really is. Since wine owes its character above all to the grape, this variation more than anything else accounts for the differences among wines. Put a modest little bunch of Pinot Noir alongside a huge compound cluster of Thompson Seedless and you would hardly think they were related, let alone of the same species.

As a matter of fact this great catch-all of a species, the Eurasian grape, breaks down into two distinct groups; and for an understanding of the gross and subtle differences to be found among wines it is necessary to understand the distinctions between the two groups and how they came about.

The members of both do have certain common characteristics. They interbreed freely. They are deciduous. They lack resistance to various parasites, notably phylloxera and nematodes, and to certain fungus diseases. They require a good deal of heat to ripen properly. They are not very winter-hardy. The parts of the earth where they will thrive and produce wine are large in total but nevertheless restricted, so that they do beautifully in California but not in Colorado, well in Chile, South Africa, and Odessa but not in Brazil, the Congo, or Vladivostok.

Acknowledging the common characteristics, we turn to the differences between the two groups; and for this purpose the map of the European viticultural homeland on pages 18–19 will help.

Note the lower line, which divides Europe into two distinct winegrowing areas, running roughly east and west across the map. The line is only an approximation on this map but could be drawn with considerable precision on a larger one. It represents the division between temperate-climate Europe and the area of Mediterranean influence. (The upper line merely signifies the northern limits of viticulture.)

The Mediterranean basin has a two-season climate with mild, rainy winters and hot, dry, almost rainless summers. Its characteristic flora is exemplified by the olive and the cork oak, citrus and melons, the oleander and a host of succulent plants. It also has its own distinctive group of grapevines. As one might expect, this climate and the common parentage of the vines that have evolved in it confer a strong family resemblance on all Mediterranean wines. As a rule they are bland, soft, low in acidity, relatively high in alcohol, not very fruity, and with a somewhat earthy background to their flavor.

North of this line is a quite different world. Here in an irregular band stretching across Europe is the four-season temperate climate in all the variations that will support the grape, with cold winters, highly variable temperatures during the growing season, and rainfall scattered throughout the seasons. The soils are different too, since soil tends to be a function of climate. The flora is distinct from that of the Mediterranean basin, though of course there is some overlapping.

And the grapes are also distinct; they look different, taste different, and produce different wines. Generally speaking, these wines are fruitier, lower in alcohol and higher in original acidity, and more delicate and subtle in flavor. Some of the differences in the aromatic constituents defy even such a sensitive tool as gas chromatography, but they are real and the market reflects them in spite of occasional deceptions.* Although the area of Mediterranean influence has its superior wines, such as Châteauneuf-du-Pape and Hermitage and the Piedmont and Alpine wines of Italy, most of the wines which have acquired distinguished reputations are the temperate-climate wines such as Bordeaux, Burgundy, Champagne, the Rhenish wines, and Beaujolais.

The general nature of the wines produced on each side of this line is determined, then, by a combination of the prevailing climate and the adapted grapes and, only to a lesser extent, the soil. The refinements of wine quality within the two broad groupings, which make the study and comparison of wines so endlessly absorbing, are determined by micro-climates and micro-adaptations of the grapes.

The Burgundy region of France offers an apt illustration. All of the great and famous Burgundies are grown on the sunny and protected southeastern and southern slopes of the Côte d'Or, from certain subvarieties (known as *clones*) of Pinot Noir and Chardonnay grapes. In the valley of the Saône a few hundred yards to the east the micro-climate is different, different grapes are used, and the wines are quite ordinary. The same is true up and over the Côte d'Or escarpment to the west.

Another illustration of the subtlety of this close relationship between climate and grape is produced when the Pinot Noir of Burgundy is transplanted south of the line. In places

---

* The 1974 Bordeaux scandal involved the strengthening of thin Bordeaux wines with headier Mediterranean wines, but only the cheapest grades. In fact, such blending has gone on in Bordeaux since the fourteenth century. It was to bring down the heady wines from Cahors that the Lot River was originally made navigable by Colbert. Such blending yields a wine better than its component parts, usually: the deception enters when it purports to be something it isn't.

WINE-PRODUCING REGIONS OF EUROPE.

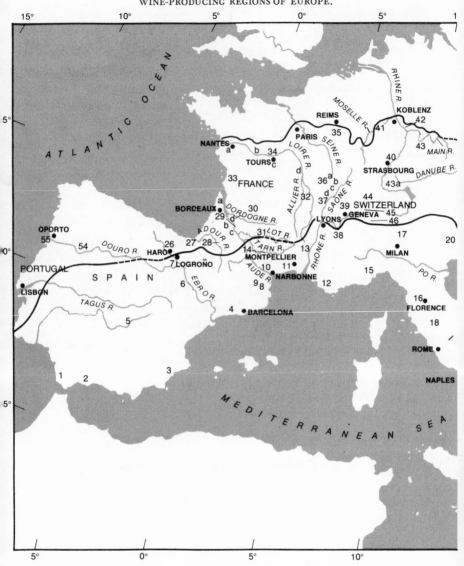

MEDITERRANEAN CLIMATE

SPAIN
1. SHERRY
2. MALAGA
3. ALICANTE
4. TARRAGONA
5. VALDEPENAS
6. ZARAGOZA
7. BAJA RIOJA

FRANCE
8. ROUSSILLON
9. CORBIÈRES
10. MINERVOIS
11. LANGUEDOC
12. CÔTES DE PROVENCE
13. CÔTES DU RHÔNE
14. GAILLAC

ITALY
15. PIEDMONT
16. TUSCANY
17. ALPINE
18. ORVIETO
19. VERDICCHIO
20. VENEZIA
21. NAPLES

YUGOSLAVIA
22. DALMATIAN
23. SERBIAN

U.S.S.R.
24. CRIMEA
25. GEORGIA

TEMPERATE CLIMATE

SPAIN
26. ALTA RIOJA
FRANCE
27. JURANCON
28. ARMAGNAC
29. BORDELAIS
   a. MÉDOC
   b. GRAVES
   c. SAUTERNES
   d. ST. ÉMILION

30. MONBAZILLAC	d. MONTRACHET	**AUSTRIA**
31. CAHORS	37. BEAUJOLAIS	47. DANUBIAN
32. AUVERGNE	38. SAVOIE	48. BURGENLAND
33. COGNAC	39. JURA	**YUGOSLAVIA**
34. VINS DE LA LOIRE	40. ALSACE	49. SLOVENIAN
a. MUSCADET	**GERMANY**	50. CROATIAN
b. ANJOU	41. MOSELLE	**HUNGARY**
c. VOUVRAY	42. RHINELAND	51. TOKAY
d. POUILLY	43. FRANCONIA	**U.S.S.R.**
35. CHAMPAGNE	a. BADEN	52. MOLDAVIA
36. BURGUNDY	**SWITZERLAND**	53. UKRAINE
a. CHABLIS	44. NEUCHATEL	**PORTUGAL**
b. NUITS	45. LÉMAN	54. PORT
c. BEAUNE	46. VALAIS	55. VINHO VERDE

where the Mediterranean influence predominates, the qualities that come out to perfection in the great Burgundies are lost and the end result is just another Mediterranean red wine. Likewise if the Mediterranean Grenache or Carignane grapes are transplanted to the temperate-climate side of the line, they are ill at ease and languish, if indeed they ripen at all. No southern French grower wastes his time with Pinot Noir. No Burgundian would dream of planting Grenache.

The differentiation of *Vitis vinifera* into two groupings came about through an evolution that has been traced back to the glacial period and before. The story is much too long and intricate to be told here. But the result is evident: two broad categories of wine, the one altogether characteristic of the Mediterranean basin and similar climates elsewhere and made from grapes beautifully adapted over the millennia to such conditions, the other reflecting temperate-climate areas and having its source in greatly different grapes equally well adapted to their particular climatic conditions. An experienced wine taster can separate these two categories if not unerringly at least with a high degree of success, and if he is sufficiently knowledgeable can even spot blends of the two sorts, as when Algerian or Rhône Valley red wine is used to strengthen a thin Beaujolais.

Most of the Mediterranean grapes are what the French call *cépages d'abondance*, yielding heavy crops of quite ordinary wine, food wines rather than works of art. These grapes are spread throughout the basin and have often picked up local names. They traveled with traders and accompanied every migration of the human population: often, as seems to have been the case with the grape called Aramon, they were camp followers of military expeditions.* Some of the most familiar and widely grown are Carignane (Cariñeno and

---

* The areas where this heavy producer is grown today coincide in striking fashion with the outline of the conquests and short-lived empire of Les Rois de Mayorque, or the Kings of Mallorca, a historical episode known to every French school child but generally unknown to Americans.

Mazuela in Spain, Gragnano in Italy), Grenache (Garnacho in Spain), Cinsaut, and Syrah (which seems to have migrated all the way from Persia to the valley of the Rhône). All are red-wine grapes. There was a similar diffusion of the whites: the Italian Trebbiano, which was a Roman grape in the beginning and in southern France has become Ugni Blanc, the Clairette tribe, the Muscats. Most often today these are brought together in blends, as for instance Carignane for firmness and good color, Grenache for alcoholic content, Syrah for oomph and nose, Aramon for sheer quantity.

Endless numbers of local variants, genetic throw-offs, or accidental recombinations provide individuality and occasionally superior quality. But in our world of instant communication and compulsive standardization these increasingly take on the character of poor relations: vines clung to stubbornly by certain individuals and communities but in the not-so-long run doomed to disappear. Works of ampelography are full of references to half-forgotten varieties that really don't matter any more and in many cases have disappeared altogether. It is the nature of evolution to leave much by the wayside.

The temperate-climate areas have their *cépages d'abondance* too, varieties that mean bread and butter to the grower and are as fondly cherished as members of the family but are unknown to the connoisseur or indeed to anybody beyond the viticultural brotherhood. Who has ever heard of Grolleau, which is the twelfth most widely grown grape in temperate-climate France and might almost be called the Concord of the Loire Valley? Its name reflects its role. Grolleau is a corruption of *gros lot*, French slang for a winning ticket in the lottery. Grolleau may not produce great wine, but for many a grower it provides the difference between mere subsistence and affluence. It is rustic, productive, and reliable, its wine is sound if unexciting. Think of it the next time you have an Anjou rosé or find a carafe of red wine on your table in Orléans or Tours.

Grolleau has its counterparts elsewhere, white and red; in

the Bordelais, in the huge viticultural area stretching from there to the Pyrenees, on the wrong side of the road in Burgundy, in Poitou and the Centre, in Savoie and the Juras, and in nooks and crannies everywhere.

The following table puts this matter of grape varieties in a more realistic perspective than is conveyed by most wine-appreciation books, at least so far as French wine production is concerned. The left-hand column lists the thirteen most important grapes of the Midi together with the acreage devoted to each. The right-hand column lists the thirteen most important temperate-climate grapes, with their acreage.

MEDITERRANEAN		TEMPERATE-CLIMATE FRANCE	
Grape	Acres	Grape	Acres
Carignane	456,950	Gamays	101,270
Aramon	395,200	*Sémillon	74,100
*Ugni Blanc	118,560	Malbec	41,990
Grand Noir	98,800	Gamays Teinturiers	39,520
Alicante Bouschet	86,450	Cabernet Franc	34,580
Grenache	79,040	*Folle Blanche	29,640
Cinsaut	39,520	*Chenin Blanc	27,170
Terrets	37,050	*Colombard	27,170
*Clairettes	34,580	*Muscadet	27,170
Morrastel	27,170	*Sauvignon	27,170
*Mauzacs	16,055	*Jurançon	24,700
Valdiguié	12,350	Grolleau	24,700
Syrah	8,151	Pinots	19,760

* Those with asterisks are white-wine grapes; those without are red.

It is instructive to read these lists along with the accompanying map showing the main concentrations of French wine-growing. The names of many of the grape varieties included are only vaguely familiar to most wine drinkers. Note that certain grape names of immense reputation, such as Cabernet Sauvignon, Merlot, Chardonnay, Traminer, Riesling—names

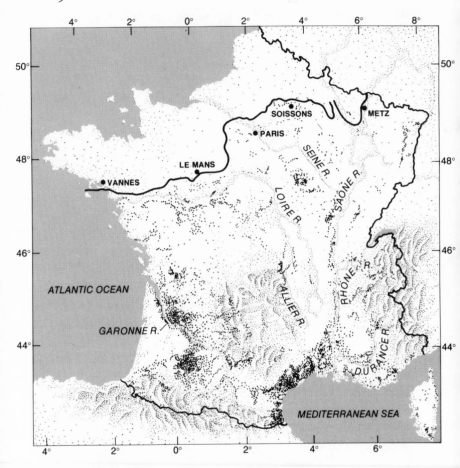

CONCENTRATIONS OF WINEGROWING IN FRANCE.

that trip off every connoisseur's tongue—don't even make the list. Which is not to belittle their importance, but rather to emphasize the truism that great quantity and high quality rarely coincide. The wines of greatest distinction are frequently associated with a single grape variety, what has come to be called a "varietal" in this country. Thus, Pinot Noir and Chardonnay for the red and white Burgundies and the Champagnes; Cabernet Sauvignon for red Bordeaux; Sémillon and

Sauvignon Blanc for Sauternes and white Graves; and Riesling for the Rhenish wines. There is some justification for this association, because some few wines are quite literally "varietals." But it can be misleading.

It can be misleading because these famous "varietal" names convey a false impression of precision. For example, there is no such thing as *the* Pinot Noir. If we want to be accurate, we can only speak of *a* Pinot Noir; for Pinot Noir stands not for a unique and unvarying plant but for what the French call a *cépage*, which is to say a group of similar and closely related but not absolutely identical individuals sharing the same genetic background: a group of brothers and sisters, cousins and aunts, so to speak. Thus the Pinot *cépage* includes some strains (technically known as *clones*) with a place name added, such as Pinot d'Aunis and Pinot d'Ambonnay. The names of others introduce some special characteristic along with the place name (Gros Plant Doré d'Ay) or the name of the popularizer (Pinot Renault). Dozens of Pinots

Delivering grapes at the cuverie *of Château Lafite.*

A *corner of the* Hospices de Beaune.
An efficient small contemporary hospital is part of the complex,
supported by the annual wine auction.

are found in the Champagne district, dozens more in the Côte d'Or and no fewer than forty in the German-speaking area of Switzerland alone. The total easily reaches 1,000, all of which are entitled to be called Pinot Noir. In areas where Pinot Noir has not been isolated from the background of native material, but has been deliberately introduced as in California, variation within the *cépage* is always more restricted. Yet even in California there are definitely two Pinot Noir clones that are widely grown, and probably more, and the process of broadening and enriching the Pinot Noir *cépage* will undoubtedly continue with further introductions. Winegrowers are and always have been absorbed in selecting what they deem the best clone of Pinot Noir for their purpose and propagating it, and the process is without end.

So it is with Riesling, Chardonnay, and all the other *cépages nobles*. At the Viticultural Institute in Colmar, I once saw a dozen newly harvested clones of Pinot Blanc, each transplanted from a different part of France. Their differences, standing in their separate baskets, were as conspicuous as their resemblance. Near Cahors the principal cooperative maintains an experimental vineyard containing no fewer than 200 different clones of the variety known locally as Auxerrois but in other parts of France as Malbec or Côt. José Baudel, the director, has been trying for years to decide which one is best for his area.

A similar situation exists in the vast region straddling the Gironde estuary, where the red Bordeaux are grown. In the minds of many, Cabernet Sauvignon is practically synonymous with red Bordeaux. But that is an error. Many of the most prestigious Bordeaux reds—notably those from Saint-Émilion and Pomerol (Châteaux Petrus and Cheval Blanc, and Clos Fourtet, for example)—contain none of it. Cabernet Sauvignon is essentially a vine of the Médoc and Graves subdistricts, and even there it is in the minority. Normally it is blended (usually to its advantage) with such related grapes as Merlot, Petit Verdot, Gros Verdot, Cabernet Franc, and Carmenère. The name Cabernet Sauvignon does not ordinarily appear on a bottle of red Bordeaux, and when it does the wine is likely to be of inferior quality and lacking the warranty words *appellation contrôlée*. The red Bordeaux derive not from a single variety, then, but from a complex of related and congenial grapes which are native to that climate and do well in it, and from the way these are handled during fermentation and aging. One cannot expect to obtain the equivalent of a red Bordeaux simply by planting a few vines of Cabernet Sauvignon in Saginaw, Michigan, or Williamsburg, Virginia, or Delano, California.

So much for the "varietal" question. All the grapes we have mentioned up to this point (except one, Alicante Bouschet) and most of the other *cépages* so familiar in the literature of viticulture and winemaking originated spontaneously over thousands of years, from wild native plants. Man's role was simply to pick and choose, singling out the best, propagating them, and so bringing them into cultivation. With one or two exceptions, the actual circumstances of their selection are lost to history.*

But there is more to be said about the grapevines used in winemaking. For better than a century now, man has been deliberately intruding in the genetic process and creating new varieties by deliberate cross-fertilization, sometimes between already familiar members of the Eurasian species† and sometimes between V. *vinifera* and other species that by themselves are worthless for wine.‡

The inspiration for this plant breeding was a succession of calamities that struck the vineyards of Europe during the mid-nineteenth century and all but wiped them out. The first was the appearance of a fungus disease called oidium, or powdery mildew, brought in by accident from the New World. It attacked both foliage and fruit with devastating effect. This was followed by another called plasmopara, or downy mildew, and by yet another called black rot, which reduced the unripe fruit to hard, black mummies. (A sardonic Frenchman once said that these were among the unfortunate results of Columbus's discovery of America.) Means of coping with the diseases were discovered in due time, principally by spraying and dusting with copper salts and sulfur; but as the *vinifera* have little or no resistance to the diseases, prevention places an onerous and never-ending burden on all winegrowers. In some districts and for some varieties there must be as many as twenty sprayings or dustings a year.

Then came the deadliest blow of all: the appearance of the insect called phylloxera, which was likewise an immigrant from North America, where it exists almost everywhere east of the Rockies. This baffling insect attacks the foliage to some

---

* One of the exceptions is Gewürztraminer. It is a clone of the ubiquitous Traminer of northeastern France and central Europe that was singled out and propagated by M. Oberlin, director of the Alsatian experiment station at Colmar.

† Alicante Bouschet, mentioned above, is one of these.

‡ Intraspecific crosses are known as *métis*; interspecific crosses are hybrids. However, the word "hybrid" is loosely used for both.

extent, but more importantly the roots. The *vinifera* have no immunity to it, and so the vine dies.

Oddly enough, phylloxera was first spotted and identified on the European side of the Atlantic in 1863 in a garden in a then stylish suburb of London. But its arrival in France was probably independent of its presence in England, since during this period many American grapevines were also coming into France as curiosities. Some of them undoubtedly gave the phylloxera a free ride. It was a time of two-way traffic—between the New World and the Old—in novel plant materials and inevitably for the diseases they carried. In exchange for the phylloxera, Europe gave us the chestnut blight, to cite but a single illustration.

From the time when it was first noticed in French vine-yards of the Bas-Rhône, the phylloxera spread with frightful speed, from vine to vine, from vineyard to vineyard, from region to region. French wine production was 2,216,258,000 gallons in 1875. Four years later, in 1879, it had shrunk to 679,000,000 gallons. Another illustration: Portugal, where it struck later, had 1,500 infected hectares in 1882, which had jumped to 15,433 by 1885.

The social consequences were appalling. Winegrowing was wiped out in one region after another as the winegrowers stood by helplessly. (Some regions have never resumed wine production.) No means of subduing the insect could be found —and none has yet been found. The destruction of vineyards took away the livelihood of hundreds of thousands, reducing large areas to poverty. It inspired wholesale migrations: as from the Bordeaux district over the Pyrenees and into northern Spain, where the Rioja people were taught how to make red wine Bordeaux fashion; and from the Rhône Valley and other parts of the Midi to Algeria in search of land that phylloxera had not reached. The planting of French civilization in North Africa, where the French population trebled between 1866 and 1901, was indirectly the work of this insect.

The story of the full impact of this insect invasion on the

course of Western civilization is still to be written.* For our purpose, however, it is sufficient to know that in the affected vineyards an indirect way of coping was finally found. Though the fat, soft roots of *vinifera* vines are soon destroyed by the insect, the tougher and more wiry roots of certain wild American species were found to be resistant, or at least sufficiently so. The fact is obvious, when you think about it: otherwise the stream banks and hills of eastern North America would not have been festooned with wild grapevines.

The answer lay in grafting the classic vines of Europe on phylloxera-resistant American rootstocks,† much as apple scion wood is grafted to different rootstocks for various purposes. But finding rootstocks that were compatible and also adaptable to European conditions entailed the deliberate crossing and recrossing of likely species and varieties until eventually the whole range of contemporary grapevine rootstocks came into being, capable of accepting grafts, sufficiently phylloxera-resistant, and adapted to a wide range of growing conditions. It is on these rootstocks that the classic *vinifera* vines of Europe are now grafted wherever phylloxera is present or a threat.

The need for suitable rootstocks turned the attention of plant breeders to the grapevine. Once their attention was turned, another and different solution suggested itself, which was to breed entirely new grapes, hybrids between species, that would combine the fruit and wine quality of the Eurasian grape with the winter hardiness and phylloxera resistance of the alien species, and perhaps introduce resistance to the mildew diseases as well. Conceivably such hybrids could not only extend winegrowing into new areas but replace some of the less satisfactory ancient varieties, while at the same time eliminating the need for grafting and reducing the need for

---

* Although George Ordish has made a fine beginning with his book *The Great Wine Blight*.

† Feminists might well look into the role played by Marguerite-Auguste-Marie, Duchesse de Fitz-James, née Lowenhjelm, one of the leading "Américanistes," who preached, nagged, and fought for this solution with equal fluency in French, English, and Swedish.

spraying. But such efforts raised immediate hostility, and for a number of reasons the antagonism persists to this day.

For one thing, the vested winegrowing interests had no wish for competition from new areas; and the important viticultural areas have ample political clout to back up their objection. In terms of quality, the regions of *grand appellation* were well satisfied with the vines they had, thank you, since these could survive on the new rootstocks—and continue to produce the wines on which their reputations depended. This was a more valid reason to resist the introduction into their delimited areas of new grapes having other wine characteristics.

Further complicating matters, hybridization yielded rather dreadful results in the beginning, recalling Bernard Shaw's warning to Ellen Terry that a child of their union might inherit her brains and his beauty rather than the reverse. Hardiness and disease resistance were improved in these early hybrids, but at the cost of wine quality.

The work nevertheless persisted, being done in the main by a little band of dedicated men caught up in a dream, not scientists but amateurs whose lives were bound up in the métier of viticulture. All the pressure of the established commerce, of official agricultural science, of the viticultural press, and of political opposition was not able to divert them from their goal.

A good thing, too, for as one generation of hybrids succeeded another the results improved. There exists today a range of hybrids, some of exceedingly complex ancestry, which yield good wines under conditions hostile to V. *vinifera*. Good wines—not great wines. So far no hybrid can challenge the most famous *cépages*. But then, most of the world's wine is made from *vinifera* grapes and nine-tenths of it is mediocre. There is a tendency always to compare the worst hybrids with the best *vinifera*, not the other way around.

During this effort to develop good hybrids, the European winegrowing establishment, even including many of the viticultural schools, has been implacably hostile. The hybrids are "mules" and "bastards"—strangely unscientific terms to issue from the mouths of men who call themselves scientists. The attitude is blindly anti-scientific and—considering the great gifts that applied genetics has brought to other branches of the world's agriculture and to animal husbandry—perverse as well. What is the contemporary "green revolution" in the production of new wheats and rices and other grains but a triumph of applied genetics?

By a twist of fate, the work of creating new hybrids, which has been carried on amid such hostility in France and other European countries, was just what was needed in the United States, where the future of winegrowing in many regions quite clearly depends on them. I will go into this aspect more fully later on. Sufficient to state that the classic Eurasian grape is not really at home in many parts of North America, because of the continental extremes prevailing in most of our temperate-climate areas. Not until the coming of the better French-American hybrids, with their superior hardiness and disease resistance, was it possible in those parts to produce wines that meet European norms with consistent success.

Now that is being done, and in the most unlikely places, where the hope of successful winegrowing had long since been abandoned, if indeed it had ever existed. Today American plant breeders have picked up where the Europeans left off, in the search for grapes that may come closer to the ideal. No ideal hybrid yet exists, and maybe it never will—but the future is wide open.

CHAPTER 3

The American Connection

 THE EURASIAN HEARTLAND, then, is the birthplace and home of the wine grape. We have seen how in the long stretch of time since the glacial period this single species, V. *vinifera*, evolved into subspecies and groupings, each consisting of numberless varieties uncannily adapted to local requirements of climate as well as to human preferences.

Why is the story of wine in this country so different from Europe? What is the connection between the grapes that grew in the New World and the V. *vinifera* of the Old, and once the gap was recognized how did we manage to bridge it?

Grapevines are indigenous to many parts of our country. We have a dozen or more native species, each with its own area of adaptation, and nowhere do they flourish more conspicuously than along the Atlantic littoral. Beginning with the original visits of the Norsemen, no feature of the landscape impressed the early explorers more than the abundance of wild grapevines. The name the Norsemen gave this new land, as we all know, was Vinland the Good. With few exceptions the records of those preliminary reconnoiters and tentative landings, and then of the first semi-permanent and permanent settlements, refer to the grapevines encountered everywhere and to their fruit. The report of Amadas and Barlow, after visiting Roanoke Island in 1584, is typical. It speaks of a land "so full of grapes as the very beating and surge of the sea overflowed them. . . . In all the world the like abundance is not to be found." To find the material of a vintage ready at hand and waiting only to be picked and made into wine seemed almost too good to be true.

And so it was, too good to be true, as one settlement after another discovered to its sorrow, though each was slow in admitting it. Captain John Smith lost no time trying his hand as a winemaker, and in 1606 he wrote: "Of vines great abundance in many parts that climbe the toppes of highest trees in some places, but these bear but few grapes. Except by the rivers and savage habitations, where they are not overshadowed by the sunne, they are covered with fruit, though never pruined nor manured. Of those hedge grapes we made neere twentie gallons of wine, which was like our French Brittish wine, but certainely would prove good were they well manured. There is another sort of grape neere as great as a Cherry, this they [the Indians] call Messamins,* they be fatte, and the juyce thicke. Neither doth the taste so well please when they are made in wine."

It is not hard to read between those lines. There was a good deal of the promoter in these early venturers, and their reports were sometimes suspiciously like the prospectus of a real estate development. Captain Smith was not about to say that he was disappointed and these grapes had no future. But neither would he state that the wine from the wild grapes was much good. And this was the universal experience with wild grapes: first the high hopes, then the disillusionment. They were grapes, no doubt of that; but for anyone with a taste for wine, something important was missing and something objectionable had been added.

---

* Undoubtedly what we now call Muscadines, the Scuppernong being the best known.

Hindsight sheds some light on what to the explorers was a mystery. Our numerous wild species are related, however distantly, to the Eurasian grape. The flower structure is the same. With one exception they have the same number of chromosomes (thirty-eight) and, as remarked earlier, they therefore interbreed freely. They are not of independent origin but products of diffusion. What evidently happened is that during distant periods of terrestrial upheaval the forebears of the Eurasian grape migrated eastward across south-central Asia, submitting on the way to natural selection. Out of that migration there emerged a number of Asian species that are very different from V. *vinifera,* especially as regards hardiness and fruit characteristics—for example, V. *amurensis* and V. *coegnetiae.* In the course of time the migration continued over land masses very different in conformation (and climate) from those of today, until the vine reached North America at last, by way of Asia, just as the original Americans did. And so by degrees the many American species of the genus V*itis,* from the inedible V. *californica* to the edible V. *labrusca,* or fox grape, of the American Northeast, came into being.

Similar phenomena are observable everywhere in nature. The skeleton of a dog has many analogies with the skeleton of a dolphin, thus indicating drastic differentiation from a common mammalian ancestor. It is not surprising that the many American grape species should share morphological characteristics with the single European species while showing such pronounced differences. Many of the American species have their uses, as we have seen, but these do not include making good wine from the wild fruit.

Having made one false assumption and found it to be false, the early settlers then proceeded to another. Where the wild grapevine flourishes, they reasoned, then surely the cultivated vines of Europe would flourish too. And so a long series of ambitious winegrowing enterprises began. At the urging of proprietors and other leading settlers along our East Coast, cuttings of choice European varieties were sent across the Atlantic, often accompanied by experienced vignerons. Some of these enterprises were communal and haphazard, each householder participating. Others were undertaken much more systematically. One way or another, efforts were made in every colony: in Georgia, the Carolinas, repeatedly in Virginia, in Massachusetts, Pennsylvania, Maryland, New Sweden (on the Delaware), and New Netherland (on the Hudson and also on the lower Delaware).

The invariable result was failure. By 1679 a traveler reported that the Dutch effort had failed lamentably, and that the colonists "have not yet discovered the cause of the failure." Every conceivable explanation was offered but the right one. The colonists were reported to be ignorant of the essentials of winegrowing, to be lazy, to have been seduced away from the vine by other and more immediately successful crops such as maize and tobacco. But along with these explanations the reality was reluctantly admitted, soon or late, by all who participated. The cuttings might root well. The vines would grow for a few years, often to the point of producing a crop or two, usually meager. But then they would go into a decline. It was an unaccountable affliction that took various forms. The vines might blossom and set fruit, but then the developing bunches would wither away into mummies. Or in midseason the foliage would begin to mottle, turn brown, and finally fall away, leaving the vine starved for nourishment. Or vines that went into dormancy seemingly healthy and vigorous would be dead to the ground the following spring when it was time for them to resume growth. Or the vineyard would simply begin to languish, gradually or abruptly, and in the end all the vines would die.

The efforts continued nevertheless. A letter dated 17 March 1772, from Charles Carroll of Carrollton (later to be one of the signers of the Declaration) to an English friend tells of a vineyard set out by his father at Doughoregan Manor in Maryland. Carroll goes on to say: "If we live a few years longer, you may depend on tasting the wine of its growth, & doubtless y^r prejudices in favor of ye owner will make you fancy it excellent Burgundy, equal to the best wine of France. The vineyard is planted with several sorts of grapes, that we may learn by experience which sorts are best suited to our climate." The varieties planted were, according to Charles Carroll, Sr., "Rhenish, Virginia grape, Claret, and Burgundy." Alas, nothing came of the effort.*

The experience of Thomas Jefferson's friend from Tuscany, Philip Mazzei, was equally disappointing. In 1773 he planted a considerable vineyard of European vines near Monticello, bringing in sixteen experienced Italians to help him and planning an ambitious expansion. But each year something went wrong, not least the outbreak of the Revolution. With that, Mr. Mazzei gave up trying. "And thus ended," wrote Jefferson to Albert Gallatin, "an experiment which, from every appearance, would in a year or two more have established the practicability of that branch of agriculture in America."

Again by hindsight we know that the trouble was nothing so temporary as a war for independence. Just as fruit of the native grapes lacked the qualities essential for making good wine, so the European vines lacked the qualities that enabled the native vines to survive and flourish. Wherever the European vines were brought in and tried, whether in Massachusetts colony or tidewater Carolina, they found themselves in a hostile environment. Fruit and foliage were ravaged by the endemic fungus diseases, and in the deep South by the virus-like ailment called Pierce's disease. Roots were riddled and destroyed by the phylloxera insect, against which the wild native vines had been armed by natural selection, and by numerous nematodes. And if disease didn't get the vines there was still our continental climate, so different from the mari-

---

* The vineyard was planted in 1771. By an odd coincidence Charles Carroll's descendant, Philip Carroll, planted a vineyard on the manor only a few hundred yards away from the original site in 1971, just 200 years later. The vines are French hybrids. The vintage of 1974 was excellent, and the vineyard is currently flourishing.

time climate of western Europe or that of the Mediterranean. Through natural selection the native vines had acquired winter hardiness: the immigrant vines lacked it.

The situation is somewhat improved today. Resistant rootstocks, then unknown, are a help. Fungicides are to some extent a substitute for natural disease resistance. But Mark Twain's saying still applies: there isn't much we can do about the weather except talk about it. Even today climate has the last word, and those who propose to challenge climate should fully understand the risk.

In spite of the disappointing performance of the alien vines, hopes for winegrowing in the United States did not die, and toward the end of the eighteenth century and into the nineteenth, interest turned again to the possibilities of the native grapes. As early as 1683 William Penn was saying that it might be better "to fall to Fining [that is, improving] the Fruits of the Country, especially the Grape, by the care and skill of Art" than to send to Europe for "foreign Stems and Sets." He announced his intention, "if God give me Life, to try both, and hope the consequence will be as good Wine as any European Countries of the same Lattitude do yield."

There were several good reasons for turning back to the wild native vines. The first was obvious: the European grape had been a failure and hence there was no other way to turn. A second was the realization, available to any serious amateur, that no two wild grapevines are quite the same, as no two human beings are quite the same. A sufficiently diligent search might conceivably discover a wild vine meeting or approximating the wanted fruit characteristics. A third was the observation, already made by Captain John Smith in the case of the Messamins, that among the wild grapes there were what today we would call species differences. Some of our species such as the familiar *labrusca*, of which Concord is an example, have that pronounced aroma and flavor which is called "foxiness."* Others such as the northern V. *riparia* and the southern V. *aestivalis* lack foxiness though they have other undesirable qualities such as high acidity. This fact broadened the search and increased the theoretical possibility of finding something worthwhile.

The fourth and most compelling reason was that certain native grapes were beginning to show up which could survive and indeed could also yield tolerable wine, though still a long way from the European ideal. Some had been found growing wild. Others, such as the famous Alexander grape, were supposed at the time to be true V. *vinifera* which had somehow acquired, or carried within them, the power of survival; but there always turned out to be gaps in the pedigrees.

We now know that none of those supposed to be *vinifera* actually belonged to that species and that the ones found growing wild were not in fact full-blooded Americans. What happened is easy to understand, and the story of the Alexander grape (also known as the Cape, the Vevey, Clifton's Constantia, Schuylkill Muscadel), which has been fairly well worked out, illustrates what undoubtedly occurred over and over again. John Alexander, who was Governor John Penn's gardener, was interested in grapes. He had been through the usual unsuccessful effort to grow European grapes. Before he gave it up, the vines had survived long enough to spread free-floating pollen and pollinate some nearby wild grapes accidentally. A seed of one of these accidental crosses eventually germinated. By a happy chance it carried the hardiness and disease resistance of its native parent but bore fruit considerably ameliorated in quality by its European parent. John Alexander found the vine and either transplanted it or rooted a cutting of it in John Penn's garden. So the Alexander grape came into being.

---

* In French, *goût de fox*, or *goût de renard*. Aromas and flavors defy verbal description. The way to fix foxiness in the memory is to compare the flavors of fresh Concord grapes and any fresh California table grape. In this form, and also in Concord grape juice and jelly, most people find it sprightly and delicious. But when foxy grapes are used to make dry table wine the flavor becomes obtrusive and even disagreeable to habitual wine drinkers.

This was followed by other such accidental hybrids, all of uncertain ancestry—the Catawba and Isabella, Norton, Clinton, Lenoir, and ever so many others. Most of them, alas, carried the foxy *labrusca* parentage, because most of them were found in that part of the country where the *labrusca* is the predominant wild species. But the *labrusca* foxiness was somewhat attenuated in them; and in the case of some, such as the still widely grown Delaware, certain non-foxy American species intervened, attenuating the "wild" flavor still more. Drinkable wine could be made from them. An answer of a sort had been found, and on the basis of these grapes an Eastern winegrowing industry came into being, the principal areas of production being the Finger Lakes district of northern New York, the southern shore of Lake Erie from west of Buffalo to Sandusky, Ohio, and beyond, the islands of the Lake Erie archipelago, the valley of the Ohio River, especially around Cincinnati, where the innovative drive of the first Nicholas Longworth brought forth the first American champagne, the Valley of Virginia, the valley of the Missouri River upstream from St. Louis, and New Jersey around the town of Egg Harbor. The American connection was thus established by a series of accidental marriages between the indigenous wild grapes of the United States and the *vinifera* of Europe.

In the midst of all this, something occurred which, for good or ill, settled the course of Eastern viticulture for a full century. It was the planting of a grape seed in 1843 by Ephraim Bull, of Concord, Massachusetts. With due local loyalty he named the resulting vine Concord and when it was exhibited for the first time, it was an instant sensation. In terms of vigor, hardiness, disease resistance, productivity, and beauty of fruit, it outshone anything else then in cultivation.

The development of the Concord grape had many good results: it made grape growing profitable; it provided a reliable and easily cared for source of fresh fruit as delicious as any table grapes grown in Europe, though altogether different in flavor; it made excellent jelly and provided the material for an easily stabilized, storable, and flavorful fresh fruit juice on which a large industry was built.

The ill effect, from the point of view of anyone who enjoys good wine, was that the Concord promptly took a place of dominance in the Eastern wine industry and has continued to hold this place, though its pronounced flavor and aroma, delicious as these are in the fresh fruit, do not come through well in dry table wines. In sweet wines, yes. And with appropriate manipulation it can serve as a base for fortified wines of the port and sherry types, or for the heavily sweetened nonfortified wines called kosher, or even (when picked while still unripe, decolorized, and somewhat deflavored) for a material out of which white and sparkling wines may be made. Though culturally ideal for the Northeast, its fruit is far from ideal in the winery.

The introduction of this grape had one other effect. Persons with some background in botany had long since come to realize that the cultivated native grapes were in fact accidental hybrids. But they had not taken the next step, which was of course to hybridize deliberately, choosing the parents with the conscious purpose of combining their characteristics. When he introduced the Concord, Ephraim Bull believed, and announced, that it was a cross between a wild *labrusca*, or fox grape, and the then widely cultivated Catawba. He may or may not have been right about that: it didn't really matter. What did matter was that the possibility of creating entirely new sorts of grapes by the hand of man was dramatically advertised and instantly seized upon. The grape is so malleable genetically that the possibilities are endless. Hybridizing the grape is indeed a little bit like playing God, and in the mid-nineteenth century it became a lifelong vocation for some and a sort of gentleman's hobby for many more. Every year saw the introduction of dozens of new hybrids, hundreds of them eventually described and illustrated in color (and for all practical purposes embalmed) in U. P. Hedrick's monumental tome *The Grapes of New York.**

The queen of these native hybrids was the Delaware, not a deliberate cross but nevertheless a hybrid of complex ancestry. It seems to have originated not in the state of Delaware but near the town of Delaware, Ohio, and can yield a white wine of very good quality. Its runner-up was the Dutchess, a hybrid introduced by A. J. Caywood, of Marlboro in the Hudson Valley of New York, and still grown to some extent. Other hybridizers who gained fame (though few of their productions have survived) were E. S. Rogers, of Salem, Massachusetts, and Jacob Moore of Brighton, New York. Unfortunately, the Eastern hybridizers depended for their American parentage mainly on the foxy *labrusca*, so that their productions, though often improvements, were almost invariably touched by the tail of the fox† and so rather less than ideal from the winemaking point of view.

Three other hybridizers whose work was of immense value not only for American viticulture but for European winemaking as well were Hermann Jaeger and Jacob Rommel, who lived and worked in the Missouri River Valley, and T. V. Munson, of Denison, Texas. These men had the advantage of working with a range of grape species unknown to Easterners, species whose potential was even greater than they perhaps realized. Their work coincided with the catastrophe of the phylloxera epidemic in France and it fell to their lot to provide much of the hybridizing material for the rootstocks on which Europe's vineyards were re-established. For his part in that lifesaving enterprise Munson was awarded the Ordre du Mérite Agricole by the French government.

However, the efforts of these men to replenish the vineyards of Europe remained secondary to their interest in pro-

---

* Hedrick's book has long since become a collector's item. But the color plates somehow escaped and continue to lead lives of their own. Reproductions from them are often to be seen on papier-mâché wastebaskets, trays, and other such humdrum items.
† In fact, a volatile compound called methyl anthranilate.

ducing new grapes of value for this country. Of the three,* Munson's work proved to be of the greatest permanent value, as Denison is in the Red River country, which turned out to be a sort of center of diffusion for grape species. He was first and last an outdoorsman and a tireless explorer, the perfect type for his vocation since much of the grapevine material in the unsettled country thereabouts had never been studied and described, let alone used for breeding. The hybrids he introduced, with their fanciful names like Lomanto and Manito and Wapanuka, ran into the hundreds and are illustrated and described in his book, *The Foundations of American Grape Culture*, which he published himself and which has lately been reprinted by the Denison Public Library. Not many of Munson's hybrids are grown extensively today, though a few have special value for the Southwest and for land bordering the Gulf of Mexico. In honor of his centenary an effort is under way to reassemble a collection of those Munson hybrids which still exist—the one monument that could have had meaning to him. Alas, his own experimental vineyard, his collection, and his nursery—a priceless storehouse of genetic material—went the way of all such things after his death. His chief work, however, was not his introduction of this variety or that but his discovery and identification of hitherto unknown species and his original classification of species. When Pierre Vialla was commissioned to make his famous *mission viticole* to the United States at the height of the phylloxera crisis, the man he most wanted to see was T. V. Munson. It would have been a privilege to be present when Munson and the urbane Frenchman met. They had much in common and much to discuss, language barrier or no.

In due course the "craze" for grape hybridizing died out, like the mulberry-silkworm craze and various other manias which

---

* And there were others who worked and corresponded with them, exchanging seeds and breeding material. One thinks of Bush and Meissner, whose comprehensive nursery catalog, in translation, has become a French classic.

have periodically swept American agriculture. The Eastern wine industry had accommodated itself to its limitations and settled down, reasonably content with its reliable Concords and Catawbas and Delawares. An entirely different viticulture emerged in California, where, blessed by a Mediterranean climate, the European grapes and especially those from the Mediterranean basin found conditions rivaling those of their origin. This is a separate story and will be discussed in the next chapter. After a two-hundred-year struggle to become established, Eastern winegrowing found itself confronted by a competitor it was entirely unprepared for and could not hope to match. A wealth of information on the early development of American agriculture can be found in the series of Annual Reports of the Department of Agriculture, the first of which was published in 1847 as a supplement to the Report of the Patent Office. Problems involving grapes and winegrowing were regularly treated. But California was not even admitted to the Union until 1850, and so as late as the Annual Report of 1861, California's potential for winegrowing was still not mentioned. By 1880 California shipments of wine had already begun to challenge the Eastern industry. Before the turn of the century California was producing 85 per cent of all our grapes, and an even greater percentage of all American wines.

Winemaking in California

 WE HAVE SEEN in the previous chapter how the connection was established, with so many frustrations and disappointments along the way, between the Old World grape and the indigenous grapes of the New. The story began with the pre-Columbian explorers and led eventually to a viticulture and a modest wine industry based on grapes quite different from those of Europe.

But there was a parallel development, beginning back in the sixteenth century, equally laborious but entirely different, which established a much more direct connection with the viticulture of Europe—indeed an extension of it.

California has what is technically a Mediterranean, or two-season, climate in which the rainfall is concentrated in the mild winter months and the long summers are hot, dry, and flooded with sunshine. The resemblance to the Mediterranean area proper is instantly apparent to anyone at all sensitive to environment, and it is supported by numerous analogies of temperature, rainfall, and humidity with stations in southern France, Italy, Spain, Greece, and Algeria. The

Old World grapes, and especially those native to the Mediterranean basin, find California conditions congenial. Therefore, California wines have a kinship with Mediterranean wines.

There is one important difference between viticultural California and the Mediterranean area. As one can see from the map on pages 18 and 19, the latter area is east-west in orientation and borders an inland sea. Viticultural California is a north-south region separated only by the unstable coastal ranges from the ocean. This produces variants of the "Mediterranean" type of climate unknown in the Mediterranean itself. So do the range of altitudes in California and their placement as well as the presence of that arid but enormously fertile inland basin known as the Central Valley, which is as though the Mediterranean Sea were a dry plain.

The coast counties yield California's best dry wines, red and white. These counties have the Golden Gate and San Francisco Bay as their hub. The rule is that those counties running directly into the bay produce the best wines, and that the farther one gets from the tempering maritime influence, the hotter the climate and the less fine the wines. The chief beneficiaries are Sonoma, Napa, and Alameda counties, with Santa Clara and San Benito pushing them closely.

Two other important gaps in the coastal ranges provide a tempering maritime influence not unlike that of the Golden Gate: the Russian River gap north of San Francisco, leading back into Sonoma and Mendocino counties, and the Salinas River gap, with the Salinas River flowing up from the south just east of the first coastal range and emptying into Monterey Bay. The areas behind these two gaps have lately been scenes of large new plantings of the better wine grapes.

The vineyards of the coast counties, though extensive, are dwarfed by comparison with those of the Central Valley. This immense basin lying between the coastal ranges and the Sierras is divided into the Sacramento Valley at the north, the San Joaquin Valley at the south, and the Central Valley proper in between. It is the greatest raisin-producing region of the world and the leading table-grape region of the United

States. The San Joaquin Valley is also the principal growing region for the Sultanina, or Thompson's Seedless—the seedless raisin grape and also the chief table grape of our supermarkets, which enters in vast quantities into the cheaper grades of wine. So its growers have a shot at three quite different markets, which is a comfort. This grape is immensely productive, hence cheap, and its effect on the wine industry is to lower quality.

There is little rainfall in the San Joaquin, and not many years ago it was a baking desert. The valley is still blistering hot, but under irrigation its rich soil is enormously productive. It is an awe-inspiring experience to fly the length of the valley in summer and note the abrupt divisions between green and brown that signify the borders of the irrigated parts.

Unfortunately, desert heat combined with such unremitting sunshine, and the production of truly superior wines, do not go hand in hand. In this inland valley large quantities of the more prolific wine varieties are grown, for sweet fortified wines and for table wines, primarily the same ones that have been cultivated for years in the south of France, Algeria, and elsewhere in the Mediterranean basin.

To the south, around Los Angeles, lies California's third viticultural region, much less important than the other two. Though least important today, it was in this southern region that California's first vines were planted, two centuries ago. But to tell the California story from its beginning one must go back further than that.

Vines and cuttings are known to have been brought from Spain to Mexico as early as 1524, when Cortez was Governor of Mexico, on the initiative of the Spanish mission fathers. The padres had a more powerful incentive for doing this than most of the settlers along the Atlantic seaboard. As mission priests they had to have wine for the celebration of the mass. If they couldn't grow their own wine, it had to be brought for them all the way from Spain, not an easy thing to do in those days. And being Spaniards, they considered wine as essential a part of daily fare as bread. Much of Mexico was hardly more congenial for the Old World vine than the North Atlantic coast, but they had strong motives for trying.

The credit for succeeding, which happened, of all places, on the bleak and barren peninsula of Baja California, is traditionally given to the strong-minded and strong-muscled Jesuit padre Juan de Ugarte. One source says that he got across to Baja from the mainland in 1697; another, that he did not make it permanently until 1701. No matter. What does matter is that he got a vineyard going at the mission of Lareto at a time when the colonies on the Eastern seaboard had hardly begun to be filled out. His vineyard was soon providing wine for the other missions of the peninsula as well as his own. The Jesuit historian Father John F. Bannon states that by the time the Jesuits were expelled in 1767, the surplus was often used for barter with mainland Mexico and some had even found its way back to Europe.

As the chain of missions spread northward, grape cuttings went with them and new vineyards were established. And so it is that the Old World grape eventually reached Alta California, where it was first grown at the Mission San Diego. The date usually given is 1769, the founding year of that mission, and the man responsible was the redoubtable Father Junípero Serra, throughout his lifetime the dominant figure in the California mission system.* From then until now California has never seen a year without a vintage of a sort. Such difficulties as were encountered in the expansion of winegrowing, and there were many, had no parallel with those encountered on the East Coast because here, on the West Coast, the Eurasian wine had found an ideal second home.

Here enters an ampelographic puzzle. The vineyard at Lareto, and those of the other missions as the system spread north into California proper, was based on a single *cepa*, or

---

* Junípero Serra was a Mallorcan born in the village of Petra, where his birthplace has been restored and a museum and library relating to his career have been established. A visit there is a delightful and rewarding pilgrimage.

grape variety—a variety subsequently known appropriately as the Mission (Criolla, in Spanish). It is most definitely a *vinifera*, yet nowhere in Spain, nor anywhere else in the Mediterranean lands, does this identical grape exist. The conclusion must be that it was not brought from Europe as a rooted vine or cutting but that it had its origin in the New World from an Old World seed—seeds travel much better than living vines or cuttings. The seeds of grapevines rarely if ever come true. Thus the Mission need not have a European counterpart to be a true *vinifera* of strictly European parentage.

From Father Serra's mission, San Diego, the chain of missions continued to extend northward along the coast and into the inland valleys behind the coastal range. By 1805 all twenty-one of the missions of the Spanish period had been established, from San Diego to Sonoma. At all of them the vine had been planted and cultivated diligently (by the local Indian subjects, to be sure, not the fathers). In all but a few it succeeded.

But to say that the vine succeeded is not to suggest that the missions did much more than a hit-or-miss job. The quality of their wine was indifferent. The virtues of the single variety they grew, the Mission, are vigor, fruitfulness, and dependability, not high wine quality. The surplus beyond the fathers' own needs was bartered or sold, some of it even exported. But no real effort was made by them to exploit California's viticultural potential systematically or even intelligently, and the quantities of wine produced were never large by commercial standards. To its end the mission system was only fitfully commercial and only incidentally concerned with much beyond the glory of God and its own perpetuation, and wine remained basically a subsistence crop even though prices had to be set by the government.

By the decade of the 1830's the missions were in decline. Doomed by the rise of the secular spirit, the missions began to fall apart. The vineyards and the winemaking premises deteriorated along with all the rest. The missions had shown the way, but viticulturally and in every other respect they had had their day.

Not until that time did secular or purely commercial wine-growing begin; and as one might expect this took place in the area where the mission fathers had been most successful, close to the pueblo Los Angeles. Just who was the "father" of this phase is a moot question. The first secular winegrower, and the first American one, was probably Joseph Chapman, but he disappeared swiftly from the scene. A better claimant to fatherhood at this turning point was Jean Louis Vignes, an appropriately named Frenchman. He saw, as perhaps only a Frenchman would, the geographical correspondence between California and the Mediterranean region. He knew the difference between superior wine and ordinary wine. He knew well that there were better grapes for such a climate than the productive but mediocre Mission. He broadened the *encépagement* (as the French call it) by bringing in some other and better varieties, though not a great many. He was a cooper too; and let us not underestimate the ability to fell a tree and make a tight cask out of it. In this country today coopering is a dying trade.

Vignes, who came to be known as Don Luis, made a very good thing out of his enterprise and became a leading citizen. He brought in two diligent and accomplished nephews, the Sansevaine brothers, founders of one of the historic California wine houses. Another picturesque character, William Wolf-skill, moved in and provided competition.

The swift success of these and a few others had its effect. This was a buoyant and free-spending time, thanks to gold. The mood of California's surging population was speculative. Soon these first successful enterprises set off a cheerfully chaotic grape-and-wine boom quite as frenzied in its way as the Gold Rush.

The wine boom was not confined to the southern area. The potential of the Santa Clara and Sonoma and Napa valleys became a subject first of rumor and then of action. There was an expansion of vineyards in the foothills of the Sierras next to the prospectors and their takings. As the sea of vine-yards planted in the fifties began to bear, Ohio's modest 1860 claim to primacy disappeared, never to reappear. Which is not to say that the expansion of winegrowing in California went smoothly. What was needed in this anarchic situation was an energizer with a personality forceful enough to put across the necessity for standards of quality and for finding better grapes and planting them in the right places.

Such a man did emerge in the person of Ágoston Haraszthy de Mokcsa, a cultivated man and a member of the minor Hungarian nobility but a frontiersman at heart. There is a current tendency to denigrate his accomplishment, and with some reason, for he was by temperament a promoter, an un-disciplined character, and to put the best face on it a "poor businessman." But he provided a focus of attention that the young industry badly needed.

He was a native of a corner of Hungary that is now part of Yugoslavia, an army officer and a civil servant. But he broke with the establishment (not for the last time in his life) and was forced to flee the country in disguise; in the spring of 1840 he finally reached a site on the Wisconsin River, now called Sauk City, which he named Haraszthy in honor of himself and where he proposed to make wine. After a char-acteristically frenetic decade his interest waned; and by 1850 we find him transplanted with his progeny (his three sons were named Géza, Attila, and Árpád) to San Diego, then still a fairly uncouth place. In no time flat he became a leading citizen, and within the year he had been appointed sheriff and busied himself subduing the Indians. Two years later he was elected to California's General Assembly, in which body he promptly made himself a conspicuous figure. But like Sauk City, San Diego failed to hold him: his attention was diverted to San Mateo County (what choices there were in those days!), and it was then, apparently, that he began to consider seriously California's winegrowing possibilities. For such individuals, to think is to act—in this case, to bring in cuttings of grape varieties from Europe. If it is true that the

Count/Colonel Ágoston Haraszthy.

The 1870 vintage at Buena Vista, founded by Ágoston Haraszthy.
(Eadweard Muybridge photograph)

Muscat of Alexandria was among these, and it seems to have been, then he must be accounted the "father" of California's present raisin industry. Other cuttings followed. Just what they were is now lost to the record, but it was long thought probable that one of them was the Zinfandel, which in a comparatively short time ousted the Mission as the staple variety and is still a mainstay. How it acquired the name, no one knows, nor had its European origin been determined until fairly recently. It appears now that Zinfandel was not one of Haraszthy's importations but reached California by another route, possibly via the nursery of William Prince on Long Island, where various *vinifera* had been tried without success, including one called Zinfandel. Dr. Austin Goheen, a U.S.D.A. plant pathologist stationed at the University of California at Davis, places its origin in southwest Italy near Taranto, where an apparently identical grape is grown as Primitivo di Gioia.

Whatever the origin of the Zinfandel, Colonel Haraszthy's contributions (he dropped the title of Count) were numerous and important if disorderly.

His main accomplishments were to persuade the state to appoint a Viticultural Commission to guide the development of the industry, and to send Haraszthy himself on a *voyage d'études* to Europe. In the course of this journey he sent back more than 100,000 vines and cuttings of many hundreds of varieties; a good proportion of these somehow survived the hard trip to California. Thus in one massive importation much of the viticultural capital of a thousand years of European winegrowing was made suddenly available to Californians.

By this time the restless colonel had moved from San Mateo to a piece of land in Sonoma Valley, a change perhaps inspired by the knowledge that the best of the Franciscan wines had come from there. Here he had established his nursery, his vineyard, and his winery. From here the results of his European trip were disseminated. It would be pleasant to say that these riches were systematically distributed and studied. They weren't. To begin with, the state refused to repay Haraszthy. And for all his enthusiasm, or perhaps because of it, Haraszthy was not a methodical man. The vines were dispersed helter-skelter. Many lost their identity. Many were lost in mishandling. Yet much of this enormous range of material did get planted. And if it has taken another century to bring order out of the chaos and reduce California's *encépagement* to the thirty or forty best-adapted varieties, much of the material out of which these choices could be made was there mainly because of Haraszthy's energy and enthusiasm.* Having made a substantial contribution, he disappeared from the scene almost as abruptly as he had appeared, and under something of a cloud at that; the ambitious winemaking enterprise he founded was a commercial failure. But his original Buena Vista cellars near the town of Sonoma have been restored and are in production today.

The expansion continued, and California wines began to go East in some quantity. In 1862 for the first time the *Annual Report* of the U.S. Department of Agriculture acknowledged the existence of a California winegrowing industry by devoting a few pages to it. But there were clouds on the horizon. These burst in the slump of 1876, indirectly the result of the Eastern panic of 1874 but complicated by other factors such as the continued absence of quality standards—a failing that by then had built up a substantial backlog of dissatisfied customers—the prevailing ignorance of sound winemaking techniques, overproduction, and the prevalence of dubious trade practices, including much outright falsification.

* Of course, this importation was supplemented before and after from many other sources and by many other persons, with much duplication. To cite a single example, Louis Mel, a Frenchman from Bordeaux and a pioneer in Livermore Valley, brought in the Sauvignon Blanc and Sémillon from Château d'Yquem, doing much to establish Livermore Valley's reputation for white wines.

*Inglenook, built to last by Captain Gustave Niebaum in 1887,
re-established after prohibition by John Daniel,
and now part of United Vintners.*

These accumulated difficulties led finally to action. The
better winegrowers banded together and in 1880 got the state
legislature to pass the Pure Wine Law, with teeth, to end the
grosser types of fraud. This law had its positive as well as its
purely regulatory purpose. Its title, "An Act for the *Promotion*
of the Viticultural Interests of the State," indicates as much.
A Board of Viticultural Commissioners was charged with
bringing order out of the commercial chaos. At the same time
the State Agricultural Experiment Station, headed by Dr.
E. W. Hilgard, and the University of California were charged
with a parallel task in the combined areas of viticulture and
enology.

Thanks to the wisdom and the personalities of Charles A.
Wetmore (the leading commissioner) and Dr. Hilgard this
tandem arrangement worked well in spite of a fair bit of
feuding along the way—the one concentrating on the "practical," or business, aspects and the other concentrating on
production know-how, without which, of course, there isn't

much point to staying in business. Both were working toward the same end: the improvement of California wines. (It is pleasant to record, also, that since the repeal of prohibition the university and the contemporary trade organization, the Wine Institute, have continued to work in harmony.) Under the law, and with the cooperation of a sufficient number of growers and wineries, Professor Hilgard was able to carry out investigations into many aspects of winegrowing, especially the problems peculiar to winemaking in hot climates, and to begin sorting out the varietal confusion.

Quality standards and commercial standards were established and enforced, and by degrees the right grapes were fitted to the right districts—varieties and districts not greatly different from those dominating the scene still. To read those early reports of Hilgard, giving the results of innumerable small fermentations of countless grape varieties harvested from every reachable part of the state, is to behold a powerful and original mind at work and to realize how much a region, a people, and an industry can be indebted to a single man. He spoke to an industry, and the industry listened. California winegrowers rewon the faith and credit of the consuming public, and continued to expand in a more orderly way. The memory of this dedicated man is perpetuated in *Hilgardia,* the journal of the California Agricultural Experiment Station.

The Californians were beginning to discover, in the meantime, that they had another enemy to put down besides their early reputation. That was the phylloxera. No one knows precisely when or how this native of the East got over the Rocky Mountains. But it got there, most likely by grapevine importations from the East, perhaps the Zinfandel—just as it had gotten to Europe. And it was greeted as it had been in Europe. First it mystified, then it was dismissed as a passing blight, then it was fought with oratory and indignation, and finally it aroused something approaching panic. But the panic never reached the intensity that it reached in Europe, for the phylloxera has never worked its destruction so rapidly in California. In fact, there are important areas that are phylloxera-free, notably parts of the Salinas, San Benito, and San Joaquin valleys, where ungrafted vines are grown and still being planted.

Because the phylloxera spread slowly, the fight against it (by grafting, as in Europe) could be launched in sufficient time to save the infected vineyards. But the counterattack against the phylloxera had no sooner been mounted than a major diversion appeared in the neighborhood of Anaheim, then a big grape-growing center lying south and east of Los Angeles. The Anaheim district had its beginning as a quasi-religious cooperative in the 1850's.* But piety did not keep the symptoms of a mysterious new disease from appearing suddenly in the 1880's in these vineyards. It was not the phylloxera, nor could its source and identity be established, and no satisfactory treatment was discovered. It was swiftly fatal, and so contagious that in the ten years between 1884 and 1894 no less than 30,000 acres of vines were wiped out and the district plunged into ruin. Fortunately the Anaheim disease, after raging for a decade, began to lose its virulence and hence did not cause great losses in other areas. Yet it is recurrent, and under its contemporary name of Pierce's disease it is in the ascendant again in parts of the Central Valley and in the Napa Valley. Pierce's disease appears to be indigenous to a broad belt bordering the Gulf of Mexico and stretching all across the southern states, and in parts of that area is a decisive obstacle to grape growing. Its symptoms resemble those of the French virus disease *court noué*. The best current opinion is that it is not a virus but a virus-like disease. The distinction is important.

Around the turn of the century a new source of anxiety began to emerge, a threat potentially more damaging to the young industry than phylloxera and Pierce's disease put together. This was the growing sentiment for prohibition. The center of the bull's-eye was hard liquor, personified as the

* V. P. Carosso, *The California Wine Industry, 1830–1895*. Berkeley: University of California Press, 1951. This monograph has been drawn upon at numerous points in this chapter.

demon rum; and there is no doubt that the misuse of strong
drink was then a social problem—as it always has been and
always will be. But the full target soon came to include alcohol
in any form, and so of course wine found itself in the line of
fire, even though its contribution to the alcohol problem was
negligible in an essentially non-wine-using culture.

The winemaking fraternity treated the threat of prohibition just as they had the phylloxera: first telling each other
that the movement was largely an affair of fanatics and of too
little importance to matter, then speaking of it with indignation, and finally developing symptoms of panic. They found
state after state closing the door to what they grew and made.
By 1915 they had their backs to the wall, like condemned
men facing a firing squad. They made statements denouncing
prohibition as "virtual confiscation of property without pay-
ment," as indeed it was. The long and honorable place held
by wine in the history of mankind was cited with pathetic
eloquence. The ultimate futility of sumptuary legislation, pit-
ting the police power against the will and habits of any significant proportion of the population, was argued with equal
eloquence. But to no avail. In due course the highly organized
political power of the prohibitionists prevailed. The Eighteenth Amendment was ratified and took effect January 16,
1920.

Thus after a short and eventful life of little more than
sixty years, the secular wine industry of California was destroyed, or so people thought, as was the Eastern wine industry. Some 700 wineries were affected by this act of destruction,
most of them rather small but a few of very large capacity.
Some held on for a year or two as bonded wineries and
warehouses, then passed out of existence. A few stuck it out,
keeping body and soul together by the legal production of
sacramental wine; for though wine on the dining-room table
had become profane and illegal, it was still sacred in the
churches—the ancient symbol of the blood of Christ.

Now, better than half a century later, the grotesqueness of
prohibition in practice is hard to evoke, even from personal

memory. Socially, the effects were wholly deplorable and an everlasting discredit to those who brought it into being. It failed to prevent the use of alcoholic beverages, it fostered a vast illegal liquor industry, destroyed standards of taste, and, far more serious, corrupted both public and private morality. Without broad public consensus to back it up, the police power was useless—as is always the case in a country that considers itself free. The age of the bootlegger is one of the blots on American history and I shall not dwell on it further except to mention one unexpected way in which it perverted the grape-growing industry.

The vineyardists of California, with no wineries to sell to, began to ship their grapes all the way to Eastern markets for amateur winemakers. But in this curious trade the desideratum was not wine quality but shipping quality. The profitable grapes were those that could survive the transcontinental trip, not those best for wine; and so after all the effort to improve the California *encépagement*, prohibition degraded even that. Superior vines were abandoned or uprooted in favor of inferior ones. It was not the most destructive thing about prohibition, but it was surely one of the most ironic. Only the conscientious growers of superior vines were penalized. Under prohibition California's annual production of wine grapes doubled, and toward the end enough were being shipped east each year to produce approximately ninety million gallons a year.

There is no point in lingering any longer over this episode in our social history. It is enough to say that the end of prohibition found California with its head bloody, yet eager to rebuild what had not quite been destroyed. How well it has succeeded is a matter for the next chapter.

CHAPTER 5

The Contemporary Scene

 ANOTHER DAWN finally broke with the repeal of prohibition in 1933—the beginning of the contemporary period of American winemaking. East and west, the wineries that had survived were in wretched condition. The rest were in ruins or been had diverted to other uses. Worse, the ranks of experienced winemakers had been severely depleted by old age and death and no new generation had been trained to succeed them. The California growers, though they had survived well and profitably thanks to thirsty amateurs, were no longer oriented toward wine quality. For Eastern growers there had not even been the solace of that amateur market for grapes, and viticulture was in a state of collapse.

Short of know-how, short of equipment and capital, and short of the grapes it needed, the winegrowing industry had to be born all over again. And I think no one will be offended when I write that much of the early post-prohibition production was poor stuff. How could it have been otherwise? The saving grace, I suppose, was that a generation reared on what

Al Capone and his kind had to peddle didn't know the difference.

But the speed of recovery (and having watched this recovery closely from its beginning I can say this with authority) was nothing short of miraculous. The few surviving Eastern wineries, principally the sparkling-wine producers of New York State, soon found their bearings again, in some cases bringing in European winemakers to supply the needed expertise. In California, Professor Frederic Bioletti, who had succeeded E. W. Hilgard and had presided over most of the long moratorium, did not live to participate in the rebirth. But he left behind several dedicated contemporaries and a remarkable group of students, whose competence in their several fields was strengthened by their personal compatibility and a shared conception of the job that lay before them. They remained the core of the faculty at the experiment station and department of viticulture and enology at Davis until the mid-1970's, though the time for their retirement had arrived, and one by one they began to step aside.

The department at Davis was and is well supported by the state and by the industry; no praise is too high for the work that has been done there since the repeal of prohibition—in original ampelographic, genetic, and enological research and in disseminating the results. The Davis department is one of the great specialized schools of the world, ranking with those of Bordeaux, Montpellier, and Geisenheim. The experiment station at Geneva, New York, is its Eastern counterpart.

In California the industry-supported Wine Institute and its affiliated Wine Advisory Board soon took up the work of the old Viticultural Commission and much more besides. These were the educational and protective arms of the industry in its relations with government and the public, and at the same time the agencies for the encouragement and support of research and for the enforcement of quality and other standards within the industry itself. The Eastern wineries and growers have had nothing quite like them, but they have nevertheless found an effective modus operandi.

In spite of the mediocrity of the first post-prohibition

wines, there was a good public response. In the first full year of repeal, consumption of all wine in the United States (excluding the continuing output of homemade wine) amounted to about 38 million gallons, of which about 4 million gallons were imported. By the year of our entry into World War II, 1941, consumption of tax-paid wine had jumped to about 104 million gallons, the fraction of imported wine remaining at about the same figure of 4 million gallons. The largest total consumption in any one year before prohibition had been 54 million gallons. Of the 1941 consumption of 104 million, 88 million were made in California, and the state has continued to hold this dominant position.

The war created exceptional conditions for the wineries. Imports were practically eliminated, and the conversion of whisky distilleries to war production of alcohol broadened the market for wines. These conditions led to an "invasion" of the liquor interests into winemaking, which naturally caused apprehension, for the liquor business is in certain respects the antithesis of the wine trade. Yet the effects of the invasion were by no means wholly bad. It brought financial strength to an industry still badly in need of it. It brought skill in advertising and distribution. And the industry was by no means swallowed up. The main interest of the whisky people was the mass production of "standard" wine and in particular of the cheap fortified sweet wines. For the most part, the smaller wineries concerned with producing quality wines were not affected. The invasion touched none of the old Eastern producers of still and sparkling wines and only a few of their counterparts in California. By the time the war ended, more than one of the "invaders" had found that they weren't really so very interested in wine, and withdrew. (Some returned to winemaking later, as we shall see.)

California Today

In the mid-1960's California had something under 500,000 bearing acres, yielding 3 million tons of grapes a year more or less, making them the state's largest agricultural crop: more important than oranges and lemons, plums and prunes, pears, peaches, nuts, lettuce and other vegetables, cotton, rice, sugar beets. . . .

Grape growing can mean several things in California: table-grape growing, raisin growing, winegrowing. At the time when these figures were compiled, roughly one-half of the total grape crop ended up in the wineries, for the production of 130 to 180 million gallons of wine a year.

That's a good bit of wine. But a closer look at the totals for those years yields an unsettling discovery. Only one-third of the production was of still table wines. The rest, definitely not for the family dinner table, consisted of cheap, high-alcohol dessert wines, plus about 1 per cent of champagne and a miscellany of specialties such as vermouth. The California wine industry was, and to a degree still is, two industries. Many table-wine producers make or at least market dessert wines, sometimes including a brandy, to complete their commercial "line," and the big dessert-wine people offer a reverse selection. There is no sense pretending that cheap dessert wines and brandy are not part of the liquor industry, and to the extent that the winemakers served this market, they were held in the same defensive posture as liquor manufacturers.

But then a heartening thing happened. Year by year the production and use of table wines began to creep up on that of the fortified wines in response to a change of public taste. In 1966 production of the two types was almost equal. In 1967 or 1968 (depending on whether the base is production or actual consumption) the halfway mark was passed. In those years, from the point of view of the proponent of table wine, the tail stopped wagging the dog as far as the domestic wine industry was concerned. In the subsequent years the proportion of table wine kept right on increasing, even as the totals of all sorts of wine grew remarkably. The chart on page 64 traces the course of the industry quite vividly, from 1956 through 1973, in terms of the amount of wine produced each year, the build-up of inventories (which must always exceed production), and actual marketings. When one looks behind these three factors, what emerges as the most important thing about this growth is the awakening interest in table wines. Thus of the 243 million gallons shipped in 1973 no less than 165 million gallons were table wines, or nearly three times the quantity of ten years before.

This is a basic change, and there are as many ways of accounting for it as there are students of the subject. But what it adds up to is a discovery by Americans generally of the virtues of wine as a good and wholesome beverage. A nation's diet changes only slowly, but around the middle 1960's the

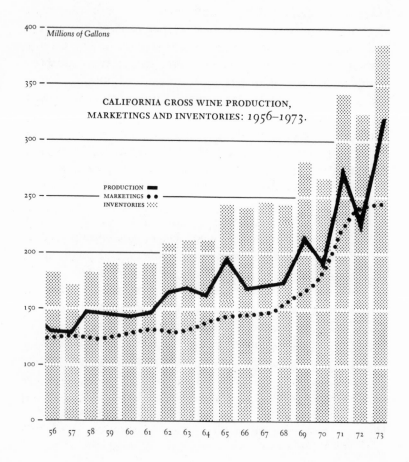

CALIFORNIA GROSS WINE PRODUCTION,
MARKETINGS AND INVENTORIES: 1956–1973.

American diet did begin to change, making a place for table wine. Some few decades ago its use was pretty well confined to two categories of the population: families in modest circumstances of Mediterranean or central European origin who had not yet broken with the customs of the homeland and for whom wine was a part of the normal food pattern; and at the other extreme the well-to-do and widely traveled. Now that division has been obliterated, and the use of wine has flowed over what were class lines.

So the United States saw the birth of what some like to call "the wine revolution." It began at the point of consumption, as it had to, but was instantly echoed throughout the industry. Better table wines need better vines; immense new plantings were undertaken, and so confidently that in some ways they recalled the grape fever of the mid-nineteenth century. Some 40,000 acres of these new vineyards produced grapes for the first time in 1974, and like quantities came into bearing in 1975 and 1976. (The unavoidable result: temporary surpluses, as the more prudent anticipated.) A few comparisons will show how badly the better grapes were needed. In 1962 there were only 150 acres of Chardonnay in all of California,* but today there are 7,368 acres, counting those not yet in bearing; similarly, in 1962 there were 300 acres of Pinot Noir and 660 acres of Cabernet Sauvignon but today 7,804 and 18,916 acres respectively. What is true of such *cépages nobles* is likewise true of plantings for wines of more modest pretension, particularly in the Central Valley: huge new vineyards with emphasis on better quality.

Naturally the question arose: Where should the new vineyards be planted? Urbanism presses relentlessly on the older premium areas, and quality wine cannot be grown just anywhere. There has been an explosive development of winegrowing in new areas possessing the necessary requirements of climate and water supply: in the Salinas and San Benito valleys, in the upper Sonoma and its tributary valleys, on most

---

* A. J. Winkler, *General Viticulture*. Berkeley: University of California Press, 1962.

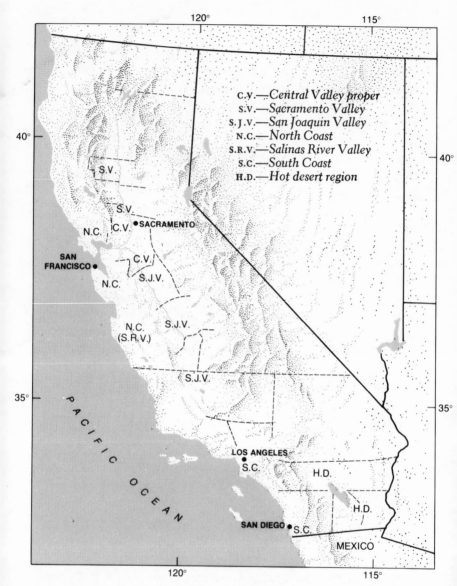

c.v.—*Central Valley proper*
s.v.—*Sacramento Valley*
s.j.v.—*San Joaquin Valley*
n.c.—*North Coast*
s.r.v.—*Salinas River Valley*
s.c.—*South Coast*
h.d.—*Hot desert region*

CALIFORNIA'S WINEGROWING DISTRICTS.

of the remaining acreage in the Napa Valley and the surrounding area, in promising new parts of southern California. A parallel expansion of winery capacity has occurred:

very large wineries and very small ones, luxurious ones and humble ones. There have been acquisitions and enlargements of famous old wineries. Established wineries have paid off their bank loans and refurbished themselves. Capital has poured in from the food, brewing, and distilling industries, and from abroad. Heavily promoted "tax loss" enterprises have been launched. Old-timers who had been through boom-and-bust episodes in the past began to shake their heads. The new prospect was exciting, but it is easy to overdo a good thing. And as a matter of fact the coming-in of the first huge new blocks of vineyard was an upsetting experience. By 1974 wine sales had leveled off somewhat. Inventories were high. The fantastic prices paid for the better grapes in 1972 and 1973 fell off drastically to more realistic levels.

For the time being caution and in some cases anxiety has replaced euphoria. Adjustments, not always painless, are in order. But behind all this lies the unquestionable truth that a fundamental change in consumption patterns has come about. And because it was so slow in coming, we may be confident that it is here to stay and may assume that after the present pause the growth in the use of wine as a normal element of the American food pattern will continue.

Many fine guides to California's vineyards, wines, and wineries are available,* so I will not go over the same ground in any great detail. Yet it may be worthwhile to touch briefly on each of the state's principal winegrowing regions—always remembering that in so changeable a situation what is written today may be obsolete tomorrow.

CENTRAL VALLEY.   This is pre-eminently the region of cheap dessert-wine production, which is concentrated in Fresno, Kern, Tulare, Madera, Merced, Stanislaus, and San Joaquin counties. The cloudless summers with their intense

---

* For some titles see the Bibliography.

heat and negligible humidity, plus rich soil and irrigation, make for huge crops and high sugar content. Sugar and alcohol are the desiderata in the production of dessert wines. But most of California's "standard" or jug table wine is also produced in the valley; and by and large the same grapes of Mediterranean origin have always been used for both: for red, Carignane most of all, then Zinfandel, Barbera, Grenache, Petite Sirah, Alicante Bouschet, Mission; for white, the ubiquitous Thompson Seedless, French Columbard, Muscat of Alexandria, Palomino, and surplus table grapes.

These inexpensive wines for everyday consumption are as a rule well made, on a highly industrialized basis. They run rather high in alcohol, are short on fruitiness, neutral to coarse in flavor, naturally low in acidity. They are typical hot-country wines, and certainly superior in quality to the run of French *ordinaire*. The red is better than the white, again a characteristic of hot-country wines. Central Valley vineyards are the main sources of the flavored "pop" wines as well, a vogue of doubtful permanence.

A proportion of the standard wine is set aside to be blended with wines of superior quality brought in from the coast counties. Most of the recent plantings have been made with an eye to producing better table wines without having to lean on the coast counties for blending. Some of the new *métis* from the university are playing an important role in this improvement, grapes like Ruby Cabernet, Carnelian, Rubired, Royalty, Emerald Riesling, as well as the best of the well-adapted older ones such as Colombard, Chenin Blanc, Petite Sirah, Barbera.

The object is to produce a range of wines that would fall between the standard wines and the elite vintages in quality and price. The first such wines, sometimes called Valley Varietals or California Country Wines, are on the market, and there will be more. They represent a good step forward. The valley production is pretty well dominated by such big names as Gallo, East Side, United Vintners, Guild, Perelli-Minetti, Franzia, and Bear Mountain.

SOUTHERN CALIFORNIA. This is where it all started, centering around what was once the pueblo Los Angeles. It is a region separated by mountains from the inner basin of the Central Valley, and its climate is somewhat tempered by exposure to wind and moisture from the Pacific. Geographically set apart, it has gone its own way, the great name being Guasti (now Brookside), which once boasted "the largest vineyard in the world." Smog and urban sprawl have raised hob with the Cucamonga district, lying east of

Outdoor crushing station and fermenting tanks;
industrial methods applied to bulk wine production.

Los Angeles, which was its center. Yet neighboring and related districts, Rancho California lying southeast in Riverside County, and parts of Santa Barbara and San Luis Obispo counties, lying along the coast northwest of Los Angeles, are participating in the current vineyard expansion. Though the standard Central Valley varieties dominate here too, they do not do so to quite the same extent; and some of the wines, for instance Zinfandel, show marked differences of character. There is some emphasis on the specifically Italian varieties, and many of the wines have an engaging roughness that somewhat recalls those to be had straight from barrel to pitcher in the *trattorias* of Italy.

NORTH COAST (*Northern Counties*).   The two counties of Napa and Sonoma, lying north of San Francisco Bay, plus the northern extension of the Sonoma Valley into Mendocino County, still produce more superior red and white table wine from more wineries than all the rest of the state. This is California's wine country par excellence.

The town of Napa is easily and quickly reached from San Francisco by the Golden Gate Bridge. But arrival there can be a letdown for the wine seeker both because a big and confusing bypass scoots around it and because it isn't a wine town anyway. The vines begin farther on along Route 29, which is this country's equivalent of the *Weinstrasse* of the German Palatinate or the *Routes du vin* that meander through the vineyards of Alsace, the French Burgundy region, and the Médoc. But Route 29 doesn't meander: it goes straight up the west side of the Napa Valley. Beginning before you reach Yountville the vineyards are much in evidence, and, interspersed with wineries, they soon are practically continuous to St. Helena and beyond. A complementary highway, the Silverado Trail, follows the east side of the valley. The diligent seeker will go up one side and down the other, though most of the wineries are still actually on the Route 29 side: such familiar names as Inglenook, Beaulieu, Louis Martini, Beringer, Charles Krug, Christian Brothers; newer names such as

Oakville, Robert Mondavi, Heitz, Hanns Kornell, Sterling, Souverain. Up in the hills and not visible from the road are Mont La Salle of Christian Brothers, a big winery, as well as modest ones such as Mayacamas, Stony Hill, Schramsberg, Cuvaison, Burgess, and Chappellet. Here is one region given over to wine and nothing else.

Two or three points about Napa Valley (and Sonoma as well) ought to be made clear. One is that this is essentially red-wine rather than white-wine country. Some good white

Mont La Salle, above Napa Valley on the west side.

Cabernet Sauvignon, California's best red-wine grape.

wines are made, to be sure, just as good white wines are made in the Italian Piedmont and Tuscany. But as in those celebrated regions, they are exceptions, stoutly though the valley wine men will dispute it. Napa Valley makes twice as much red as white, Sonoma Valley four times as much.

Another point is that not all of the wines are "fine." As a matter of fact, most of them are not. Here, as everywhere else, the heavy-producing ordinary varieties are preponderant. But the ordinary varieties produce wine of better quality here than, shall we say, in the Central Valley. Carignane from Fresno is coarse; that from Napa Valley is well balanced and far better. A Zinfandel from most parts of the Central Valley is "hot" and flat-tasting: one from Napa, when well made and cared for, is fruity and elegant—a revelation. Because the standard wines from here are consistently superior to those of other regions, they are much used in blending to upgrade the latter.

A third point is that most north-coast wineries are not at all averse to blending, as the occasion may demand, "stretching" the wines of their better grapes with cheaper and more plentiful wines of their own or their neighbors. The whole industry for that matter does a great deal of trading about. It is a practice that purists object to in principle, but it is in no sense dishonorable, providing no deception is involved. And indeed a blended wine is often superior to any one of its constituents. Most California Pinot Noir gains by being firmed up with a proportion of something else. Cabernet Sauvignon is more often than not improved by an admixture of Merlot. There exist houses of good reputation which produce little wine of their own but confine themselves to the purchase, blending, and upbringing of other people's wines.

An offshoot of the Napa Valley vineyards is the Carneros district, of recent planting, which lies south and west of Napa. Strongly influenced by the bay, it used to be thought too cool. Today its cooler climate is seen to be a key to quality. The vineyards stretch along a side road (Route 121) connecting the southern ends of Napa and Sonoma valleys.

Sonoma Valley is parallel with Napa, Sonoma lying closer to the Pacific and separated from Napa by the Mayacamas range. Unlike Napa, Sonoma is not a narrow valley that can be taken in at a glance, with the small mountains pressing in from both sides, but rather a rolling plain having twice the length, many times the breadth, and twice as many wineries, producing nearly twice as much wine. In terms of quality, each of the valleys has its partisans. A fair statement would be that Napa produces more really notable individual vintages, but that enough are produced in Sonoma to challenge the argument for Napa's intrinsic superiority. No better wine has been made in California than that from the small and luxuriously equipped Hanzell winery (a plaything of the late J. D. Zellerbach), located in that subregion of Sonoma known as the Valley of the Moon. But early circumstances in the Sonoma Valley—particularly the establishment of the Italian Swiss Colony by Andrea Sbarbaro in the 1880's in the uppermost end of the valley near Cloverdale—placed the emphasis on wines of intermediate quality. A substantial proportion of the valley's production became and still is tributary to this huge enterprise, until recently a part of the United Vintners combine. Except for Hanzell and a few others, there has not until these past few years been much emphasis on the *cépages nobles*.

Thanks to "the wine revolution," the pattern in Sonoma Valley is now changing rapidly. Traveling down the valley from north (in Mendocino County) to south, one still notes many of the old familiar names, mostly Italian: Parducci, Pedroncelli, Rege, Nervo, Simi, Cambiaso, Foppiano, Martini and Prati, Buena Vista, Sebastiani. But supplementing the old vineyards there are large new ones, many of them still not in full bearing. And there are new names, too: Château Souverain, Ville Fontaine, Windsor, and (perhaps surprisingly) Gallo, Cresta Blanca, Weibel, Widmer (the latter having come west from the New York Finger Lakes to grow and make red wine here). Some names are missing too, the one most greatly mourned being Fountaingrove near Santa Rosa: its red wines are legendary, but a combination of inept management and encroaching suburbia proved too much for its survival.

In brief, the Sonoma Valley complex (embracing the Alexander Valley, Dry Creek, and the Valley of the Moon as well as the main valley of the Russian River) is booming in terms of production. It will be a long time before its reputation for superior individual growths can catch up with Napa Valley, if indeed it ever does, though the potential is there. The real race is between Sonoma and the rapidly developing areas of the coast counties farther south, notably in the Salinas Valley.

NORTH COAST (*Southern Counties*). At this point it would be beneficial to take another look at the map on page 66, for two reasons: first, the nomenclature is confusing, and second, more than in any of the other regions, the old here needs to be separated from the new. You would think the area ought to be called "South Coast" because traditionally

The late J. D. Zellerbach's miniature Hanzell Winery
in Sonoma Valley.

it has embraced the area bordering on the long southern wing
of San Francisco Bay. But it has always been classed as North
Coast, so against all good sense, one is compelled to call it the
southern part of the North Coast.

Anyway, it has consisted traditionally of the vineyards and
wineries in two counties, Alameda, which is east of the bay,
and Santa Clara, which is at its southern end. Alameda contains two distinct districts, just to complicate matters a bit
more. One of them, the more famous, is the Livermore Valley,
which lies just east of and parallel to the bay but is separated

from it by a low range of mountains. This is a district long famous for its white wines. The names of winegrowers associated historically with it are Concannon, Wente, and the original Cresta Blanca of Charles Wetmore, the latter long since swallowed up and become a "label," but the first two are still independents. Their reputation was established on the basis of the white Bordeaux grapes Sémillon and Sauvignon Blanc, which in combination give the luscious wines of Sauternes and a quite similar wine here. Separately, these two grapes yield excellent dry white wines recalling the French Graves. Wente was among the first to introduce Chardonnay and Pinot Blanc after repeal—wines that are still among California's best whites. The reds of Livermore Valley are above the general run, especially Concannon's Cabernet.

Lying adjacent to the bay in Alameda County are several other growers of good reputation, the most important being Weibel, a substantial producer of sparkling wines marketed under its own name and also as private brands, as well as a line of still wines.

The broad and fertile Santa Clara Valley is geologically a southern extension of the rift partly filled by San Francisco Bay, cut off from the Pacific by the Santa Cruz mountains and separated from the Central Valley by another range to its east. The mushrooming metropolitan area of San Jose (which exceeds San Francisco's in size) has made heavy encroachments on the valley's two big agricultural resources, its vineyards and its prune orchards. Still, it produces three times as much wine as Alameda County, and a good proportion of it is distinctly superior, a judgment that applies especially to the vineyards along the western side of the valley. The big names are Almadén, Paul Masson, and Mirassou, though these old and well-reputed enterprises must now depend on other, newer areas for most of their grapes. Higher in the mountains above the towns of Saratoga and Los Gatos there is a gaggle of much smaller producers bent on making wines of the highest possible quality: two notable names are Martin Ray and Ridge. As one goes southward along the valley floor, the climate grows progressively hotter and the wines are correspondingly less fine. But still farther south, beginning around Hollister, the climate finds itself somewhat tempered again by access to cooling breezes from Monterey Bay.

So much for the "old" parts of the southern North Coast (here goes that confusing nomenclature again). Now for the new. The first to make the break was Almadén, as urban spread encroached on its original property near Los Gatos. In a bold decision, most of the vineyards were sold (though the winery

Typical heavy-producing blocks
of a Central Valley Vineyard.

buildings remain and are still its bottling headquarters) and exchanged for a vast territory south of Hollister near Paicenes, where an ambitious program of planting was launched and still continues, with the emphasis on the *cépages nobles*. Almadén is now a subsidiary of National Distillers—and under this ownership keeps reaching out into the Central Valley for ever cheaper bulk blending wine.

Not long afterward a number of the other well-established producers took the plunge, likewise driven by population pressure in the bay area. But they chose an entirely new district, the Salinas Valley, running north and south just behind the coastal city of Monterey. Here the climate is tempered by closer access to Monterey Bay. Its possibilities in terms of climate, soil, and water supply had been thoroughly studied by viticulturists of the university, notably A. J. Winkler, and here plantings as ambitious as those of Almadén were undertaken by Wente, Mirassou, Paul Masson, and others, beyond the range of population growth. This transplanting, or migration, from the original locations to the new is by no means completed. Much good land is still available, and as need develops, a growing proportion of California's better wines will be coming from here. An entirely new enterprise planned on a large scale from the ground up (vineyards and winery both) is the Monterey Vineyard.

The Rest of the Country

If you look at a map of the United States, California doesn't seem so very large. It covers only 158,693 square miles out of the national total of 3,615,122. Yet it consistently produces about nine-tenths of all our wine. Put it in terms of tonnage of grapes crushed: in 1973 the total crush in California was 2,475,000 tons as against only 283,000 elsewhere.

A seeming contradiction arises when one discovers that the number of bonded winery premises is almost equally divided between California and the rest of the country: 278 in California and 271 elsewhere. But this comparison gives no hint of scale. As we have seen, California possesses defined viticultural regions, the limitations and possibilities of which have been closely studied for years and are well known. The patterns of production and distribution are well established. The largest units are enormous, and even the moderate-size wineries have big production in absolute terms. California thinks big, even though there are also a fair number of small family operations and "boutique" wineries. Outside of California there are a few substantial and well-established wine producers. But most are extremely small, recently established and widely scattered in districts where the potential for wine-growing is still to be discovered and confirmed, often in districts where there has never been a winery or vineyard of wine grapes before. Their proprietors are true venturers, pioneers in the sense that no California wine man is today—as truly pioneers as those who went west in prairie schooners.

Another point is that much of the non-California wine is really something else: what were earlier called wines-by-courtesy. Such are the various fruit wines, which are essentially cordials, heavily fortified with sugar and alcohol and agreeable enough when sipped with cookies but sold chiefly as cheap intoxicants. And then there are the highly flavored wines produced in the Northeast, Middle West, and Southern states that are fermented with a large excess of sugar but without a particularly high alcoholic content. The kosher and scuppernong wines are of this sort.

Moreover, a fair bit of what comes to be classified statistically as non-California wine actually originates in California. Many Eastern wineries produce blended wines, those from Eastern grapes being extended by the use of California grape concentrate or by the addition of neutral wine brought in from California by tank car. If the addition is moderate the product may still be legitimately described on the label as, for example, New York State wine. There exist also some Eastern producers of sparkling wines who never see a grape: they simply buy California still wine in bulk and bring it east to be sparkled. These practices are legitimate, and some of the resulting wines are better for them when the object is to attenuate an excess of flavor. Yet all of them go down in the statistics as non-California wine and so distort the picture somewhat.

And then, as we have seen, non-California producers with some few exceptions (as in the Yakima Valley of Washington) are placed at a disadvantage by their climates. Yields per acre run lower than in California, and production costs are higher. Anything like a general dependence on the classic *vinifera* grapes is impractical for reasons discussed earlier, and winegrowers have been compelled until quite recently to rely on American grapes with their relatively pronounced and special flavors. Such wines have their admirers, but they are specialties that do not appeal to those whose taste in wine follows European models. These heavy handicaps are now being reduced with the help of the new French hybrids and some more recent crosses that might appropriately be called post-French hybrids, which now make it possible for the first time, outside California and the few other exceptional areas, to produce with confidence good, moderate-priced wines lacking foxiness and other pronounced "wild" flavors.

With these generalizations in mind, we may proceed to a survey of American winegrowing outside California, which will be quite brief—no more than a *tour d'horizon*.*

NEW YORK STATE. The largest winegrowing state outside of California, with 41 bonded premises, it has substantial vineyard acreage, and wineries, in four areas: the Hudson River Valley, the Chautauqua district, the Niagara district, and the Finger Lakes region. Other areas show possibilities so far unrealized.

* The whole story has been laid out in rich and fascinating detail by Leon Adams in his book *The Wines of America* (1973). This is a first-hand study and all the more impressive because Adams is California-born and has spent his entire life in the California wine industry.

Seibel 7053, also known as Chancellor, one of the new French hybrid red-wine grapes.

The Hudson Valley district had a certain importance prior to prohibition, and is now reviving. Several wineries survived that bleak period and today continue to produce dry and sweet wines in the traditional style. A change came with the establishment of the modest High Tor vineyard in Rockland County, not far north of New York City. At High Tor tradition was put aside and, starting from scratch, only the new French hybrids were planted. Farther north on the west bank, opposite Poughkeepsie, a much more ambitious enterprise, the Benmarl Vineyards, is currently under development. It is superbly situated, and its new terraced vineyards mount the hillsides in a way reminiscent of those on the banks of the Rhine. Its earliest vintages, especially the whites, show real promise.

The Chautauqua district stretches westward from Buffalo along the bench of land that borders Lake Erie on the south, continuing over the Pennsylvania line (since climate is unaware of political boundary lines) and on into northern Ohio. This geographical district has been involved in grape growing for more than a century, and the circumstance that the Concord dominates the vineyards has, since the beginning, put the emphasis on fresh fruit, grape juice, and other grape products besides wine. But there are now large and growing plantings of the French hybrids, and even a few of the hardier *vinifera* sorts; several wineries are now in production on each side of the state dividing line. Many of the Pennsylvania-grown wine grapes find their home over the border in New York wineries, since for many years the Pennsylvania wine law was written so as to prohibit the establishment of small new wineries—a piece of witlessness that has now been corrected, making such ventures possible. The Chautauqua district is undoubtedly an important winegrowing district of the future, since viticultural expertise is already abundant. (This also seems an appropriate place to mention that under the amended Pennsylvania law an equivalent development of small wineries and vineyards is now taking place in the southern corner of Pennsylvania in the watershed of the Susquehanna River

A New York Finger Lakes vineyard panorama.

south of Harrisburg. There is even a lively little publication called *The Pennsylvania Wine Letter.*)

The Niagara district occupies the neck of land between Lake Erie and Lake Ontario, which is cut by the falls and gorge of the Niagara River. Lying between the two large bodies of water, its climate is especially favorable to fruit growing. But the abundant power from Niagara Falls, the proximity of Buffalo and Toronto, and its position astride the Great Lakes shipping lane with its locks and canal also make this a favored site for electro-chemical and other heavy industry and everything that goes with a maritime entrepôt. The consequences are as menacing for fruit growing as the expansion of San Jose into Santa Clara Valley. Still, the district is Canada's prime source of grapes for winemaking, consisting until quite recently of Concord, Catawba, Niagara, and Delaware, with smaller plantings of other old American sorts. There is a pronounced trend now toward the new French hybrids, with again some experimentation with *vinifera*, the pioneer in both having been the late A. de Chaunac, for many years the technical director of Bright's Wines, Ltd. These new vineyards are yielding red and white wines of continually improving quality. The varieties include Seibel 10868, Seibel 5279, and Seibel 9110 for white; and Seibel 10878, Foch, Seibel 1000, and Seibel 9549 for red (the latter having been renamed the de Chaunac). Several new hybrids from the Vineland, Ontario, viticultural station are also finding some favor.

In terms of acreage and winery capacity, the Canadian side overshadows the American. But on the American side the tonnage of the good French hybrids is increasing rapidly, again with some hope-inspired plantings of the hardier *vinifera*. East of Fort Niagara along the southern shore of Lake Ontario to well beyond Rochester there stretches an old and famous fruit-growing district known best for its apples and cherries. A considerable wine-grape acreage is now being planted, including a block by Seneca Foods for its Boordy Vineyards winery in Penn Yan.

However, New York really owes its reputation as a wine-producing state to the vintages that have been gathered for the better part of a century from vineyards bordering the Finger Lakes. These lakes, which lie in a cluster in the west-central part of the state and have a north-south orientation, are long, narrow, and deep, with steeply rising sides. Their beauty is famous and their geology fascinating; and their configuration accounts for local climatic conditions favorable to grape growing. The largest of these lakes are Seneca and Cayuga, but grape growing and winemaking have been especially associated with Keuka and to a lesser extent Canandaigua lakes. The villages of Hammondsport, at the southern end of Keuka, and Penn Yan, at the northern end, both live by and for the vine, and most of the well-known New York State "champagnes" are produced from vineyards along both sides of this lake. The two senior establishments are Great

Western and Gold Seal, old firms whose names have long
been associated with sparkling wine. The wines are bottle-
fermented, and they derive their special characteristics from
the careful handling and blending of wines of the Catawba,
the Delaware, the Elvira, and increasingly the French hybrids.
These two companies produce still table and dessert wines as
well.

A third enterprise, Taylor Wine Company, now exceeds
them in production and in fact owns Great Western as a subsidiary. Taylor produces a sparkling wine of the same general
characteristics, and a good many still wines as well. All three
now have large plantings of the new hybrids—Taylor having
much the largest acreage and Gold Seal the biggest experimental collection—and they are expanding them as rapidly as
conditions permit. But the full effect of this will not be felt
for some time. The aggressive Canandaigua Wine Company
now produces sparkling wines in Hammondsport also, though
its bread-and-butter item, made elsewhere, continues to be a
pop wine called Wild Irish Rose.

Over a steep divide to the west of Keuka Lake lies Canandaigua Lake, with the village of Naples at its foot. Here are
the Widmer Wine Cellars, fourth of the old-line Finger
Lakes producers. The Widmers have always specialized in
still wines and gained their reputation with Eastern "varietals"
—the light, unblended table wines of such varieties as Delaware, Catawba, Elvira, Diamond, Niagara, and Vergennes—
as well as their own version of sherry. They have recently made
a partial break with this tradition and are planting vineyards
in the Sonoma Valley for the production of reds.

Alongside the old-line producers has sprung up a new
generation of small wineries, which have turned their backs
on the traditional vines. One of three based on Keuka
Lake is the Vinifera Wine Cellars, established by Konstantin
Frank. A native of the Ukraine and an expert in cold-country
survival techniques, he produces limited quantities of superior
(and expensive) wines from Chardonnay and Riesling. He is
resolutely opposed to the growing of any but *vinifera* vines,

and is the energy source of the current revival of interest in them in temperate-climate areas. The two others are Bully Hill and the Boordy Vineyards winery in Penn Yan, both concentrating on the hybrids. Others are at the point of qualifying.

OHIO. This state is next to New York in the number of bonded winery premises, with thirty. West of Cleveland, and centering on the port of Sandusky, there is a considerable winegrowing region, which is a sort of westward extension of the Chautauqua district. The vineyards are not only on the mainland but on the islands a few miles offshore; and the dominant grapes are still the Catawbas, known locally as "Cats," though, as everywhere in the East, the French hybrids have begun to assert themselves. The largest of the wineries is Meier's Wine Cellars (which has island vineyards and a winery near Cincinnati as well as at Sandusky). Numerous other small wineries are scattered among the lake-shore vineyards, most of which cater to a local trade. There is also a burst of new planting in the Ohio River Valley and in the central part of the state around Columbus, mainly of French hybrids. Each year sees the establishment of several more small bonded wineries in these areas, as well as across the border in Indiana thanks to a recent liberalization of the law. Some of their names: Tarula Farms, Valley Vineyards, Moyer, Oliver, Hafle, Mantey, Le Boudin, Banholzer, Villa Medeo, Golden Raintree, Treaty Line, Chalet Debonné (farther north).

OTHER AREAS. For the rest, we must fan out in all directions, commercial winegrowing being thinly scattered but with local concentrations here and there. Looking west into Michigan, there is one such concentration not far from Lake Michigan in the general neighborhood of Paw Paw. Michigan winemakers enjoy a substantial state tax advantage, and as so often happens the relative immunity from competition has weakened the incentive to strive for quality. The Concord is

*The entrance to a wine storage cave dug by Ágoston Haraszthy,
circa 1847, across the Wisconsin River from Sauk City.*

still the dominant grape; and here, in the hands of the chemist, it does duty for red wines, white wines, dessert wines, and "champagne." However, the established wineries have begun to find that quality does matter after all and are turning to better grapes; and they are being paced by a number of small new enterprises that do take quality seriously. Two to follow are Tabor Hill and Warner. Michigan's wineries now number eleven.

In the mid-nineteenth century, Missouri wines, chiefly from vineyards along the banks of the Missouri River around Hermann, enjoyed a good reputation. Almost completely knocked out by prohibition, this district has only recently begun to struggle to its feet. Several parts of the state show promise, however, and Missouri now has twelve wineries. Green Valley, Mount Pleasant, and Stone Hill bear watching.

An interesting reincarnation is the founding of a new winery on the site of Ágoston Haraszthy's original enterprise near Sauk City, Wisconsin. Actually the Haraszthy property, which he bought in 1847, was in what is now called Prairie du Sac, across the Wisconsin River from Sauk City. Robert Wollersheim, a young engineer, confirmed this by title several years ago and bought the property including Haraszthy's original wine storage cave and a fine building put up by the subsequent owner, a Rhinelander named Kehl, for the production of champagne. The building has been renovated as the Wollersheim Winery and flourishes in a modest way. The vineyard has been planted to the hardiest early-ripening French hybrids.

There are other winegrowing clusters in Oklahoma and Arkansas, the Wiederkehr and Post wineries and vineyards being of substantial size. South of there, in Texas, a sudden and intense interest in winegrowing has developed quite lately, in the area around Lubbock especially: we must wait to see what the results will be.

Turning eastward, one finds another cluster in southern New Jersey, several of them dating back to before prohibition; and there are scattered small wineries in other parts of the state as well, mostly very young. Maryland has three wineries, with the prospect of others. Virginia has five, and there is much interest; but there is also the obstacle of a pointlessly obstructive state law. A small established winery exists in New Hampshire. And before ending this brief summary, I must note an anomaly. The state of Illinois stands first after New York in Eastern wine production, yet its acreage of grapes is negligible. This is accounted for by the big Mogen David plant in Chicago, now owned by the Coca-Cola Bottling Company of New York, which brings its grapes (and grape concentrate) from elsewhere.

And then there is the Northwest, meaning the states of Washington, Oregon, and Idaho. Washington and Oregon have a sprinkling of wineries, including Ste. Michelle and a third Boordy Vineyards regional winery. Those in the cool and rainy coastal parts have to be content with the old Eastern grape varieties, but they also produce berry wines. Over the Cascade range to the east in the valleys of the Columbia, the Yakima, and the Snake rivers the situation is altogether different. In a way this great inland area recalls the Central Valley of California—a sort of extension of it but with differences attributable to its higher latitude. Rainfall is negligible, a few inches a year at most, and yet the sources of water for irrigation are almost limitless. Disease problems are unimportant. The deep wind-blown loess soil is incredibly fertile, making it hard to keep a vineyard from overbearing, and yields of fourteen tons an acre and more have been known. The summers are cloudless and the heat is abundant, but the season is frequently cut short by early autumn freezes, and spring frosts are frequent. What keeps the area from being a viticultural Eden is its vulnerability to periodic winter freezes of great intensity, flowing straight down from the North Pole (as in the Ukraine) and doing damage to the vines. For regular and consistent production, hardy grape varieties are necessary.

Because of this combination of circumstances the Concord grape has found a western home here. Production in the Yakima and Snake river valleys will soon exceed that of New York State if it doesn't already. Because of climatic conditions, however, there is still confusion about the region's winegrowing possibilities. The area has a considerable planting of *vinifera*, but for the most part this *encépagement* has been a carbon copy of the vines grown in California, which are inappropriate here. If there is to be a future for the *vinifera* in inland Washington, it surely lies with hardier sorts. There are also modest plantings of some of the hybrids, better able to withstand winter cold, but again the business of determining the best ones for the region has barely begun and is handicapped in both Washington and Oregon by an embargo on the importation of new experimental varieties (except from California) and by the doctrinaire rigidity of the local agricultural bureaucracy. Nevertheless, some very good wines have already come out of the region in small quantities.

The Role of the Amateur

One of the paradoxes of the California wine scene is a relative scarcity of serious amateur winegrowers. Conditions in much of the state are so hospitable that grapevines practically beg to be allowed to grow. Nothing is easier than to set out a mini-vineyard in the garden or along a fence and have the satisfaction of one's own annual family vintage. Yet it isn't done to any great extent. Good jug wines are plentiful and inexpensive; this dampens the incentive, and so most Californians remain innocent of one of the healthiest, most agreeable, and most rewarding of all avocations.

The reverse is true in other parts of the country, where vineyards and commercial winegrowing are so much less familiar and where heavy transportation costs and capricious state laws make store-bought wine unduly expensive. There are thus powerful incentives to make one's own. And in the mysterious way these things happen, millions today are curious about winemaking and want to give it a try.

The first step, available even to apartment dwellers, is winemaking with the use of wine-grape concentrate. After a try or two, what starts out as something only slightly more romantic than canning beans or putting up a batch of jelly becomes a challenge and an adventure.

The logical next step is to find some grapes of the right sort or, failing that, to plant some; and with that the amateur is caught for fair. A whole new world unfolds, and he begins to discover what it is about the growing of grapes and the making of wine that has seized and held mankind through countless generations. He becomes part of a tradition and a brotherhood.

What we are seeing in this country today is an immense expansion of this fraternity. Barring some utterly hostile regions, its members are everywhere: small growers with a modest vineyard, a few dozen vines perhaps, or a quarter-acre —planting, observing the results, taking disappointments in their stride, gradually accumulating a body of knowledge of what is possible and what isn't.

I have mentioned already those early U.S. Agricultural Yearbooks, the first of which appeared in 1847. It was the custom then for the leading farmer in every part of the young United States to take pen in hand during the winter and write an account of his successes and failures of the previous season: the new crops he was experimenting with, the new strains of sheep and cattle that he had imported, the vagaries of the weather, the special characteristics of his soil. These communications were brought together in the annual yearbooks. At that time the outlines of American agriculture, which is today the marvel of the world, had not yet been established. Those articulate farmers were in the process of establishing it.

We see the same thing happening today in viticulture, everywhere but in California, where that fundamental labor has already been done. There is intercommunication on an informal basis. The word spreads. The agricultural press discovers that things are happening. Here and there a state experiment station enters the picture, sometimes to help and as often to hinder. From time to time a backyard winegrower takes a deep breath and leaps overboard to have his try at winegrowing as a full-time occupation. Some will sink. Some will swim. Out of all this, and in the most surprising places, amateurs today are beginning to make winegrowing a far more generalized part of American life than it has ever been in the past.

Establishing a Small Winery

Needless to say, the big plunge from amateur winegrowing to the establishment of a small winery is something that must be planned with great care. The way to success is strewn with assorted obstacles and booby traps, and it is important to know what these are. The following paragraphs may help in charting the course.

Classic white oak cooperage in a small eastern winery.
(Boordy Vineyards)

The new way. Vertical stainless steel tanks for either
red-wine or white-wine fermentation and later
for wine storage. (Boordy Vineyards)

1. Begin as a grape grower. Except where the potentials of different varieties are already firmly established, as in the older regions, begin with experimental plantings, relying on the best advice available. Out of such plantings certain varieties will emerge that are culturally well adapted and that meet your winemaking standards; others will fall by the wayside. Conclusions cannot be reached in a hurry. As the vines come into bearing, the vineyard may become self-sustaining through the sale of grapes, to a neighboring winery (if there is one) or, better, to the eager army of amateurs. The huge size of the market among amateurs is only beginning to be appreciated. While catering to it, a grower can take his time in planning the next step.

2. Be sure of your technical competence as a winemaker, by study and practice. This does not mean a degree in biochemistry, though a short course at the University of California Department of Enology at Davis, or at the New York Experiment Station at Geneva, or perhaps before long at the experiment stations at Wooster, Ohio, and State College, Pennsylvania, can be tremendously valuable. It does mean thorough practical competence or competent technical assistance. The public is a heartless judge and will not be indulgent about defective wines.

3. Study the alcoholic beverage laws, both federal and state. Every winery must have a basic federal permit, is required to submit monthly reports of its operations, and is subject to periodic inspection and auditing. Obtain a copy of "Wine: Publication 146" from the nearest office of the Bureau of Alcohol, Tobacco, and Firearms of the Treasury Department or from the U.S. Government Printing Office (price $0.55). This is the "Bible" for establishing and maintaining a federal bonded winery. The bureaucratic prose at first seems formidable, but you will get used to it. Qualification and subsequent compliance are somewhat tedious but basically not difficult. The regulatory personnel are extremely literal-minded, but generally on your side. Their interest is in the federal tax equity in the wine you will produce.

Having reconnoitered the federal situation, check in with your state authorities, because you are not qualified to make and market wine until you have met their requirements too. Here more likely than not you will encounter most of your frustrations and aggravations. The reason is that there are fifty different sets of state regulations, all different. Taxes, for example, vary. Some states exact exorbitant taxes and licensing fees, others don't. Some states allow sales direct to consumers, others allow sales to retailers but not to consumers, and still others allow sales to wholesalers only. Some state regulatory agencies are chronic nit pickers and obstructionists, others may be lived with in tolerable harmony. Some few states have regulations so stringent and arbitrary that they have you licked before you start. Without any question the balkanization of state regulations is the biggest single obstacle to the expansion of winegrowing, and of wine consumption, in this country. It is vital to know what one is up against legally before making any serious plans.

4. Know your market. The basic market of any small winery is local, for many reasons. The *vin du pays* always has a certain amount of built-in acceptance, provided it is good. Moreover, the local market can be reached; and it is the maker who must always go forth and find his market—it will not come to him. A new wine must, to put the matter bluntly, be *sold*. The necessary task of spreading the word, of arousing interest, of establishing a reputation, is least difficult and least expensive close to home. Successful marketing comes down to getting that bottle of wine on the table of the person who intends to use it, and the most accessible consumers are those who are closest, or at any rate no farther away than the nearest population center. The more broadly anything is distributed, the more expensive and difficult distribution becomes.

This brings us back to the law under which you must operate. If your state law allows wine sales only to a wholesaler, then you must first catch your wholesaler. Having caught him, you must still make an end run around him and create

Vines planted to approximate contours
in north-central Maryland. (Boordy Vineyards)

the demand yourself. He won't, and can't, do much about distribution until the demand is there. You are your own salesman.

It is no accident that the establishment of small new wineries is more frequent, and the odds for success are greatest, in states where the law allows the producer to sell direct to consumers. Wine is not sold if it goes to a wholesaler and sits in his warehouse. It is not sold if it goes to a retailer and just stands on his shelf. It is sold only when a consumer buys it and takes it home. Wholesaler and retailer can *help*, if they are so minded, but it is not their job to create the demand.

There is another immense advantage in selling direct to

the consumer, especially important in the beginning, when production is very small. It gives the producer the benefit of the wholesaler's and retailer's markup as well as the normal winery profit. Actually no real conflict exists between direct sales and conventional distribution by way of the wholesaler-retailer pattern. Sales at the winery are the one best way of creating demand; and it is the demand thus created that eventually makes the sale of your wine desirable and profitable to wholesaler and retailer as well. But there is one important rule to observe: you don't create friendly and sympathetic retailers by underselling them at the winery. If you do that, you will find yourself selling at the winery and nowhere else.

Let no one suppose that establishing a small new winery is easy. It is laborious and at times disheartening. It is not a road to riches, and it requires resourcefulness and a certain kind of doggedness, not to mention a conviction that the transformation of grapes into good wine is a matter of high seriousness. But for the right temperament it offers a challenge that comes close to being compulsive, and accomplishment is singularly satisfying.

Part II

THE
WINEMAKING
ART

CHAPTER 6

Fundamentals of Winemaking

WINE ISN'T at all hard to make if you aren't too fussy about its quality. It will make itself if given half a chance, which is why wine was known, used, and appreciated long before history began to be recorded.

If you want to emulate the neolithic winemaker, just dump some grapes into a clean container that doesn't leak, mash them up a bit with a blunt instrument or your feet, cover, and let stand in a warmish place. Stir once in a while. Soon they will begin to throw off an intriguing odor and will heave and gurgle as gas escapes when you stir. When fermentation dies down, drain off the yeasty liquid and press the solid material to extract the rest. Pour the liquid into a large jug of some sort, filling it full and stoppering it lightly. When there is no further sign of activity, stopper it tightly and put it in a cool place. After more waiting, separate the naturally cleared wine from its sediment, and begin to use it. Given clean receptacles, suitable ripe grapes, and a bit of luck, one may thus obtain drinkable wine, though it had better be drunk up before something else happens to it. It isn't going to stay drinkable indefinitely.

The vintage is frequently a family enterprise.

The contemporary art of winemaking is only an elaboration of this rudimentary method. The microbiologist and the biochemist seek to understand and explain the natural process and to guide it by providing a congenial environment both externally and within the evolving mass of the wine itself. The technician seeks to reduce the labor. The difference between primitive winemaking and enlightened winemaking is that one is laborious and uncertain in its result, the other less laborious and more certain.

Yet it will not do to overemphasize the simplicity of winemaking. That would be misleading. If a man comes down with a bad cold, his doctor gives him aspirin and some cough medicine and tells him to go to bed. If he takes his medicine and stays in bed, he is well again in a few days. Simple enough. But that is not to say that the process by which his body throws off infection and heals itself is simple. It is in fact a complicated biological melodrama that the doctor knows all too little about.

The process by which grape juice becomes wine is no less complicated. We say that the juice "ferments." What do we mean? It wasn't until the mid-nineteenth century that anyone had the least inkling of the nature of the process. Pasteur himself, who stumbled on the big clue, was only partly right. The biochemist of today would still hesitate to give a flat answer. The more he learns, the more he realizes how much there is still to learn. In a manner of speaking, the advances in the understanding of fermentation have served mainly to complicate our ignorance. The secret keeps retreating. Yet every advance toward the ultimate explanation has helped in one way or another, and many have direct practical applications. Slowly winemaking becomes less an art and more an applied science, even though the subjective judgment of the winemaker is still indispensable. The purpose of this chapter is to sketch out as simply as possible what is known of the winemaking process, so that the practical winemaker, before proceeding to explicit instructions, will have some insight into what he and nature are up to.

The Raw Material

Having given a good deal of attention so far to the differences between grapes, let us now see what they all have in common. Grapes grow in clusters, or bunches. Each grape is attached to the main stem or one of its branches (technically, the *rachis*; in French, *rafle*) by a small individual stem called the *pedicel*. The essential parts of the grape itself are the *seeds*, the *skin*, and the *pulp*.

The parts of a grape berry.

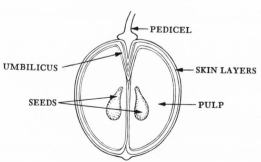

Depending on the grape variety and growing conditions, there are differences in the proportions of these four elements. Taking a rough average, the proportions by weight of stems and fruit are:

Stems	3 per cent
Fruit	97 per cent
	100

Forgetting the stems for a moment, by weight the grapes themselves consist approximately of:

Pulp	75 per cent
Skins	20 per cent
Seeds	5 per cent
	100

Stems become woody and hard in some varieties and remain soft and herbaceous and easily broken off the vine in others. This matters in the picking. They contain some water and about 3 per cent tannin, the complex of substances which gives astringency to wine. The current practice is to remove the stems prior to fermentation in order to keep down astringency. But depending on the grapes being used, an experienced winemaker may prefer not to remove them, or to remove only a portion. In crushing and pressing for white wine the stems are not removed since their presence improves draining of the juice during pressing; but they are then discarded along with the skins.

Seeds are normally four in number, and in seedless grapes are either nonexistent or so rudimentary as not to be noticeable. They contain 3 or 4 per cent of tannin and about 10 per cent of an oil. In making red wine they may contribute a bit of tannin to the wine. They drop to the bottom of the fermenter, and in large-scale industrial winemaking they may be salvaged and pressed for their oil, which is used for fine cosmetics and is greatly valued for its siccative properties by certain artists who work in oils.

Skins, which are more or less waterproof while the grapes are intact, contribute a great deal to wine, much more, as I have indicated, to red than to white. They contribute the coloring matter (though there is also pigment in the juice of a few varieties), aromatic substances, and most of the wine's tannin. The velvety-looking bloom which develops on the surface of ripe grapes consists of a number of waxy substances, is somewhat protective, and has a role in snaring and retaining yeast cells. Some of these waxes are slightly aromatic, but otherwise they have nothing to contribute.

The coloring matter is not a single substance but an assortment of complex compounds related to the tannins, the assortment varying from one species and variety to another. These compounds develop after the grapes begin to ripen. Nothing is to be gained by reciting a list of them, which would be incomplete anyway since they are not yet all deciphered. But it is important to know that they are divided into two groups, the monoglucosides and the diglucosides. Monoglucosides are generally characteristic of *vinifera* grapes and diglucosides of the principal American species used in hybridization. Since the two types are quite easy to distinguish, chemical analysis provides a ready means of identifying wines of the hybrids and has become a handy device for excluding the importation of hybrid wines where that is deemed politically or economically desirable—as for instance in Germany, where the importation of cheaper wines from elsewhere is resisted by the high-cost local industry. But despite their ease of identification there is nothing inherently undesirable about diglucoside pigments. And the controversy about them has been made somewhat laughable by the discovery that a good many hybrids do not carry diglucoside pigments after all, and that a number of highly regarded *vinifera* varieties do.

Whichever type they are, these pigments are only slightly soluble in fresh juice at moderate temperatures. They may be dissolved by the alcohol when wine is fermented "on the skins," and sometimes by preliminary heating, which is the way commercial grape juice and some wines get their color.

Each pigment has its own way of behaving, which helps to explain the evolution in any wine's color and the appearance of precipitates in the bottle. Some of the pigments which give a new wine its deep color soon polymerize and precipitate out. Some become insoluble in the presence of oxygen or a diastase. Less vivid but more persistently soluble pigments then have the field to themselves, which accounts for the color changes we associate with aging.

As with the red pigments, the related tannin is not a single substance but an assortment. Though the stems may have been eliminated, they are still the source of the agreeable astringency, or puckery effect, so characteristic of such red wines as Chianti and Bordeaux, and of the slight background of bitterness which is normal in all wines. Tannin contributes to what may be called the "body," or "substance," of a wine. It also helps to induce the precipitation of certain constituents present naturally in grape juice and wine which tend otherwise to remain in suspension and prevent wine from clearing. A wine that contains adequate tannin becomes clear and bright with relative ease and stabilizes more rapidly. White wine is naturally poorer in tannin, and hence clears less easily. For this reason a small dose of tannin is sometimes added to the juice, or must, before fermentation.

Likewise the aromatic substances are located almost entirely in the skins. The aroma of most *vinifera* grapes is slight. But there are exceptions, such as Riesling, Traminer, and the Muscats. As I have mentioned, many of the American species and standard American grapes are overly aromatic, a defect from the point of view of the winemaker. It is relatively easy to isolate the aromatic substances for smelling purposes by separating some skins from pulp and seeds, steeping them for a week in a 16-degree alcohol solution slightly acidified with a bit of tartaric acid, and decanting the liquid. But analyzing and identifying them is something else, owing to their extreme complexity and the minute amounts that are present. A hardly quantifiable bit of aromatic material in grape skins goes a long way.

The *pulp* in some grapes is crisp and compact; in most, soft and juicy. It represents three-fourths or more of the weight of the grape and is the source of the juice, or must, which eventually becomes the wine. By weight, 1,000 grams of must consists (roughly) of the following:

	IN GRAMS		
Water	710	to	800
Sugar	100	to	250
Organic acids (free)	2	to	5
Organic acids (combined)	3	to	10
Minerals	2	to	3
Nitrogenous and pectic compounds	0.5	to	1

Evidently water and sugar comprise most of the juice, amounting to somewhere around 94 to 96 per cent. But the importance of the remaining constituents is greater than one might suppose from the quantities present: these give wines their individuality.

The fermentable sugars—almost exclusively dextrose (glucose) and levulose (fructose)—are of primary interest to the winemaker. Their varying proportions are of scientific interest but in ordinary practice they are simply lumped together as "grape sugar." During fermentation the sugars are converted into almost equal quantities of carbon dioxide gas (CO_2) and ethyl alcohol (C_2H_5OH). Roughly speaking, fresh grape juice containing 20 per cent sugar thus produces a wine having about 10 per cent of alcohol. If you know the sugar content, you can estimate in advance what the approximate alcoholic content of the wine will be after fermentation. As a rule of thumb in winemaking, *two degrees of sugar in the juice give one degree of alcohol in the wine.* This formula isn't exact, but if you remember it you are well on the way to becoming a winemaker.

But don't forget one important qualification: The yeasts responsible for converting sugar into alcohol usually slow down and eventually quit when the alcoholic solution in which they are working has reached a level of 14 or 15 per cent, even though there may still be a good deal of sugar present. Thus (remembering the two-to-one rule) a must showing a sugar content of more than 28 per cent will rarely ferment out completely. A residue of sweetness remains, and unless the objective is a sweet wine and the winemaker knows what he is doing, this residual sugar is dangerous and one of the most frequent sources of spoilage, for reasons that I will explain later on. Prudent winemakers make sure that their wine ferments out dry, which is to say that all the fermentable sugar is converted into alcohol. On the other hand, a finished wine containing less than 8 per cent of alcohol is not only thin and unpalatable but sickly and unstable. The desirable sugar content for dry table wines thus falls between 20 and 24 per cent —again based on the two-to-one rule. Under California conditions the ripening grapes approach and often exceed the upper limit: in the cooler temperate-climate parts of the country, grapes must often struggle to reach the lower limit. If the winemaker conducts no other test, he must determine sugar content.

Sugar and water aside, the remaining material in the must consists mainly of two organic acids, tartaric and malic, and their salts. Malic acid is found in many fruits. It is responsible for the tartness of green apples, for example. Tartaric acid is conspicuously the acid of the grape, present principally as the salt potassium bitartrate, which is soluble in the unfermented must but much less soluble in wine and so tends to precipitate as crystals in cask or bottle, reducing the wine's acidity. These two acids, along with small quantities of numerous others which need not concern us, provide the tartness of grapes and wine, and the winemaker lumps them together as "total acids" or "total acidity."* Some grape varieties normally show high total acidity and others low. Since total acidity diminishes during ripening, and heat promotes ripening, hot climates make for low total acidity and cool climates for high. Under California's Mediterranean conditions low

* For the more sophisticated, a complementary measure of the tartness of must or wine is the hydrogen-ion concentration, or pH value.

total acids are the rule. In the temperate-climate parts of Europe and the United States total acids are usually high. The proportions of tartaric and malic acid are in most cases a function of the grape's ripeness. In unripe grapes the malic will be high. As ripening proceeds, the malic acid is rapidly and drastically reduced (although it never disappears completely) while the amount of tartaric remains pretty much what it was when the grapes were unripe. If total acidity is in good balance, it provides a medium that is hostile to spoilage organisms during fermentation and afterward, enlivens the color, and gives freshness and body to the wine. If it is deficient, the must and wine are more susceptible to spoilage, the wine tastes flat, and color is dull. If it is excessive, the wine is harsh and too tart.

Small quantities of mineral salts (sulfates, chlorides, and phosphates of potassium, calcium, magnesium, iron, and copper as well as other metals) are present in the must. Except as the salts of iron, copper, and calcium may increase by mishandling in the course of the winemaking, they need not concern us.

The nitrogenous compounds, though ordinarily small in quantity, are important because they are an essential food in the development of the yeasts; if excessive, as sometimes happens when grapes are in poor condition, they can cause spoilage during fermentation and aging. Some pectins and gums exist in grapes and increase with ripening. In excess, they can reduce yield in pressing. For the most part, they are hydrolized by naturally occurring enzymes and thus eliminated during fermentation. Some winemakers encourage this process by adding ready-prepared pectic enzymes before fermentation. Present in the wine, these pectins and gums can contribute the softness that the French call *moelleux*, especially to wines from overripe grapes, but they also retard clarification. They have been incompletely studied.

Finally, grapes have their quota of assorted vitamins, and thiamin in particular appears to be important for yeast growth; but fermentation affects this pattern and much as one might like to say so, the finished wine does not provide a full array of vitamin supplements.

So ends our simplified description of the raw material—of the substances which all grapes have in common. Such terms as "average" and "in general" and "normally" tend to creep in because the composition of two lots is never identical and may be quite drastically different. Too much emphasis on these variations would only confuse the picture; and when it comes to the numerous minor constituents, the winemaker can do little about them anyway. The two components that he can do something about, and almost always does, are *total sugar content* and *total acidity*. As ripening proceeds, the proportion of sugar increases and total acidity decreases. If all goes well, an optimal balance between these two is reached in the fruit. This point varies from one variety to another, but ideally it is attained for dry table wines when sugar content has developed to 20 to 23 per cent by volume and total acidity has fallen no lower than 8 grams per liter, calculated as tartaric (see page 152). If and when that point is reached, pick and crush!

Timing the Vintage

Grapes on the vine should be picked when they have reached the optimal balance of sugar and acidity. Ah, it is easy enough to say, but not so easy in practice. To begin with, the grapes exposed to the sun are always sweeter and better-colored than the shaded ones; yet on the other hand these are the first to be damaged or destroyed by insects, birds, or hail. So a less than ideal average must usually be struck. In large enterprises allowance must be made for the harvesting time required, which may be several weeks. This may necessitate a premature beginning in order to avoid overripeness at the end—another compromise. In areas where the grapes must struggle to ripeness there is a chronic tendency to pick prematurely, on the principle that imperfect grapes are better than a reduced crop,

The vintage begins.

or none. In California however, there is a chronic tendency to wait too long.

Frequently there is no choice. Persistent rain in warm weather dilutes sugar content while at the same time provoking disease. Lack of sun combined with rain and cold weather reduce ripening to a crawl. Excessive bird damage may compel early picking. An early freeze ends everything.

In days gone by, winegrowing communities left the decision of when to harvest to the village elders or a committee of the best growers, and no one was allowed to begin sooner, lest the reputation of the district be compromised. Where large enterprises predominate, the situation is not greatly different today. Elaborate schedules are drawn up by contracting wineries: Growers are told where and what to pick, and when—and, indeed, when to deliver, often down to the hour. Mechanization in both the winery and the vineyard has wrought changes: a vineyard that once required ten days of hand picking and a frantic scramble for pickers is now harvested in a matter of hours by a great, lumbering grape picker with its attendant fleet of gondolas and sometimes field crushers and tank trucks; under floodlights the work goes on even at night. Of course, hand picking still prevails in small vineyards, in the choicest vineyards, and those on steep and difficult terrain. There the problem of recruiting pickers can be excruciating. But whether picking is done by hand or machine, those charming photographs of pretty girls in sunbonnets lingering over a choice bunch do not precisely reflect the reality.

It is up to the small winegrower or the amateur to weigh all the factors and make the decision on his own. Assuming that his choice is not forced by birds, disease, or some other plague, he has certain tools to help him. He knows approximately when his grapes will mature—that is, whether they are early, mid-season, or late varieties. He can tell how they are coming along by their appearance and taste. After they become convincingly sweet he follows the increase of sugar content with an inexpensive device called a saccharometer (page 148), or, better yet, with a hand refractometer. With this optical instrument he places two drops of juice on the prism, closes the little lid, and through the eyepiece takes a direct reading of the sugar content on a translucent scale; he can check the sugar of a dozen different vines in a dozen different locations in a matter of minutes. Its cost is about that of an inexpensive hand calculator.

Where adequate sugar is not a problem, the winegrower's main concern is that total acidity shall not fall too far. If he knows his grapes, he can and usually does follow this indirectly by means of sugar tests. Or he can pick a small sample of

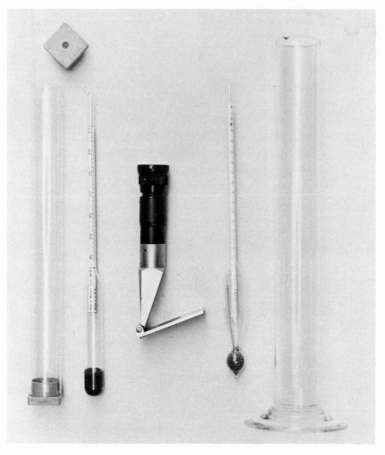

A *hand refractometer* (center)
and two types of saccharometer with their jars.

grapes, press them, and determine total acidity by titration
(see page 152). In Europe small field testing kits are sold for
this purpose.

The decision to pick is finally taken. Whether it is forced
by circumstance or a deliberate choice, this is the moment the
winegrower has been working and waiting for since the vines
first stirred in the spring. It was mostly hard work from early
spring to that mid-point in the season which the French call

the *véraison*, the turning point, and mostly hard waiting from then on. The decision, once made, brings with it a vast sense of relief, always, and of exhilaration. For good or ill, this is to be the raw material of the year's vintage: Let no time be lost in harvesting, and once the grapes are off the vines, let no time be lost in seeing them through the crusher and into the fermenter.

Fermentation

It is not until the crushed grapes are in the fermenter, skins and all (or, if destined for white wine, the juice has been pressed free of the skins), that the yeasts get down to work. The time for the business of testing and if necessary correcting the must is before they take over. This means a final and careful determination of the sugar content of the whole mass, for the field tests are only approximations. If there is a deficiency, then enough sugar is added to make it up. This practice is known everywhere in the world as *chaptalization*, after a certain Count Chaptal who rationalized and promoted it. It is based on the fact that sucrose (refined cane or beet sugar) immediately breaks down into grape sugar on contact with the juice of grapes and is almost universally used whenever a sugar deficiency occurs—in making the *grands crus* of Burgundy and Bordeaux as well as everyday wines. An alternative, not necessarily preferable, is sugar correction with grape concentrate.

Then come the test and correction for total acidity. If the acid level is too high, three means of reducing it to the proper point of balance are available: chemical, biological, and by dilution; they will be discussed later. If it is too low for quality and safety (something that rarely happens in temperate climates and need not happen in hot climates if the crop is picked at the right time), then it must be reinforced. Again a choice of methods exists. The best is the addition of some unripe grapes. The other is to add a dose of tartaric or citric acid, a legitimate and widely used procedure but rather tricky.

These corrections made (always before fermentation), the yeasts have the field to themselves. It was not until 1857, when Pasteur initiated his great series of researches leading to the isolation of the living organisms called wine yeasts and definitely linked their vital processes with fermentation, that the process of alcoholic fermentation was really understood at all. If one examines a drop of fermenting grape juice under a microscope, he beholds a great number of translucent, single-cell living bodies, so small that they are invisible to the naked eye. There may be 80 million or more per cubic centimeter. Pasteur demonstrated that in winemaking the fermentation always proceeds in the presence of these organisms. He embodied his conclusion in the famous observation: "the chemical act of fermentation is essentially a phenomenon correlative with a vital act, beginning and ending with the latter. I am of the opinion that alcoholic fermentation never occurs without simultaneous organization, development, and multiplication of cells, or the continued life of cells already formed. . . . If I am asked in what consists the chemical act whereby the sugar is decomposed and what is its real cause, I reply that I am completely ignorant of it."

Pasteur's discoveries were a clean break with the assumptions then prevailing, a fact that is well shown by a monograph on winemaking which was printed in the annual report of the United States Commissioner of Patents in the year of Pasteur's first great discovery, 1857. Nowhere in the essay is it suggested that organisms are involved; the word yeast is not used. Pasteur's discoveries were the real beginning of the understanding of fermentation.

From then on the mystery has slowly yielded to study, and much has been learned of the nature of fermentation. However, there still remain intermediate steps in the process which are not understood. Pasteur had focused his attention upon the organisms always present in fermenting liquids. Another forty years later Eduard Buchner carried things forward by showing that fermentation is caused, not by the yeast itself, but by a substance that the yeast secretes. What he did was to crush and filter yeast cells and from them obtain a liquid entirely free of living matter. This liquid caused fermentation in a sugar solution even though no active yeast cells were present. He showed that the active agent is a secretion of the yeast cell, not the yeast itself, and he called this *zymase*, now understood to consist of numerous enzymes. These enzymes are substances secreted by molds and bacteria and are the effective agents, or catalysts, of numerous reactions in nature. The enzymes do not themselves enter into combination with the material of the reaction but in an unknown manner achieve their effect by contact; the contrast between their own small mass and the drastic changes they bring about is awe-inspiring.

Stated at its simplest (in the Gay-Lussac formula), alcoholic fermentation consists of the breaking down of the sugar molecule into alcohol and carbon dioxide in the presence of yeast enzymes:

$$C_6H_{12}O_6 \xrightarrow{\text{(enzymes)}} 2\ C_2H_5OH + 2\ CO_2 + \text{(calories)}$$

(sugar)	(alcohol)	(carbon dioxide)
100.00	51.34	48.66

Buchner's discovery opened the way to the special field of study known as enzymology, and we now know that alcoholic fermentation involves a series of different enzymes working in relay, so to speak. The molecules of sugar are not simply broken down into molecules of alcohol and carbon dioxide. Instead there is a series of reactions, of which at least thirty have been studied, each presided over by a different enzyme. These successive reactions follow "pathways" along which intermediate products are formed, only to be used up in subsequent steps.

Moreover, what goes on in the winemaker's fermenter is more complicated than a controlled laboratory fermentation, since grape must is variable in its composition and includes the many other substances besides sugar and water that have previously been mentioned. Other kinds of fermentation proceed alongside the alcoholic, often becoming entangled with it. Crushed grapes bring to the fermenter a large population of microorganisms other than wine yeasts, the latter usually being a minority. The others are yeast-like organisms and also bacteria of numerous species, some of which are benign so far as alcoholic fermentation is concerned, and some of which, the spoilage organisms, may cause fermentations that are harmful. There are ways of dealing with these aggressors. But fermentation in winemaking may be summed up without much exaggeration as a struggle between the bad guys and the good guys.

Carrying the complexity a bit further (but trying not to overdo it), there is no single wine yeast but a whole tribe of them, each behaving differently. The genus *Saccharomyces* is the most important. Of this genus the three species that matter most are *S. apiculata*, *S. ellipsoideus*,* and *S. oviformis*. They are distinguishable without too much difficulty under the microscope. In alcoholic fermentation *S. apiculata* is more numerous in the beginning and usually the first to take hold, but then drops out of the running when alcoholic content has attained 3 or 4 per cent. By that time *S. ellipsoideus*, the real workhorse, has multiplied tremendously and in fermenting for dry table wine usually carries through to the finish. Some strains of *S. ellipsoideus* may ferment as high as 16 per cent, but in general its activity begins to slow down at about 11 or 12 per cent. Toward the finish it is often given a boost by *S. oviformis*, which has the valuable ability to work in higher concentrations of alcohol, sometimes as high as 18 per cent. It is the "finishing" yeast species for wines normally rich in naturally-produced alcohol, such as the great Sauternes and the sherry-like Spanish Montillas, and is useful as well in the secondary fermentation of champagnes.

A half century ago it was thought that a massive inoculation with a single strain of "selected yeast" following the elimination of "wild yeast" from the juice with the help of SO_2 was the one sure way of obtaining a clean fermentation, and a cult was built on that assumption. Yeast inoculation is still correct practice, especially in hot countries, where danger

* Sticklers call it *S. cerevisiae* var. *ellipsoideus*.

of spoilage is always greatest. But the doctrine has been qualified. The participation of more than one yeast strain, and of certain bacteria as well, is acknowledged to be not only desirable but in practice almost unavoidable. In the cooler regions many experienced winemakers today are content with encouraging the naturally prevailing yeast flora.

This is as good a place as any to explode a myth. Yeasts that have been selected and propagated as pure strains are frequently named for the region where they were isolated, as for instance Montrachet or Sauternes or Steinberg. From this, the innocent too easily conclude that if they buy and use a yeast culture carrying one of these names, their wines will resemble those of Montrachet or Sauternes or the Rhineland, no matter what the raw material. This is not so. It is the grape, and only the grape, which determines that. The yeast strains that prevail in a given region may be found on whatever grapes happen to be growing there, whether white or red, Pinot Noir or one of the hybrids. No yeast strain is associated with a given grape variety.

The Fermented Result

When the turmoil of the primary fermentation is concluded, what we have in the raw, new wine is something very different from the original material. The most conspicuous difference is the transformation of the sugar. Again resorting to rough averages, the sugar has become, by weight:

Ethyl alcohol	48.4 per cent
Carbon dioxide	46.0 per cent
plus	
Glycerol	
Succinic acid	
Acetaldehyde	
Volatile acids	
(Material consumed by the yeast)	

Virtually all of the carbon dioxide is thrown off during fermentation. No proportions are given for the lesser compounds because the quantities, small in any case, are extremely variable. The glycerol, heavy and sweetish, partly accounts for the "tears" showing on the side of a wine glass. Glycerol and succinic acid together contribute to the softness and "body" of the wine. (An old Burgundian "secret" is to add a half wine glass of glycerin to a *pièce*, or barrel, of wine.) The acetaldehyde and volatile acids contribute to the wine's aroma and flavor but can be sources of trouble too.

As for the original acids and their salts, a part of the potassium bitartrate has precipitated and precipitation will continue as the new wine cools. Free tartaric acid carries over though part of it has entered into secondary reactions. The malic acid is reduced in quantity and some will have been converted into the milder lactic acid (see page 169).

Most of the nitrogenous matter has been used up as food by the yeasts. Some has entered into the composition of the *higher alcohols*, which in small quantity play a role in the development of the wine's bouquet. Minerals, pectins, and gums are still present in small quantities, and of course the tannins and pigments have been transferred from the skins to the wine. There are numerous volatile compounds, especially esters formed by the action of the acids on the alcohol. One of these, ethyl acetate, is the bane of winemakers, being the principal source of *piqûre*—the hot, sharp, vinegary odor and taste that spoils more wine than anything else.

The Cultivation of Yeasts

Since a rapid and continuous multiplication of the yeasts has first priority, the winemaker does everything he can to encourage it. The old empirical method takes advantage of the quite different behavior of yeasts in the presence of abundant air and when air is denied them. When they have plenty of air, the yeasts reproduce with great speed and vigor (the population doubling every two hours under ideal conditions) but make little alcohol; when air supply is reduced, they do not reproduce so rapidly, but their efficiency as makers of alcohol is increased.* During crushing, or the more primitive treading, there is maximum contact with air. It was to increase this contact that in times past the freshly crushed or trod grapes were tossed into the air with shovels and forks before being put into the fermenters. For the same reason the must in the fermenters is further exposed to air in various ways during the early part of fermentation.

This is also why the first fermentation of the vintage is always the slowest to get started and to be finished: the yeast must start from scratch. But soon the entire fermenting area, including equipment, is so well supplied with yeast that later fermentations get a big boost even as the grapes go through the crusher.

Yeasts have other needs besides the oxygen of the air. Their rate of growth is responsive to heat and cold. For reproduction they require some sugar, some nitrogen and phosphorus and other substances as well as vitamins. Sex is not involved: yeasts reproduce by fission and sporulation.

They readily survive extreme cold, but show small reproductive activity below 60° F. and do their best work between 65° and 80° F. Their rate of reproduction (and hence of alcohol production) slows down sharply beyond 95° F. and ceases entirely at about 105° F. At that temperature they are killed in about an hour, and at 140° F. in about ten minutes. These temperatures, again, must be taken as approximations because different strains behave differently. But the important point, for the winemaker, is that excessive temperature stops yeast growth and is a source of extreme danger. The reduced activity or death of the yeast leaves the field open to the spoilage organisms, which function well at higher temperatures. The winemaker therefore does whatever he can to hold the temperature of fermentation within the range which favors yeast growth but discourages growth of the spoilage bacteria, which is to say between 65° and 90° F. This upper

---

* Pasteur defined fermentation as "respiration without air."

limit is not itself harmful but it is the red flag that calls for cooling action.

The food which the yeast requires is normally available in ample quantity. But in special circumstances the nitrogen supply may need a bit of boosting.

I have made references earlier to the importance of the grapes' total acidity in promoting a clean fermentation—low acidity being a source of danger and high acidity a form of protection. The point here is that the saccharomyces are relatively indifferent to the acidity of the must, but that the harmful bacteria must have a neutral or only slightly acid medium for development. Therefore if the must is sufficiently acid the latter are held at bay.

Winemakers, then, encourage yeast growth in every possible way: by aerating the must, by controlling temperature, by assuring proper acidity. If these things are done, the naturally occurring yeasts will do the job nine times out of ten. But to make doubly sure of a good send-off most winemakers today take the precaution of adding a "starter."

Here we return to the subject of "selected yeast" inoculations. A strain of yeast is isolated under the microscope at the end of a successful fermentation and cultivated under sterile conditions. This culture is held dormant by refrigeration from one season to the next; several weeks before the vintage it is added to some fresh sterilized must and its rapid reproduction encouraged. A yeast "generator" is then put to work (in large wineries) producing fresh supplies of pure yeast starter for each successive fermentation, the starter being normally about 1 per cent of the volume to be fermented. Other yeasts may creep in, but the starter strain predominates. In recent years this rather difficult technique has been modified by the industrial propagation of wine yeast, just as bread yeast is produced. Wine yeast is equally available for mass production in large cakes of pressed yeast or for amateurs in dehydrated form in 5-gram envelopes.*

* In discussing yeast populations, one deals in fairly staggering figures. This dehydrated yeast averages 18 billion yeast cells per gram; a 5-gram packet therefore contains about 90 billion cells. (Communication from Dr. K. H. Steinkraus)

Another sort of starter is what the French call a *pied de cuve*. A *pied de cuve* is made by selecting a quantity of sound, ripe grapes a week before the vintage, crushing them into a crock, stirring in a small dose of SO_2, covering the crock, aerating occasionally, and so encouraging the spontaneous reproduction of the resident yeast flora. It will be in full fermentation a week later, is dumped and stirred into the first fermenter of the vintage proper, and off it goes. Some of the wet pomace from this fermenter, once it is in full fermentation, is used to start subsequent fermentations. The method was used, no one knew why, long before anyone was aware of the existence of yeasts; and in temperate climates, where the acid level is safe, it still is.

The Uses of Sulfur

Sulfur in the form of the gas sulfur dioxide (SO_2) is indispensable in winemaking, a versatile tool of many uses. It is an antiseptic, an antioxidant, a defense against unwanted enzymes and aldehydes, a preservative.

Sulfur dioxide is the gas formed when elemental sulfur is burned:

$$S + O_2 \rightarrow SO_2$$

The practice of burning sulfur wicks or candles in empty wine containers to keep them "sweet," that is, to prevent mold growth and souring, is very old, and sulfur is still used universally for this purpose. Its more sophisticated uses came along later; and the first of these to concern us is its use in primary fermentations.

When added to the freshly crushed grapes, or must, sulfur acts as a selective antiseptic or disinfectant, inhibiting or destroying the unwanted molds and bacteria that may be present but not injuring the wanted yeasts. Introduced at this point, it does no more than stun the yeasts. After a brief interval the partially sterilized material is aerated by stirring or pumping. This revives the yeasts, which promptly get to work. At this point the *pied de cuve*, or other yeast starter, is added, and a correct fermentation is off to a good beginning.

The other uses of sulfur occur after fermentation. When the wine is subsequently "racked" (pumped or siphoned) from its sediment, or lees, a small added dose of so₂ combines with the oxygen inevitably picked up and so prevents the oxidation that might otherwise affect flavor or cause browning. It also destroys enzymes responsible for oxidation and hazing; and it combines with the acetaldehyde which otherwise has an adverse effect on the aroma, the "freshness," the flavor, and the lasting power of wine.

Without its use, any prolonged aging of the wine is practically impossible. Dry table wines conforming to present standards did not exist prior to these applications of so₂, the reason being that in nature wine is not an end product but an intermediate product which if left to itself goes on to become vinegar, or worse. The unique function of so₂ is to halt the natural sequence of reactions at midpoint, when wine is wine, and conserve it as wine. The ancients had resort to other preservatives, such as the pine gum which gives the denatured flavor to Greek retsina; but for the most part whatever wine they had left by midsummer following the vintage was hardly drinkable.

Another valuable characteristic of so₂ is that if properly used its free, or active, form conveniently disappears when it has done its work. Some escapes by evaporation. What remains behind in the wine exists, unnoticed and inoffensive, in what is called a "combined" state—sulfites and sulfates in traces. It goes without saying that the excessive use of sulfur or its use at the wrong time is as bad as the excessive or un-timely use of anything else. Too much so₂ in the beginning can prevent complete fermentation even by the good yeasts; too much of it used afterward harms both aroma and flavor, and in really massive doses it is not good for you. Legal limits prevail wherever wine is made. An over-sulfured wine is in-stantly recognized by its acrid, sneeze-inducing odor, its pallid color, its dried-out taste. One cannot assume that because a little sulfur is a good thing, a great deal of it is a better thing.

There are several sources of SO_2. Though burning sulfur wicks or pastilles remains a standard method of keeping cooperage in condition, it is not an accurate way of introducing SO_2 into wine because most of the gas is forced out as the wine enters the sulfured barrel or tank and the amount picked up by the wine cannot be premeasured. Large wineries use compressed liquid SO_2 which comes in cylinders. Some use a dilute aqueous solution, but the preparation is onerous. The best source for the small winery, the laboratory technician, or the amateur winemaker is the salt known as potassium metabisulfite ($K_2S_2O_5$). This is a white, crystalline powder soluble in water. It keeps well in a closed glass or plastic (never metallic) container. The salt, commonly called "meta,"* contains 57 per cent by weight of SO_2, which is released when the salt comes in contact with the mild acidity of the must or wine.

For practical purposes, then, a given weight of "meta" salt provides one with half its weight in SO_2. If 1 gram of SO_2 is the correct dose, all one has to do is to add 2 grams of the salt, dissolved in a bit of warm water, and stir in thoroughly. The correct dose of the gas is instantly released, as your nose will inform you. Aside from the accuracy of this method, an advantage is that nothing else is added to the must which would not normally be found there, the other products being mere traces of water and cream of tartar, both normal constituents.

The Fundamentals Applied

We have had a look at what is involved in vinous fermentation. Now a few words on the management of this process. (We will assume that red wine is being made.) Very little time elapses after crushing and stemming before the fermenter

---

* And so called throughout this book.

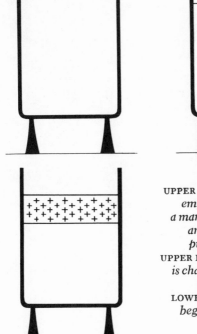
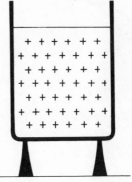

UPPER LEFT: *An open fermenter, empty. Large ones require a manhole close to the bottom and assorted fittings for pumping and draining.*
UPPER RIGHT: *The open fermenter is charged with crushed grapes but is not filled full.*
LOWER LEFT: *As fermentation begins, skins and stems rise to form the cap.*

begins to show signs of life. There is that distinct and beguiling odor. A separation takes place in the mass, the solid matter of the grapes rising to the surface and forming what the French call the *chapeau*, meaning hat or cap. If a hole is poked through the cap, the liquid beneath (which has begun to pick up color) gushes and foams up through, looking like the gay part of a strawberry ice cream soda. Fermentation is under way.

The mass gathers force. The liquid beneath the cap is in convection, like boiling water. It gives off a sound reminiscent of a swarm of bees, the odor becomes more insistent, and the force of the gas as it seeks escape packs the cap more densely.

Pumping over in a large open fermenter.

Remember that nearly one-half of the *weight* of the sugar is converted into gas, an immense volume at normal pressures. The gas is not toxic, but it is heavier than air and in a closed room soon displaces the air from the floor up. Persons entering a poorly ventilated fermenting place do so with caution or they may be suffocated: the traditional precaution was to carry a lighted candle, which goes out if the gas is too dense for safety. Large wineries have ventilators to carry it off.

The system of *cuvage*, which is to say the actual conduct of fermentation, differs from one winemaking region to another. The traditional method, and in small-scale winemaking still the best, is the "open" system, in which the cap floats unimpeded on the surface in an open fermenter. The cap is broken up at least twice a day, an operation called punching down. In this way the cap is given maximum access to air during the

crucial beginning when the yeasts need it for rapid development, and the punching down distributes the multiplying
yeast throughout the whole fermenting mass. It also brings
all the liquid into contact with the skins, for good color
extraction.

The ancient practice was for one of the winemakers to
strip, climb onto the solid cap, and work his way down into
it (always hanging onto the edge of the tank), thrashing about
until he could stand the fumes no longer, then being hauled
out and replaced. This method may be, and has been, justly
criticized on sanitary, aesthetic, and humanitarian grounds,
and today would bring hordes of FDA and OSHA (Opera-
tional Safety and Health Administration) inspectors on the
run, but it does a splendid job and is probably still used here
and there in places where the writ of OSHA does not run.
The amateur usually punches down by rolling up his sleeves
and stirring the mass with his arms, first putting on an apron.
If the fermenter is too large for that, he may put on a pair of
long rubber boots reserved for the purpose, sit on the edge,
and do it with his feet. When wine is fermented in larger
quantities, punching down ceases to be feasible. The fermenter may be of the open kind or partially closed. The
equivalent of punching down is accomplished by the process
called pumping over, or *remontage* in France. The free-run
must, meaning the fermenting juice beneath the cap of skins,
is drawn off into a sump through a valve at the base of the
fermenter, pumped back to the top, and sprayed over the cap,
thus providing the needed oxygen for the yeast and extracting
color from the cap by percolation.

We have seen that in fermentation some form of heat
control is necessary. During fermentation the temperature of
the must rises—faster and higher in a large tank than in a
small one because the radiating surface in a large tank is proportionately smaller, and more in a concrete tank than a wooden
one. Thus radiation from small, open-top wooden, stainless
steel, or plastic fermenters provides a certain amount of auto-
matic temperature control. But frequent temperature readings
are as routine as in a hospital. Before temperature reaches the

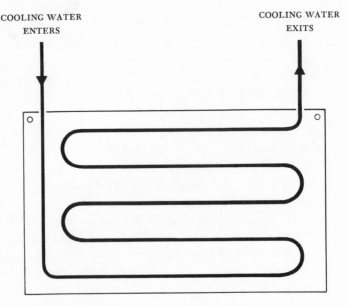

COOLING WATER
ENTERS

COOLING WATER
EXITS

Drapeau, for warming or cooling.

danger point, measures are taken to bring it down. There are
various ways of doing this. In large commercial operations,
the usual practice is to pump over, running the must through
a heat exchanger to cool it. The most elegant solution is a
stainless-steel-jacketed tank: a coolant circulated through the
jacket provides precise temperature control all the time, auto-
mated with the help of a thermostat. In moderate-size operations such as in the Burgundy region of France winemakers
use a device called a *drapeau* (meaning flag). It is essentially
a flat "coil," or a pair of formed metal plates either coated
with or made of stainless steel bonded together to create a
serpentine canalization running between. The *drapeau* is suspended in the fermenting mass and cold water is circulated
through it (or for that matter hot water if the fermentation
is a slow starter). For the amateur, a quick substitute is a
plastic bag filled with ice cubes. In extreme situations the
free run is drawn off and the remainder pressed from the skins
before fermentation is finished, the half-finished wine being

transferred to small containers and allowed to finish at a more leisurely, and hence cooler, pace.

Progress of the fermentation is followed by checking the loss of sugar with the saccharometer, and by tasting. Assuming that all goes forward smoothly with no trying interludes, the violence begins to subside after a few days. The humming is reduced to a whisper; the cap, no longer supported by escaping gas, begins to sink.

When red-wine fermentation proceeds normally, the sugar is transformed into alcohol at the rate of about 4 per cent a day, so that a must of 20 per cent sugar is fermented out dry in about five days, although the period may vary from three days to ten or more. When fermentation is finished, or preferably when it has 1 or 2 percentage points of sugar to go, the free run is drawn off and the pomace (solid residue) is pressed. The precise time for doing this is a matter of regional or individual preference but should not be postponed much beyond the point when the wine has reached the desired level of dryness. In this operation (called *décuvage* in French), the free run is drained off first. The saturated pomace is transferred mechanically or by hand to the press. The pomace, after the first pressing, is usually loosened and pressed again. The press wine is always darker in color than the free run and higher in tannin and other extractives but usually a bit lower in alcohol since small quantities of alcohol may be drawn back into the skins. In large operations the two are often kept separate, the free run being considered superior and the wine from the final pressing being sent to the distiller. On the other hand, the extra oomph of the press wine may be just what the free run needs for "completeness," in which case it is added back. Much depends on the nature of the original raw material, and this is one of the places where the judgment of the winemaker comes in.

The exhausted pomace may be used for making sugar wine or *piquette* (page 216) or for the distillation of neutral fortifying alcohol or one of those ardent and indelicate spirits called *marc* in France and *grappa* in Italy. But amateur distillation is illegal in the United States.

Bailing the last of the pomace from small open fiberglass fermenters into a small horizontal French wine press.

In the course of drawing off and pressing, the new wine is transferred to casks or other appropriate vessels which are filled full and lightly stoppered, often with a fermenting valve or "bubbler." There it undergoes a much quieter secondary fermentation, during which all remaining traces of sugar are fermented, and various other inconspicuous but important changes take place which will be dealt with later. These changes transform the new wine from a merely muddy and somewhat alcoholic liquid into something worth all the trouble.

The foregoing description of fermentation was based on the making of red wine. The making of white wine is different in two ways: first, the grapes are pressed immediately or soon after crushing and the fresh, sweet juice is fermented by itself, *off* the skins; and second, the course of fermentation is usually slower, less likely to impose heat problems, more likely to impose yeast-growth problems. Details of procedures for red wine and white wine are dealt with in Chapters 8 and 9 respectively.

CHAPTER 7

Premises and Equipment

 DURING AN EIGHT-HOUR working day, an average man puts out about one-twenty-third of a horsepower, which is equivalent to thirty-seven watts. That explains the most conspicuous characteristic of commercial winemaking—the substitution of machine power for human muscle. The first steps are modest: power multipliers like jacks and levers, fractional horsepower motors, gravity, small pumps, and simple conveyors are brought in to do most of the heavy work. Larger operations resort to specialized material-handling equipment and automation coupled with precise control in the winery and in the laboratory, all the way from crushing to bottling. Engineers and food technologists take over.

Yet what happens in the big fermenters and storage tanks of an industrial winery is not essentially different from what happens when a competent home winemaker goes to work. The principles are the same no matter how large or small the quantities involved. The gains from volume production are in efficient handling, control, and uniformity. The loss is in individuality.

The preceding chapter laid down the fundamentals of winemaking and offered a glimpse of the practical art. The chapters that follow go into detail and are mainly devoted to what might be called mini-winemaking. But it is only right to say that the mini-winemaker follows an ancient tradition and is in good company.

Throughout most of history wine was made only in small lots by hand (and foot). Many of the world's great wines are still made in quantities one or two men can manage in what are no more than farm outbuildings and with minimal mechanical equipment.

Most of the significant insights into the winemaking process have been gained by men working with mini-fermentations and small lots. Pasteur was working and thinking small, exceeding small, when he made his epochal discovery of the role of yeasts, and so was the chemist Buchner. The same was true of L. Ferré in Beaune and J. Ribéreau-Gayon in Bordeaux when they unraveled the secret of malolactic fermentation. E. W. Hilgard laid the groundwork for the modern California wine industry on the basis of hundreds of small fermentations of small lots of grapes grown in all parts of the state. Years later his basic work was confirmed and extended by Maynard Amerine and A. J. Winkler in the same way. In experimenting with new grapes lots are necessarily small, since in the beginning there may be the fruit of no more than a single vine to work with.

Wherever research on winemaking is done—in Bordeaux; Montpellier; Geisenheim; Davis, California; Geneva, New York—small fermentations, hundreds of them, provide the material. Visit the fermenting rooms of such research centers and what you see is hardly more than a refinement of any amateur's premises. The same is true for that matter in every large winery that prides itself on its technology: the small fermentation precedes the large; the small blend comes before the large. And there is gustatory satisfaction as well as insight to be had from such work with small lots, as anyone knows who has ever had access to the wine "libraries" at Davis or Geneva.

As for the army of amateurs, their motives are as various as the motives of amateurs always are. Most of them both in this country and abroad have no loftier goal than to put good wine on the family table. Yet they often find as much pleasure in the making as in the drinking. Every field of knowledge owes a debt to amateurs and the amateur spirit, and winemaking is no exception. What these amateurs all have in common is that they work in miniature.

The Premises

The amateur winemaker must fit his labors into whatever space he has, and into his budget. If he is lucky enough to live in the country, he may be able to adapt part of a farm building as a small winery; if a town dweller, he will make do with laundry, basement, garage, or even a corner of the kitchen or pantry if he can get away with it. Almost always compromises have to be made.

Since crushing and pressing are messy operations, a slightly sloping concrete or tile floor with a drain in it is a big advantage. In the absence of that, the best solution to the cleanup problem is to do the crushing and pressing on the back porch or in the backyard.

Running water is a necessity, preferably hot and cold. There should be some means of holding the temperature of the fermenting place at around 65° to 70° F. during the vintage period and into November. Basement temperatures are usually satisfactory, except near a boiler. If an outbuilding is available, it should be sufficiently insulated and in cold climates should have some source of heat, for instance a small stove or portable electric heater. It is important to maintain this moderate warmth for a month after the primary fermentation is done, for reasons to be discussed later. After that, cold temperature is needed for clearing and stabilizing the wine. A temperature as low as 25° F. is helpful, not harmful. Well-equipped wineries use cold rooms and heat exchangers for this purpose. Older wineries in cool climates use nature for a heat exchanger by opening the doors of their primary storage cellars.

Ventilation and excessive humidity or dryness must be taken into account. Lighting must be adequate, and power outlets will come in handy. There has to be storage space for equipment, empty bottles, and the wine itself. Sanitation is important because wine is easily contaminated. There should be a sink, preferably a double one, a well-lit table next to it for tasting and analysis, above it a shelf for records and references, and nearby a cabinet or more shelves for glassware, testing equipment, reagents, and other small items.

Essential Equipment

Most domestic winemakers ferment between twenty and one hundred gallons a year,* using grapes of their own growing or grapes bought in the market, often supplemented with concentrate. Smaller quantities may be successfully made but good results are less certain, and twenty to forty gallons require hardly more labor than five gallons. Whatever the quantity to be made, certain items of equipment are necessary:

Small crusher	Metabisulfite or sulfur strips or pastilles
Small press	Funnels
Saccharometer	Laboratory scale
Pails and tub	Kitchen scale
Fermenter	Assorted Pyrex or plastic measures
Wine storage vessels	Absorbent cotton
Siphoning tube	Thermometer
Corker or capper	Stoppers

* The maximum allowable for home winemakers is 200 gallons. Federal regulations require that the nearest office of the Bureau of Alcohol, Tobacco, and Firearms be notified on a small form provided for the purpose, but the requirement is treated quite casually. This is a *notification*, not an *application*, as home winemaking is a civil liberty under the Constitution.

A simple hand or power crusher.
(Geneva, New York, Experiment Station)

A portable, peasant-size crusher-stemmer, an elevator,
and 260-gallon fiberglass fermenters.

CRUSHER. Whether hand driven or motor driven, the grapes are passed between the rollers, stems and all, into a bucket or tub or directly into the fermenter. A crusher is often shared by several winemakers or rented. Lacking a crusher, a well-washed bare foot or rubber boot in a tub will do as good a job. Really. In making red wine, some or all of the stems may be removed by hand after crushing. There are lightweight, hand-operated crusher-stemmers for home winemakers. These are considerably more expensive than a simple crusher and are almost always shared or rented.

PRESS. The classic Italian press with a heavy screw running up the middle is illustrated, in several sizes and styles. A second-hand cider press will also do the job. With a bit of imagination, a homemade press using either a ratchet or hydraulic truck jack for power can be devised.

In commercial winemaking the classic Italian model still has a place in small European establishments. It has generally been replaced in larger enterprises by hydraulic, pneumatic and semi-automatic horizontal screw presses as well as continuous presses, some of which are illustrated just for the record.

A small Italian-type screw press being used
for some experimental lots. This style comes in many sizes,
some with a hydraulic pressing unit.

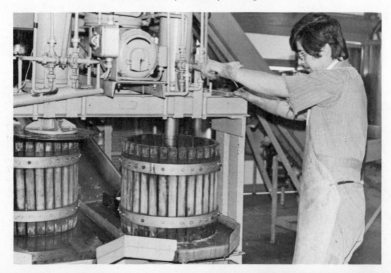

TOP LEFT: *Filling the press basket.*
TOP RIGHT: *Pressure provided by hydraulic unit.*
BOTTOM LEFT: *What it's all about.*
BOTTOM RIGHT: *Opening basket to remove pomace.*

*A homemade rack-and-cloth press powered by a hydraulic jack.
It may also be adapted to a press basket.*

*Thousands of experimental lots have gone through
this small hydraulic press at the Davis station.*

SACCHAROMETER. This instrument, with its cylindrical jar, is indispensable, inexpensive, and available from any winemakers' shop. The sugar content of the grapes must be known, since alcoholic content of the finished wine is related directly to it. The saccharometer provides this information. It is a calibrated glass spindle weighted at one end so that it will float upright in the juice to be tested. It is in fact a special form of hydrometer that measures the specific gravity of the juice. A liquid containing dissolved sugar and other solids is heavier than water and thus causes the saccharometer to float higher than it would in plain water. In plain water the instrument will float so that zero on the scale is exactly at the level of the fluid, reading at the top of the meniscus. If the juice contains, say, 20 per cent sugar by weight, then the instrument, floating much higher, will give the appropriate reading at the level of the liquid. It is as simple as that.

Pressing red wine in a small winery.
Horizontal Vaslin screw press.

Saccharometers are made in various lengths (the longer the spindle, the more accurate the reading), and they are fitted with scales that differ according to the convention of the country. In the United States the Brix, or Balling, scale (different names for the same thing) is usual. This scale gives a direct reading of the proportion of "total solids" dissolved in the must; and of course most of these "total solids" are sugar. Often the spindle has two parallel scales: one showing Balling degrees, the other showing specific gravity. American saccharometers are calibrated for a juice temperature of 60° F., and the meticulous take a temperature reading along with the

A simple French alcohol-testing still.
A diagram of the standard lab set-up on page 287.

Balling reading and make an appropriate correction (a thermometer is enclosed in some saccharometer spindles). French
winemakers use a scale that indicates the *potential alcoholic
content* of the must sample. The Germanic countries use still
another, the Oechsle scale. The French scale is perhaps simplest to use; but all of these scales are referable to the specific
gravity of the must (see table, page 149). In taking the sugar
test it is important to use a representative sample of must.
For accuracy the saccharometer must be scrupulously clean
and float free, and the must sample should be strained to clear
out extraneous matter.

An alternate instrument is a hand refractometer, which
needs only a drop or two of must for a quick reading. One
must take care, however, that the sample is representative.

PAILS AND TUB. Grape must and wine are mildly
acid and hence interact with most metals, especially iron,
causing "metal pickup" problems later. For this reason, one
should use ten- or twelve-quart plastic pails, which are cheap
and available everywhere; or stainless steel pails, which are
expensive. The smallest operation requires two or three pails,
plus a shelf to drain them on. The tub is for crushing into and
all sorts of miscellaneous uses. It should be of wood, fiberglass,
or sturdy plastic. Two good oak tubs of twenty-five-gallon
capacity may be made in about five minutes by sawing a
second-hand barrel in two. The interior of such tubs should
be scraped and scrubbed and then coated (using a cheap new
paintbrush) with melted household paraffin or jelly wax. The
tub should be soaked tight before using, and the paraffin coating renewed as necessary.

FERMENTER. For small lots of red wine, the half-
barrel oak tub makes a good fermenter, as does a plastic
garbage pail or a large, old-fashioned dairy crock. For larger
lots, a used fifty-gallon barrel with one head knocked out is
satisfactory. To make such a fermenter, loosen the top
hoops, knock the head into the barrel with a mallet, pulling

it out edgewise, then replace the hoops and drive them tight. The interior should be scraped clean and given a coating of hot paraffin.

For white wine fermentations of must only, five- or twelve-gallon glass carboys of the kind used for chemicals or spring water are ideal. They are easily cleaned, and they let you observe the action. Large plastic jugs, jars, or bottles are also suitable.

WINE STORAGE VESSELS.   These are for handling and storage following the primary fermentation. Again, the novice will do well to begin with five-gallon glass bottles. They are sanitary, they continue to let you see what is going on, they are easily moved about even when full. For a twenty-gallon vintage the winemaker will require not four but five or six such containers—a spare is needed for racking or siphoning into. He will also want a few bottles of smaller sizes (three-gallon, two-gallon, and several one-gallon) since containers must be kept full once the fermentation is over and quantities never come out even.

This is the appropriate place for a word of warning about wood cooperage, the traditional storage material. Beware of it. Wood cooperage ranges in size from five-gallon kegs through barrels, butts, puncheons, bilge casks, and ovals on up to great tanks holding thousands of gallons. White oak, the customary wood for cooperage, has one substantial advantage and many disadvantages. The advantage is that just the right amount of extractive from a white oak barrel contributes to the special bouquet and flavor that is associated with Bordeaux and certain other red wines. Years ago the Bordelais discovered empirically that a *barrique* of 225 liters, which is about the size of our fifty-gallon barrels, gives just the right ratio of wood surface to volume of wine to yield this result, if proper care is taken. But the minute one moves to larger cooperage that ratio disappears, so that in larger casks one is left with most of the disadvantages of a white oak container, minus its one indisputable advantage.

As for the disadvantages: small cooperage (meaning any-

*Soaking, tightening, and sterilizing
a small cooperage prior to the vintage.*

thing with a capacity of fifty gallons or less) is responsible for more spoilage and loss in winemaking than anything else, once the original fermentation is over. The reasons include its tendency to shrink and warp and spring unexpected leaks, and above all the difficulty of keeping it clean when empty. Rinsings won't do this. If you don't believe it, try rinsing a barrel six times with hot water. The drain water from the sixth rinsing will still not be clear. A freshly emptied wine barrel contains in the pores of the wood up to a gallon of wine, which is released only gradually. The pores and interior surface are an ideal habitat for molds and bacteria. Not even regular sulfuring can be relied on to control these, and once mold gets into the wood you might as well cut up the barrel for firewood. Stronger agents such as hypochlorite or quaternary ammonium compounds are hard to rinse out completely and any residue is deadly to wine quality. Finally, wine shrinkage, leakage, and evaporation leave an open space for the development of aerobic bacteria if routine topping (that is, filling that empty space called "ullage") is neglected. Also, a charred whisky barrel puts things into the wine that ought not to be there. A waxed barrel eliminates the one virtue of cooperage, which is its oakiness. Even the oakiness injures the wine unless the barrel is of *white* oak. Small kegs are the worst offenders. So unless you know very well what you are doing, keep away from oak cooperage.

SIPHONING TUBE.   This should be a six-foot length of good-quality rubber or transparent plastic laboratory tubing, three-eighths-inch or one-half-inch inside diameter. It is used for racking (that is, siphoning) the young wine at various stages of its development and also in bottling. The intake end should be notched for free suction. For the squeamish there are racking tubes with bulbs to start the suction.

CORKER OR CAPPER.   Straight-sided wine corks, being larger in diameter than the neck of a wine bottle, need a device for compressing them and driving them in. Two inexpensive types of hand corking machines are illustrated on page 200. If screw-cap bottles are used instead of cork-finish bottles, obtain a supply of new caps from a glassware supplier. Crown caps are feasible, and cappers are available at all winemakers' shops.

MISCELLANEOUS.   The uses of SO_2 have been mentioned and will be returned to repeatedly. The sources are sulfur strips or pastilles (for burning) or metabisulfite. Potassium metabisulfite is preferable to the sodium salt, but the latter will do. One needs several sizes of funnels, plastic or stainless steel. A small scale such as photographers use for measuring in grains and fractions of ounces is useful, as is an ordinary kitchen scale for weighing sugar. Pyrex or plastic measures come in handy in all sorts of ways, as does absorbent cotton. The thermometer must be immersible.

Desirable but not Indispensable

When the novice winemaker begins to get the feel of things and finds that he really can make good wine, he begins to cast about for ways of doing the job better: reducing the labor and improving control. The following notes may prove helpful when that point is reached. Some of the items of equipment about to be mentioned come close to being necessities for the really serious amateur. Not many years ago they were hard to find. But with the astonishing increase of domestic winemaking, shops dealing in such items have sprung up. Some dealers are franchised, others are independents. Generally speaking, the latter are preferable as the proprietors are more likely to know what they are talking about.

LABORATORY EQUIPMENT. The saccharometer, as we have seen, is a *sine qua non*, as is a good immersible thermometer. But the careful winemaker wants to go beyond them. He wants to know the *total acidity* of the must before it begins to ferment, and of the new wine, and of the wine as it evolves. For this he needs a simple titrating set (illustrated on page 287) or one of those acid-testing tubes that small French winegrowers use, with the appropriate reagents—the actual test is extremely simple. He will also want to test his wine for *volatile acidity*, this being the indicator of infection and disease. This calls for a more complex apparatus (see page 149). He may also want to test for both free and combined SO_2, especially if he takes to making sweet wines, which require a constant level of free SO_2 to inhibit refermenting in bottle. The standard test for *residual sugar* is rather complex; but there now exists a shortcut in the form of prepared "sugar pills," devised originally for testing sugar in urine, which come with instructions and give an instant if not exact reading.

The serious amateur knows in advance what the approximate *alcoholic content* is going to be, and that is usually enough to know because the precise content is less important than an alcohol/acid balance that pleases the senses. But if he wants to know the result precisely, he will need a laboratory alembic, or distilling outfit. This consists of a small flask and heat source (either a Bunsen burner or an alcohol lamp) for distilling off the alcohol, a cooling coil for condensing the distillate, an alcohol hydrometer, an appropriately graduated flask, and a table for interpreting readings. These are available as kits, or may be assembled. An alternative to the alembic is an ebulliometer (page 289), which indicates alcoholic content by boiling point. It is easy to use, but expensive.

In addition to the tests that can be conducted with these basic analytical instruments, there is no limit to the range of inquiry (and accompanying laboratory equipment) into the composition of must and wine, including the microscopic examination of the life that goes on in them. But such matters are beyond the scope of this modest treatise.

BOTTLING EQUIPMENT.   Stiff brushes are needed for cleaning used wine bottles, longer ones for the five-gallon bottles, dairy brushes for other equipment. Simple bottle rinsers that may be screwed onto a sink faucet can be purchased. A draining device for rinsed bottles is necessary, the simplest being a piece of board with neck holes bored into it, the next simplest being some sort of A-shaped rack with perforated cross pieces to hold the necks of the inverted bottles. Small lots are easily bottled with the siphoning tube, with or without a small stop-start valve that can be inserted into the filling end. For larger quantities there are siphon fillers fed by gravity from a bottling tank, with from two to eight spouts.

WINE TRANSFER.   Buckets, funnel, and siphoning tubes give way to more pretentious equipment when the scale of operations increases. A bronze spigot with cone provides an easy way to drain fermenters and barrels and casks. There are various sorts of hand pumps for the transfer of crushed and stemmed grapes and new wine. A small bronze mail-order pump with a neoprene impeller is useful, mounted on a home-made base and driven by a one-quarter-horsepower motor and using half-inch or three-quarter-inch transparent tubing. Pumps that expose the wine to iron should never be used.

CLARIFICATION. This is done by the addition of *fining* materials, of which there are many. The best and simplest for the small-scale winemaker are powdered tannin and ordinary grocery-store gelatin, added in correct doses during a racking. More about this later. Filtration by primitive methods (as through filter paper or a bag filter) should never be done as this exposes the wine too freely to air and promotes oxidation. There exist perfected filters of every capacity, which avoid exposure to air and are universally used in commercial winemaking. The small laboratory sizes do a beautiful job, but their cost makes them a luxury: some winemakers' supply shops have them available for rent.

MISCELLANEOUS. As time goes on, the small-scale winemaker will feel the need for a range of other small items —fermenting valves or bubblers, paper towel dispenser, roll of wax paper, corks and rubber stoppers of various sizes, a bench or wall corkscrew, an assortment of broad scrubbing brushes and stiff brooms, galvanized or plastic washtub for soaking used bottles and many other purposes, rubber gloves, rubber boots, rubberized or plastic apron, platform or hanging scale for weighing grapes, spade or shovel for handling pomace, dolly for moving filled tubs or five-gallon bottles, heavy wooden and rubber mallets, file cabinet, homemade *drapeau* for cooling or warming fermentations as needed, electric plate or Bunsen burner, plastic sheeting to cover fermenters, insecticide fogger for coping with fruit flies, penlight for peering into opaque fermenters and wine vessels, graduated glassware for making blends, side-illuminated black box for examining wine clarity, metal siphon, "wine thief" for taking samples. Of such things there is no end, and winemakers' shops can supply lots of tempting gadgetry.

CHAPTER 8

Making Red Wine

 THE GRAPES are on hand. A Californian will be using *vinifera* grapes presumably. An Easterner will be using the common California varieties that are shipped east, or else either the standard American sorts (in which case his wine will have the "foxy" flavor) or the newer French hybrids. Particulars on grape varieties are to be found in Appendix A. Or he may be trying his hand with canned grape concentrate (see Chapter 13 for details).

What follows in this chapter assumes a domestic vintage of modest size, using as a fermenter a fifty-gallon barrel with one head removed or a plastic or fiberglass equivalent. The maximum quantity of grapes to be handled in an open fifty-gallon fermenter is seven good bushels or a dozen California "lugs" (the standard shipping box), either of which will yield somewhere around twenty-five gallons of wine.

Crushing

Check the fermenter for cleanness and (if a barrel) for tightness. Mount it on three bricks or blocks. Place the crusher across the open top. Empty grapes into the hopper and crush them. The crushed bunches, dripping juice, will plop directly into the fermenter. Do not wash the grapes in advance. Discard badly rotted bunches, but a bit of rot will not hurt. Fill the fermenter no more than three-fourths full.

When the crushing is done, remove and rinse the crusher immediately. Using both hands scoop out let's say one-half of the stems from the fermenter (the fewer the stems, the less tannic the finished wine). When that is done, clean up before things get too sticky.

Then remove about a pint of the juice for use in testing sugar content and possibly total acidity.* Set aside, covered, to settle. After the sample has been taken, dissolve a bit of potassium metabisulfite (meta) in a glass of warm water, pour it into the fermenter, and stir it in thoroughly. You will smell the SO_2 as you mix it in, added at this point to kill or immobilize spoilage organisms and give the good yeasts their chance. Correct dose: ⅛ oz. (3.5 gm.) per 100 lb. of grapes. A bushel of grapes weighs about forty pounds, a "lug" about twenty-four pounds. The meta dose is essential if California grapes are used and a wise precaution in all cases. After the meta is well stirred in, cover the open top of the fermenter with a piece of plastic sheeting or a clean cloth to keep out dust and fruit flies.

Preparing the Starter

If a yeast starter has not already been prepared, this is the time to do it. Before covering the fermenter, bail out a half-bucketful of mixed skins and juice. Wipe off the outside of the bucket, add a "pinch" of meta, place the bucket in a washtub half-filled with warm water, and cover it. Open a 5-gram envelope of dehydrated wine yeast (the little metallic packet containing 20 billion yeast cells, usually the Montrachet strain, and available from winemakers' shops), empty the brown

---

* Few people know how delicious fresh grape juice is. Draw off a bottle of it, put it in the refrigerator to settle, and have it for breakfast next morning. In some parts of Europe grape juice "cures" are popular during the vintage season.

granules into a measuring cup, and cover with an ounce or two of warm water to rehydrate the yeast. In a few minutes it will have taken up all the water. Add more water and let stand for twenty minutes, then stir to break up any lumps: the expanded yeast will have the consistency of light cream and smell like ordinary baker's yeast. To this, add a cupful of grape juice taken from the pail and let stand, covered, for another hour. At the end of that time the swiftly multiplying starter will show signs of fermentation. Pour it all into the half-bucketful of warmed skins and juice, stir thoroughly, renew the warm water in the washtub, cover, and stir occasionally. If this is done in the morning, the mass will be in full fermentation by late afternoon and ready to use. If done in the evening, it will be ready the next morning.

Testing and Correcting the Must

Now for testing the sugar content, and the total acidity also if this is to be done. The time for these tests is during the intervals in preparing the yeast starter.

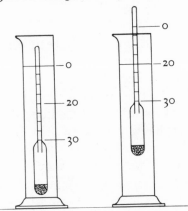

Saccharometer and hydrometer jar.
Floats at zero in plain water;
floats higher according to the sugar content of must.

TESTING AND CORRECTING FOR SUGAR

| | | | | TO MAKE WINE OF 10% BY VOL.‡ ADD | | TO MAKE WINE OF 12% BY VOL.‡ ADD | |
| | WHAT THE SACCHAROMETER SHOWS | | | | | | |
Specific Gravity	Crude Balling*	Potential Alcohol (Dujardin scale)†	Sugar per gal. (in lbs.)	In pounds per 10 gal.	In ounces per gal.	In pounds per 10 gal.	In ounces per gal.
1.039	10	4.5	.6875	7.426	11.80	10.125	16.19
1.044	11	5.1	.7765	6.436	10.13	9.234	14.77
1.048	12	5.7	.8663	5.539	8.86	8.337	13.33
1.052	13	6.2	.9568	4.634	7.41	7.432	11.90
1.056	14	7.2	1.0480	3.722	5.94	6.521	10.43
1.061	15	7.8	1.1399	2.903	4.64	5.601	8.92
1.065	16	8.4	1.2326	1.876	3.00	4.675	7.47
1.069	17	9.2	1.3260	.942	1.50	3.740	5.98
1.074	18	9.8	1.4202			2.798	4.31
1.078	19	10.5	1.5151			1.849	2.95
1.082	20	11.2	1.6106			.894	1.42
1.087	21	11.9	1.7073				
1.091	22	12.6	1.8047				
1.095	23	13.4	1.9027				
1.099	24	14.1	2.0016				
1.103	25	14.9	2.1014				
1.107	26	15.5	2.2020				

* The indication when the Balling saccharometer is floated in grape juice. It indicates the proportion by weight of total solids (most of the solids being sugar).

† The indication when the French, or Dujardin, saccharometer is floated in grape juice. Direct reading shows potential alcoholic content by volume of the unfermented juice.

‡ Remember that the result is not precise—the yield of alcohol varying under the conditions of fermentation. To make wine of 11% by volume, add quantity halfway between.

Note that all columns are referable to the specific gravity scale.

SUGAR TEST. We know, as explained earlier, that to be stable and palatable a finished dry wine should have an alcoholic content of from 10 to 12 per cent by volume, and that 2 degrees of sugar yield 1 per cent of alcohol. If the sugar is too low, it should be corrected by an appropriate supplement before fermentation. Strain a sufficient part of the sample through a piece of cheesecloth and pour the strained juice into the hydrometer jar, filling it about three-fourths full. The temperature should be between 55° and 75° F. for a reasonably correct reading. If it is not within this range, cool it or warm it. Be sure that the saccharometer is clean and dry and insert it carefully by the tip into the sample. When it is floating freely and has come to rest, take a reading at the top of the meniscus. Having taken the reading, consult the table, "Testing and Correcting for Sugar." This will tell you whether the must needs sugar correction or not, and if it does how much sugar is to be added. The table is equally applicable to a Balling, Brix, or French (Dujardin) saccharometer or a specific gravity hydrometer calibrated within the range indicated by the table.

> EXAMPLE 1. The reading shows 21° on the Balling or 11.9° on the Dujardin scale. Referring to the table, we see that no correction is required.

> EXAMPLE 2. The reading shows 16° on the Balling scale or 8.4° on the Dujardin. Refer to the table. To make a wine of 10 per cent alcohol by volume add 3 oz. of sugar per gal. of juice; to make a wine of 12 per cent alcohol by volume, add 7.47 oz. of sugar per gal. of juice.

CORRECTING SUGAR. In making the sugar correction, use standard granulated cane or beet sugar (sucrose). On being dissolved and mixed with the must, sucrose is converted immediately into grape sugar (dextrose and levulose), which is indistinguishable from that occurring naturally in the grapes. Such a correction of a natural sugar deficiency is an all but universal practice. The Cistercian monks had stumbled on it by the eighteenth century and prior to 1790 were regularly treating the wines of the Clos de Vougeot in this way when in their judgment the grapes were insufficiently ripe (but using honey, as refined cane and beet sugar were not then available). Today its use is authorized when necessary in the Côte d'Or and indeed in every winegrowing part of France including Bordeaux but excepting the five mass-producing *départements* of the Midi (where it is done anyway). Most German wines are made with its help. If sugar correction to make up a natural deficiency is sound practice for such wines as these, it is sound practice in making American wines.*

In correcting the red-wine must, assume that the twelve lugs, or seven bushels, will yield approximately twenty-five gallons of juice. Thus, using the table, compute the approximate amount of sugar to be added.

> EXAMPLE. *The saccharometer indicates 18° Balling or 9.8° Dujardin. The table shows that the correct amount of sugar to add for a 12% wine is 4.31 oz. per gal. of must. Then 4.31 times 25 equals 107.75 oz., or 6.73 lb.—the proper amount of sugar to add.*

The sugar may be added in several ways. The simplest is to sprinkle it in and dissolve it by stirring. The best is to take out some of the juice, dissolve the sugar in that, and return it. A third is to dissolve it in a minimum quantity of warm water: this requires an increase of sugar to account for the volume of water used (1.7 lb. per gallon). Whatever the method, the correction should be evenly distributed by stirring. As the amount of correction is based on an *estimate* of the amount of wine the batch is going to yield, the sugar

---

* California regulations prohibit the use of sugar but they allow the use of grape concentrate for the same purpose. Thus if fine Napa Valley Cabernet grapes are picked promptly in order to retain a proper total acidity, they may sometimes require sugar correction. In this case concentrate must be used. But most California concentrate is made from cheap Central Valley grapes and in a sense "adulterates" the Cabernet. The use of pure sucrose would be more rational.

should be tested again following the correction. The estimated volume should also be checked when the still-fermenting wine is pressed: a small deficiency can be made up even then.

If sugar content proves to be too high, as may sometimes happen when California grapes are used, there are three choices. The first possibility is to adjust by mixing in some low-sugar grapes, if they are available. Or you could try your hand at making a natural sweet wine (see Chapter 15). The third choice is to bring the sugar content down to normal by diluting with water. But since excessively sweet grapes also have excessively low acidity the acidity must be corrected too.

TOTAL ACIDITY TEST.   California grapes often have an acidity rather lower than the ideal, and Eastern grapes an acidity rather higher. Home winemakers tend to skip the test for acidity and count on luck. But this test is so simple that once the idea is grasped, it can be done quickly and easily without any background in chemistry; then one knows what one is working with.

For this purpose the several acids (mainly tartaric and malic) and their salts are simply lumped together as total acidity and expressed in terms of an acid of known strength, usually tartaric acid. Thus one says that a given must has a total acidity of 0.9 gm. per 100 milliliters expressed *as tartaric* (or 9.0 gm. per *liter*, which is the same thing with the decimal point moved over one digit). This is of course an arbitrary unit of measure. What it means to the chemist is that the total acidity of the must is such that the quantity of basic, or alkaline, substance required to neutralize it is the same as would be necessary *if all the acid in the must were tartaric acid*. The known strength of any other acid would do as well for a measuring unit, but tartaric is the commonly accepted standard in the United States. (In France it is sulfuric acid. To convert to sulfuric, multiply the tartaric acid reading by 0.653.)

The total acidity is determined by titration. A simple

titrating set that can be either assembled or bought as a kit consists of:

---

50 ml. burette graduated in 0.1 ml., with stand
Small glass jar or water glass
5 ml. pipette
Glass stirring rod
Dropper bottle of phenolphthalein indicator
N/10 (0.1 Normal) sodium hydroxide (NaOH) reagent
Distilled or boiled water

Two types of burette graduated in milliliters.
Used for titrating total acidity.

The steps in the titration are as follows:

1. Fill the burette with NaOH, running a few drops through the stopcock to make sure it functions. Record the level of the NaOH in the burette.

2. Place about 3 oz. distilled water in glass jar. The water should be hot.

3. To the hot water add exactly 5 ml. of juice to be tested, using the pipette.

4. Add 5 drops of phenolphthalein indicator to the mixture.

5. Using the burette, slowly add NaOH to the mixture, stirring with glass rod. Stop the instant the mixture turns pink and stays pink. That is the point indicating neutrality.

6. Record the exact amount of NaOH required to accomplish this. Multiply the quantity of NaOH that was required by 0.15. The product is the total acidity of the sample expressed as tartaric.

EXAMPLE 1: The quantity of NaOH required to neutralize the 5 ml. juice sample was 9.6 ml. Total acidity is 9.6 times 0.15, or 1.44 gm. per 100 ml. as tartaric.

EXAMPLE 2: Quantity of NaOH required to neutralize 5 ml. sample was 5.2 ml. Total acidity is 5.2 times 0.15, or 0.78 gm. per 100 ml. as tartaric.

CORRECTING ACIDITY. The acidity of California grapes ranges from about .4 to .85 as tartaric, seldom higher. Acidity of Eastern grapes is much higher, sometimes as high as 1.8. Wine men agree that the must of good wine grapes ought to have an acidity of at least .8 before fermentation and that, on the other hand, an acidity of more than 1.3 will produce a harsh or green-tasting wine. Example 1 above represents an Eastern sample; Example 2 represents a Californian.

The advantage of a fairly high acidity as an aid to a clean fermentation has already been mentioned: most microorganisms harmful to wine cannot survive such a condition (and neither can any human pathogens, for that matter). The disadvantage is that the resulting wine may be disagreeably tart. However, acidity is considerably reduced during fermentation and afterward as potassium bitartrate precipitates out. Also, much of the acidity present in high-acid grapes is malic acid, and one of the characteristics of this acid is that it breaks down into a much less "sour" acid—namely, lactic acid—when the wine is finished under suitable conditions. The effect of this breakdown is frequently to cut the effective acidity of a wine almost in two.

Even so, it may be desirable to reduce total acidity somewhat in advance of fermentation if the grapes are not fully ripe. This is usually done either by blending a high-acid must with the must of low-acid grapes or by cutting with a solution of sugar and water.

The first of these methods is the best, provided low-acid grapes are available. Cutting high-acid must with a sugar and water solution, the second way, is a traditional practice in the Eastern United States, as it is for some Alsatian and German wines, but for commercial winemaking is acceptable only within definite limits.* The method is to prepare a solution of sugar and water in a concentration of about 20° Balling, yielding a sugar solution of 1.70 (27 oz.) per gallon. The mixture is prepared by dissolving the sugar in half the quantity of water and then making up to quantity. It is then added to the must and mixed thoroughly. Of course, this sugar solution is over and above the sugar correction required by the must itself, as indicated by the table on page 149.

Obviously, such an addition alters the normal composition of the must, diluting the pigments and other ingredients that give body and character and color to a wine, and should never be overdone if one aims for a dry wine of good quality. Its justification is strictly to correct acidity, not to increase volume.

Just as Eastern winemakers must worry about excessive acidity, so California winemakers must watch out for deficient acidity. In California, as in other hot, dry regions, it is accepted practice to correct total acidity by adding tartaric

---

* U.S. Government regulations allow cutting by one-third of the volume of the original must, provided that in doing so the total acidity of the mixture of must and sugar solution is not brought below 0.5 per cent of total acidity.

acid, which promotes a more reliable fermentation and improves the quality of the wine, but this must be done with circumspection. The reason is that most of the tartaric acid in must is in the form of the salt potassium bitartrate, whereas tartaric acid conveys much more *effective* acidity, or "sourness." Titratable acidity becomes a false guide, and the domestic winemaker has to make his acid correction by "feel," adding a little bit at a time. A safe correction for a California must showing titrated total acidity of 0.6 is 9 grams of dry tartaric acid per ten gallons. The milder citric acid is much used, but *after* fermentation rather than before, because it can cause trouble during fermentation.

Fermentation

The fermenter is three-quarters full of crushed grapes which have been corrected for sugar content and acidity. They have had their purifying dose of meta and are covered with a cloth or plastic sheeting. After a wait to let the meta have its effect, the cloth is removed and the pail of actively fermenting yeast starter is poured in and thoroughly mixed. The symptoms of fermentation described at the end of the previous chapter begin to appear: fermentation odor, the formation of the cap, and so on. Bubbles begin to show around the edges. The volume of the mass begins to increase and it is soon clear why the fermenter was filled only three-quarters full.

If the symptoms are not evident after twelve to eighteen hours, remedial measures should be taken. The cause of delayed fermentation is almost always low temperature. The simplest solution is to stir the mass thoroughly and then bail out a pailful and immerse it in a tub of hot water. When it is well warmed, pour it back into the fermenter. Active fermentation in this surface layer will soon communicate itself to the mass beneath. A few hours later the surface layer is stirred in, and from then on the fermentation generates its own heat. The heat produced by fermentation is 2.3° F. for each loss of 1° Balling.

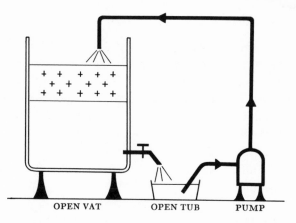

*An open fermenter. Pumping over for yeast build-up
and color extraction.*

A more sophisticated way of raising the temperature is to concoct some variant of the French *drapeau* (page 126), the simplest being a coil of thin stainless steel tubing, or of light copper tubing coated with acid-resistant paint. This is immersed in the mass and hot water is circulated slowly through it.

Once fermentation gets going, the cap is broken up and stirred into the must twice a day. As mentioned already, this access to air stimulates yeast build-up, distributes the yeast, and improves the extraction of color and the other desirable ingredients in the skins. Between these punchings-down the loose cover helps to retain the heat of fermentation, and also helps to retain a cap of carbon dioxide in the empty space above the chapeau. Remember that yeast multiplies best in the presence of air (during the first full day of fermentation), but is more efficient in producing alcohol in the absence of air.

Do not allow the temperature of the must to rise much above 90° F. Radiation is usually enough to take care of this for small-scale winemakers. A moderate ambient temperature helps greatly. If in spite of everything the temperature approaches the danger point, cool it. The homemade *drapeau* comes into play again, this time circulating cold water instead of warm. Or insert a big plastic bag containing ice cubes or a cake of ice.

Take a temperature reading and a saccharometer reading each evening when the cap is punched down. The saccharometer gives a notion of the progress of the fermentation. But don't take the reading literally, because the increasing proportion of alcohol (which has a lower specific gravity than water or sugar solutions) throws the scale off. For example, when the fermenting must registers 0 on the saccharometer, the must still contains about 2 per cent of sugar. A completely dry new wine tests *below* 0. At that point the grape sugar has all been used up except for traces. A small residue of unfermentable sugars remains, including the glycerol, amounting in total to no more than 0.4 per cent.

Drawing Down and Pressing

As fermentation approaches the end, the cap becomes less dense and begins to subside. It is dangerous to prolong the pressing beyond this time. A fermentation allowed to stand after completion loses its protective layer of carbon dioxide and there is a chance that aerobic bacteria may begin to develop on the surface. A good rule is to press when the saccharometer gives a reading between 0° and 4°—that is, when 2 to 5 per cent of the sugar still remains in the must. Normally this point is reached after about five days of fermentation. Prompt pressing helps to make a "soft" wine because it keeps the new wine from absorbing too much tannin from stems and skins. Oddly enough, it also provides deeper color: if maceration is prolonged some of the pigment material is drawn back into the skins.

Before proceeding, scrub the press with hot washing soda and rinse well in hot and cold water; likewise the containers, the pails, and the funnel.

In wineries the free-run wine is drawn off from a bung or spigot near the bottom of the fermenter, and the wet pomace is then removed by various means and pressed. In small fermentations simply bail the entire contents of the fermenter into the basket of the press. Much drains out immediately, strained between the slats of the press basket, and this may be kept separate if desired. Pour it into the waiting five-gallon bottles or other storage containers. When the press basket is full and most of the free run has drained off, press, but not too rapidly. When the flow stops, reopen the press basket, loosen the pomace, and press again. The press wine is deeper in color and more tannic. Mix the pressed wine with the free-run wine in working with small lots, unless you want to finish them separately and note the differences, which are considerable.

When the pressing is finished, wipe the mouth of each five-gallon bottle, *filled full*, with a clean, dry cloth or paper towel. The containers are not to be corked, as the wine is still fermenting and corks will be promptly blown out. Wad in a plug of absorbent cotton, or insert a rubber stopper fitted with a fermenting valve. Either way the gas is let out but impurities from the air are not let in. Remember, all bottles must be full right into the neck, since an air space provides ideal conditions for the growth of molds and bacteria on the surface of the wine. If the winemaker winds up with a container that is not quite full, he must transfer this last wine into bottles of smaller sizes, also filling them full and giving them the same subsequent care.

Then set the newly pressed wine aside, preferably on a sturdy shelf, in a place where the temperature is uniform and between 60° and 70° F., until the time for the first racking. When there is no longer any sign of fermentation, the wad of cotton or fermenting valve may be replaced by a cork or rubber stopper wrapped in a piece of wax paper, first filling any small ullage space that may have developed as the wine has cooled.

The new wine is now made. At pressing time the winemaker will doubtless have tasted it and been disappointed. At that point it will still be faintly sweetish, with a yeasty flavor, and it will be harsh and raw and muddy as well. This is normal, for though the must has been transformed into wine, it is still far from finished. A good deal more must happen to it. Patience will have its reward. Later care of the new red wine is discussed in Chapters 10 and 11.

CHAPTER 9

Making White Wine

 THE BIG DIFFERENCE between white wine and red, as we know, is that white wine is made by fermenting the sweet, freshly pressed juice. There is no maceration with the skins. The juice has no opportunity to pick up the pigments and other materials which are lodged in the skins, except as there may be a bit of leaching during the crushing and pressing. It is thus possible to make white wine from certain dark grapes. But this is rather tricky, and the small-scale winemaker, especially the beginner, will be prudent to use only white or pink grapes for his white wine.

As with red-wine grapes, those to be used for white wine fall into the same three broad categories: the *vinifera* varieties of California, the old standard Eastern varieties such as Delaware and Catawba, and the newer French hybrids or (occasionally) Eastern-grown *vinifera*. Varieties and their differences are discussed in Appendix A.

Crushing and Pressing

Assemble your well-cleaned equipment, the chief difference for white wine being that the open fermenter is abandoned for semi-closed fermentation. For small lots five- or twelve-gallon bottles or their plastic equivalents are best. For larger lots use a scrupulously clean barrel or a horizontal or vertical plastic or fiberglass drum with a bunghole or valve near the bottom and an aperture at the top that can be closed tight when the time comes.

Place the crusher over your wooden or plastic tub. Empty grapes into the hopper of the crusher and run the grapes through into the tub until there are enough to fill the press basket. Do not remove the stems, as these help drainage during the pressing.

About half of the juice, or must, is released in the act of crushing. In large operations it is usual to drain off most of this free-run must in one of several ways, a process known as *égouttage*, or dejuicing, in order to reduce the volume of material to be pressed. In small fermentations there is no need to do this. The press basket itself serves as a drain.

Transfer the crushed grapes, stems and all, into the basket of the press. The free-run juice will gush out into the waiting pail. Pour the contents into your fermenter, while a second pail is filling. When the free-run gushing has stopped, push down the contents of the press basket with your hands and more will pour out. The volume of material is thus considerably reduced, and more crushed grapes may be added until the press basket is full.

When most of the free-run must has thus been drained off, close the press basket and begin to apply mechanical pressure without delay. But press slowly. More is extracted by slowly applied pressure, up to the maximum that the press is capable of, than by trying to hasten the operation.

Pressing for white wine is much more difficult than pressing the pomace of newly fermented red wine. In the latter case the cell structure of the berries has broken down during the fermentation, releasing all the liquid, and the new wine is not viscous. In contrast, the juice of freshly crushed grapes is thick and sticky, the cell structure of the berries is by no means all broken down during the crushing, and the berries yield their juice reluctantly. Grapes of different varieties will be found to behave very differently in the press. Some press compactly and with relative ease, but others are slippery and will try to ooze out between the slats along with the juice.

Moreover, the juice within each berry is not uniform but is located in three zones: in the main part of the pulp, in the area directly beneath the skin, and in the area around the seeds. Juice from the main part of the pulp provides most of the free run; that from the other two zones is what requires the most pressure for extraction. There are variations in sugar content and acidity in the juice from the three zones, but these need not concern us as it is good practice to mix them all together.

When the first pressing is finished, loosen and stir the pomace, and press again. Because the fresh grapes are slow to yield their juice, press a third time. When the final pressing is reduced to a trickle, discard the pomace, refill the press basket with another load, and repeat the process. Home wine-makers may wish to save the pomace for some "sugar wine" (see Chapter 13).

As soon as the buckets are filled from the press, pour the must into the fermenter (or several fermenters, if five-gallon bottles are to be used). The pressed juice is mingled with the free run, and no fermenter should be filled more than two-thirds full.

As the pressing is concluded, set aside a small sample of the must for testing (a cupful will do), and a half-gallon in a gallon jug for preparation of a starter. This is also the time to add the light, prefermentation dose of meta, which is mandatory if California grapes are used. *Correct dose: 7 gm. (¼ oz.) per 20 gal.* To assure even distribution, add the dose of meta to the final pailful of must, then stir by rotating or rocking the fermenter a bit. When this is done, wipe the mouth of the fermenter and plug lightly with absorbent cotton or a stopper. A fermentation valve is not desirable at this point.

Testing and Correcting

The must is then tested for sugar content with the saccharometer. The sugar content having been determined, make any necessary adjustment by the addition of the correct amount of dissolved sugar (see table, page 149). This adjustment is easier for white wine than for red because the juice has already been separated from the skins and its exact quantity is known.

> EXAMPLE. *The saccharometer shows 17° Balling or 9.2° Dujardin. Reference to the sugar-correction table on page 149 indicates an addition of 5.98 oz. per gal. to make a wine of 12 per cent alcohol by volume. Assuming a twenty-gal. fermentation, the total quantity of sugar to add is 20 times 5.98 oz., or 119.6 oz. (7.47 lb.) Dissolve in a small quantity of juice or warm water. If water is used, add enough extra sugar to compensate for the increased volume at the rate of 1.7 lb. per gal.*

This is also the time to test for total acidity, following the instructions on page 152. If total acidity is too high, it may be reduced or "ameliorated" by adding a proportion of sugar and water solution adjusted to about 20° Balling (or 11.2° Dujardin), as in the case of red-wine must. The winemaker who is working with the relatively high-acid Eastern varieties but doesn't want to bother with the total acidity test can instead use a rule of thumb. He ameliorates with a sugar solution on a basis of ½ gallon to 4 gallons of fresh must.

White wines are almost invariably deficient in tannin, especially if the free-run must is fermented separately from the pressed must. For such a fermentation, correct with 1 gram of dry tannic acid for every 4 gallons of must, dissolved in one-fourth cup of warm water and stirred in. The additional tannic acid helps in clarification and conservation. However, if the pressed must is mixed with the free run, it is not necessary.

Fermentation

The fermenters are two-thirds full, and have been left standing lightly stoppered overnight. The added dose of meta has inhibited the start of fermentation.

At this point there is a choice to make. The process of crushing and pressing introduces a certain amount of extraneous matter into the must: dust and dirt from the vineyard, bits of stems and skins, miscellaneous debris such as bees' wings, and if the grapes were in poor condition, a population of unwanted microorganisms along with the naturally occurring yeasts. Much of this settles to the bottom of the fermenter during the overnight waiting period but is brought back up into the mass once fermentation starts.

One school of winemakers favors racking (that is, siphoning or otherwise draining) the partly cleared must from this sediment into clean containers before fermentation gets under way. The theory behind this practice is that it promotes a cleaner fermentation, which undoubtedly makes sense if the grapes have low total acidity or are in poor condition at the time of crushing. Such preliminary clearing (often these days done by centrifuge) is routine practice in the larger California and other hot-country wineries. But in recent years the practice has gone out of vogue in many areas where the grapes have a higher protective total acidity, the argument being that such clearing also eliminates various substances and organisms which can contribute to the production of a superior wine. Unless the grapes are in very poor condition, the small-scale winemaker may safely skip this preliminary clarification by settling and racking, known in France as *débourbage*.

Having made this decision, the winemaker proceeds. His first step is to add the yeast starter, prepared immediately after the pressing (see page 147) and by now in full fermentation.

There are two reasons why the fermenters were filled only two-thirds or three-fourths full. The first has to do with yeast

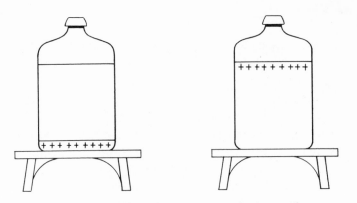

LEFT: *After pressing white-wine must, the lees settle.*
RIGHT: *When fermentation begins, the lees go into suspension
and a layer of developing yeast, known as the crown,
forms on the surface.*

build-up. Remember that a good fermentation depends on a rapid multiplication of yeast during the first several days. For this, the yeasts require air. The open space in the fermenter provides the needed air. Watching through the sides of a five-gallon glass fermenter, one can see an accumulation of yeast, the "crown," begin to form on the surface of the must in direct contact with the air, evidence of its rapid growth. As the yeast multiplies and consumes the oxygen in the air space, more air is sucked in. That's why the use of a fermentation valve during this period is a mistake: it prevents this additional intake of air. Sometimes the growing yeast forms a thick brownish-gray coating with a layer of fine bubbles beneath. Or, depending on the viscosity of the must, it may foam up like soap bubbles filling the entire space. At the same time the semi-clear must becomes opaque as the lighter material that had settled overnight mounts into the mass.

As fermentation begins to gather force, any remaining air in the open space is expelled and replaced by the carbon dioxide of the reaction. The "crown" breaks up. Denied access to air, it falls back into the liquid and begins to concentrate on the conversion of sugar into alcohol rather than self-propagation. The fermenting liquid is churned by convection. Its surface is pricked by tiny bubbles of escaping gas, which pours out of the mouth or bunghole of the fermenter. The open space has done its work of providing air for the multiplication of yeast, and fermentation valves may be inserted at this point though they are still not really necessary.

The second reason for leaving an open space in the fermenter is that there will otherwise be an overflow and a loss of both yeast and must as the fermentation becomes violent.

When the fermentation is well started, the temperature should be held, if possible, at around 65° to 70° F. This rarely presents a problem in small lots because white-wine fermentation proceeds at a slower pace than red and surplus heat is disposed of by radiation. Fermentation usually requires two to three weeks but may finish more rapidly.

If fermentation does not begin soon after the addition of the yeast starter, either of two things is wrong: the must is too cold, or the preliminary dose of meta was a bit too strong. Corrective action consists of siphoning or pouring from one container to another, sediment and all, in order to aerate it, thus reducing the quantity of SO_2 present and at the same time stimulating yeast growth; and of putting it in a warmer place. Or if the fermenter is provided with a bottom spigot of some sort the reluctant must is splashed into pails or tub and recirculated. Fermentation will begin shortly afterward.

During fermentation the sugar content is tested with a saccharometer from time to time by siphoning off a small

A closed white-wine fermenter. Pumping over for aeration.

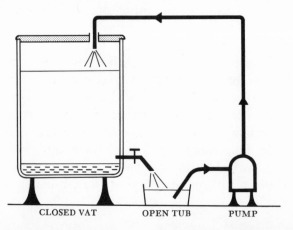

CLOSED VAT   OPEN TUB   PUMP

Aerating a small white-wine fermentation (pump not shown).

sample. Cotton stoppers must be replaced as they become damp. The end of fermentation is indicated by a subsidence of the sediment, or lees—consisting of the miscellaneous debris mentioned earlier, yeast cells that have died or ceased to be active, and various substances that have precipitated during fermentation but have been kept in suspension. It is also indicated by the saccharometer, which falls to *below* zero, and by a cessation of the sound and smell of escaping CO_2.

When the fermentation has been concluded, the vintage is brought together, which is to say that the fermenters are filled *full*.

> EXAMPLE. *If a vintage of twenty-odd gallons was fermented in five or six five-gallon bottles, each two-thirds full, the newly fermented wine in one or more of these bottles is used to fill the empty space in the others. Whatever remains goes into a smaller bottle, likewise filled full.*

The new wine is *not* racked or siphoned from its sediment at this time (for reasons that will become clear in the next chapter) but is left to rest on its lees. The important thing is that *all containers must be completely filled when fermentation ceases.* Not to fill them is to court certain spoilage because exposure to air, which was so important at the beginning, is now a deadly danger. When filled, wipe the containers clean around the mouth, and replace the absorbent cotton or loose stoppers with fermentation bungs. Then set the wine aside for its secondary fermentation. Subsequent treatment of white wine is the same as that for red wine, and will be dealt with in the next chapter.

CHAPTER 10

Malolactic
Fermentation

 FOLLOWING ITS primary fermentation the new wine, red or white, is yeasty, opaque, raw, muddy-tasting, undrinkable. A great deal must happen before it is ready to be drunk.

At this point the young wine almost always contains a residue of unfermented sugar. The yeasts have ceased to multiply, and the very alcohol they have produced inhibits their activity. Thus, fermentation of this residue proceeds at a slower pace, a sort of cleanup operation. It must be carried to conclusion because a small residue of unfermented sugar is always a source of future danger. At this point it may be desirable to aerate again by siphoning or pumping over, so reinvigorating the yeasts.

Other things that happen during this period are of a physical nature. The potassium bitartrate, which accounted for a good part of the total acidity of the must, continues to precipitate, being much less soluble in an alcoholic solution such as new wine. Some of these crystals cling to the sides of the container, and much falls to the bottom as lees. The precipitation is desirable because it reduces the total acidity of the wine, making it "softer" to the taste.

Numerous other substances begin to precipitate too in a preliminary clearing. Again it is instructive to watch this process through a five-gallon glass bottle. There is no need here for a full catalog of these precipitates. Enough to say that the materials vary greatly in specific gravity and size of particles. Thus, the heavier materials settle first, and fairly quickly. Others come down more slowly. Still others are present as colloids or finely divided particles. These remain in suspension for a long time as hazes and may have to be encouraged to precipitate. Wine clears more rapidly in a small container than in a large one, simply because in the latter the precipitates have farther to fall.

That is the traditional description of what happens during the secondary fermentation, and it is correct as far as it goes. But investigations during the past half-century have turned up some surprising facts about the secondary fermentation, which go far to explain certain important changes that take place in young wines. They also contradict Pasteur's dictum that bacteria can only cause trouble in winemaking. For it turns out that there are useful bacteria as well as harmful ones. To put the matter briefly, it is now known that the sugar/alcohol fermentation shades off into another and wholly different kind of fermentation—a bacterial one which has nothing to do with the production of alcohol but instead *modifies the acidity* of the young wine. It is called the malolactic fermentation.

Remember that grape musts contain two predominant organic acids in varying quantities: tartaric acid, which is the one peculiarly associated with grape juice; and malic acid, more widely distributed in the plant world. The proportions of these two acids vary greatly. The amount of tartaric acid is quite stable and does not change greatly as the grapes ripen. The level of malic acid is high in unripe grapes but low in ripe grapes, much of it being "burned out" in the course of ripening.

What happens in malolactic fermentation is that certain strains of bacteria which are present at the beginning of fermentation, but in small numbers and not easily perceived, begin to build up toward the end of it. When the cell population reaches a critical point,* they attack the malic (but not the tartaric) acid in the young wine and degrade it into the much feebler lactic acid plus some carbon dioxide gas. Lactic acid is not originally present in grape juice: it is the acid of sour milk and of well-ripened sauerkraut. The transformation is most simply expressed both qualitatively and quantitatively in the following formula:

$$\underset{\substack{\text{(malic acid)} \\ \text{1 gm.}}}{H_2C_4H_4O_5} \xrightarrow{\text{(lactic bacteria)}} \underset{\substack{\text{(lactic acid)} \\ \text{0.67 gm.}}}{HC_3H_5O_3} + \underset{\substack{\text{(carbon dioxide)} \\ \text{0.33 gm.}}}{CO_2}$$

During the reaction the CO_2 comes off as small bubbles. These were long thought to be the by-product of the last traces of alcoholic fermentation and so threw earlier investigators off the track. Malic acid is what the chemists call a diacid, whereas lactic acid is monoacidic and has only half the effective acidity. What the malolactic fermentation does, then, when it replaces the malic with the lactic, is to cause a sharp reduction in total acidity, amounting to one-half the acidity of the malic acid so degraded.†

This reaction is of great importance in regions where grapes ripen with the most difficulty and therefore contain a high proportion of malic acid, regions such as the Burgundy district in France, Switzerland, and much of the Eastern United States. Malolactic fermentation is what takes the "hardness" and "greenness" out of a young Burgundy and ul-

---

* Again we are dealing with big numbers. There must be at least 10^6 (1 million) cells per milliliter before a malolactic fermentation occurs, and actual numbers run between 10^6 and 10^8 cells per ml. during an active malolactic fermentation. (Communication from K. F. Steinkraus)

† The distinction between titratable acidity and *effective* acidity, or acidic force, ought logically to be followed by an exposition of the concept of pH, or hydrogen-ion concentration. Sufficient for our purposes to know that pH 7.0 stands for neutrality, pH running from 7.0 down to 1.0 represents increasingly acid solutions, and pH 7.0 up to 14.0 represents increasingly alkaline solutions. The pH of wines ranges from 3.8 (soft, flat) to 2.8 (very sour).

timately transforms it into a wine that is soft, pleasing, and well balanced. It also explains the previously mysterious and unpredictable behavior of certain wines in bottle, particularly Burgundies. If the wine was unwittingly bottled before the malolactic fermentation had run its course, this might start up again in the bottle itself and the wine would become turbid, gassy, cloudy, and unpleasant. Likewise, it explains why wines fermented in chilly cellars have a way of "coming to life" in the spring and resuming fermentation. This used to be romantically described as a response by the wine to awakening growth in the vineyards: the prosaic explanation is that the temperature of the wine rises enough to let the malolactic organisms resume the job they failed to finish the previous autumn.

There exist many different malolactic bacteria, all behaving in somewhat different ways. What they have in common is that they are sparsely present in the early stages of fermentation and do little or none of their benign work then. They increase in number and become readily visible under the microscope only after the fermentation is well advanced. This appearance of bacteria was known by the turn of the century and always taken to be a sign of incipient spoilage (following Pasteur's dictum); and indeed under the wrong conditions malolactic bacteria do cause spoilage. Any residual sugar that is present may be attacked by them with evil results.

In some cases, the malolactic fermentation is well begun and may even have been completed by the time the alcoholic transformation is done. More usually, the bacteria don't get down to the serious work of deacidification until alcoholic fermentation is finished. For the most part the work is done naturally and spontaneously, but it may be helped along by proper handling. The obvious next advance (analogous to inoculation with pure yeast starters) is inoculation with pure strains of malolactic bacteria, mainly of *Leuconostoc*, which are the ones least likely to produce unwanted and damaging by-products along with the main reaction. Such inoculation is already being done by some highly qualified winemakers, introducing the pure lactic acid culture simultaneously with the pure yeast starter.

Steps to Take

In presiding over the secondary fermentation, therefore, the winemaker takes care to establish conditions that will encourage the malolactic bacteria to do their work promptly and thoroughly.

First, make sure by tasting that the new wine is fermented to dryness, leaving no residual sugar for these bacteria to prey on.

Let the wine rest on its gross lees (what American winemakers usually call "mud") for a while. The lees are a reservoir of yeast for finishing the alcoholic fermentation and of bacteria as well.

Keep the storage place at a temperature ranging between 65° and 70° F. until the malic acid has been transformed, since the ferments work best within this range. How to tell when malolactic fermentation is over will be explained later in this chapter.

Do not treat the new wine with so₂ until after the malolactic fermentation is completed, for the bacteria will not function well in the presence of this antiseptic.

There is one sort of situation in which the malolactic fermentation requires special encouragement. This is when the total acidity of the new wine is still truly excessive. A total acidity of more than 1.1 grams per milliliter discourages growth of the malolactic organisms. To get them going it is necessary to reduce the total acidity *by chemical means* to a point where the organisms can take hold and do their job. This is done by adding a small quantity of *precipitated chalk* (to be had from the pharmacist or a winemakers' supply shop), which neutralizes an equivalent quantity of the acid present in the wine.

But there is a catch because the chalk, which is pure

calcium carbonate ($CACO_3$) acts in a very special way: it combines by preference with the tartaric acid present rather than with the malic, and if too much is used this brings about an abnormal situation in which virtually all of the acid remaining is malic. Then when the malolactic organisms carry through their work of eliminating the malic acid, the wine, far from having too much total acidity, has too little. The idea, then, is to eliminate only a part, not all, of the tartaric acid present—just enough to provide favorable conditions for the onset of the malolactic fermentation. If one must deacidify chemically, a safe rule is never to risk a dose of chalk larger than 1 gram per liter of wine. In dosing with chalk, be prepared for a rather lively eruption as the surplus CO_2, which is a by-product of the reaction between chalk and acid, seeks escape.

The two following examples, taken from the records of the late A. de Chaunac, are illustrative of the use of chalk. In Example 1 the malolactic fermentation proceeded spontaneously. In example 2 it had to be started with the help of chalk:

EXAMPLE 1		Percentage of Total Acidity
Oct. 5.	Grapes pressed for white wine	1.03
Oct. 23.	The new wine (containing CO_2)	1.05
Nov. 12.	The new wine	.90
Dec. 16.	Wine after malolactic	.69
Jan. 28.	Wine filtered and bottled	.68

EXAMPLE 2		Percentage of Total Acidity*
Sept. 24.	Grapes crushed for red wine	1.36
Sept. 28.	New wine pressed	1.18
Nov. 12.	No sign of malolactic	1.18
Dec. 4.	After addition of chalk	.92 to .98
Dec. 12.	Malolactic continuing	.72 to .96
Feb. 4.	Wine mixed to equalize and bottled	.72

* In several carboys

During the period of secondary fermentation do not bung wine containers tightly because the by-product CO_2 gas must escape. There will be some shrinkage of the wine, especially if it is stored in cooperage. The storage vessels must be topped (filled) at regular intervals, the best practice being to do this routinely on a certain day of the week. The topping is done preferably with wine of the same type, but any sound wine including store-bought wine will do. Any air space that you let develop will allow spoilage organisms (not to be confused with the malolactic bacteria) to grow on the wine's surface. The importance of this routine topping cannot be exaggerated.

The termination of the secondary fermentation, which may require a good many weeks, is signified in several ways. The small output of CO_2 ceases. Termination may be confirmed definitely by paper chromatography. The presence or absence of malic acid is indicated by placing a drop of the wine on a piece of specially sensitized paper. Paper chromatography has various uses in a wine laboratory, but will not be discussed here. It may also be confirmed by ordinary titration, as in the case of the two examples cited above. Specific tests for tartaric, malic, and lactic acids are beyond the scope of this book. What the home winemaker does is to make an end run around such techniques. He tests the young wine in standard fashion for total acidity (see page 152), then repeats the test periodically during the secondary fermentation. If he notices a sharp drop in total acidity, he infers that malolactic fermentation is under way. When acidity ceases to drop, he infers that it is finished. More primitively still, the evolution may be followed by periodic tasting.

Cautionary Note

It is now necessary to mention an important exception to what has just been written about malolactic fermentation. Broadly speaking, the lactic bacteria encountered in wine may be divided into two groups. First, there are the benign ones which do their appointed job without producing harmful by-products in significant amounts. Second, there are the dangerous ones, the ones that led Pasteur mistakenly to warn against the presence of *all* bacteria. They attack more broadly and unlike the benign ones are capable of decomposing the tartaric acid and glycerol in new wine with devastating results in terms of harmful by-products. They are true agents of disease* and must be guarded against.

A characteristic of this second group is that they work best in low-acid media, which in our context means musts from California grapes. This explains why so many California technicians continue to be suspicious of the malolactic phenomenon and are instead dead against it: their experience is that it can go wrong so easily.

In any case they have less need of it. Since they are working for the most part with fully ripe grapes, their problem is almost always insufficient acidity. The concern of winemakers using California grapes is therefore to preserve a maximum total acidity in the wine, *whether the acid be tartaric or malic.* It is to their interest, in other words, to make sure that the malolactic fermentation *does not* take place, and furthermore *will not* take place after the wine is in bottle. This is done by racking the new wine from its gross lees as soon as possible after the last sugar has been fermented out, and immediately adding a postfermentation dose of meta (4 gm. per 20 gal.).† The malolactic fermentation is thus inhibited and subsequent stability of the wine is assured by adding the same moderate dose of SO_2 at each subsequent racking, including the final one at the time of bottling. Much of the wine spoilage that occurred in California during the first post-prohibition years was caused by the harmful lactic bacteria.

---

* There is a running argument as to whether "disease" or "spoilage" is the more accurate term. The Solomon-like decision adopted for this book is to use either or both.
† Industrially there is often a first bentonite fining (see page 188) or a centrifuging as well.

CHAPTER 11

From Fermentation to Bottling

 AS SOON AS the secondary fermentation is ended, Pasteur's injunction "No bacteria allowed!" applies. The helpful bacteria have done their job; the others are a lurking menace. It is time to get rid of them all, along with the lees and the material in suspension.

The first steps are to separate the wine from its lees, to give the wine its first postfermentation dose of SO_2, and to chill it thoroughly. This is also the time for a checkup of the wine's composition.

Racking

By this point the wine will have gone part way toward clearing itself. The gross lees will have settled to the bottom, along with much of the lighter, suspended matter. Racking is simply the separation of the wine from these unwanted solids by siphoning, by draining through a bunghole, or by pumping—an act of partial purification. A wine may fall bright (which

Racking new wine from its lees.

is to say clear naturally) on its lees, but unless it is then separated, any disturbance, even a change of atmospheric pressure, brings some of the light lees back into suspension; and they can always cause trouble. Each racking carries the purification a step further.

The light aeration that accompanies racking often helps to clarify the wine by promoting the precipitation of stubborn suspensions. It eliminates any light odor of hydrogen sulfide (H_2S, the rotten-egg smell), which sometimes develops as a by-product of fermentation. But such oxidation can also be dangerous if overdone. In light white wine especially, it may cause a darkening, accompanied by the development of a not very agreeable Madeira-like, sherry-like, taste. This effect is called "maderization."

WHEN TO RACK. The first racking follows immediately after termination of malolactic fermentation. If the vintage is in early September, first racking may be possible by early October. Where the vintage comes later, racking may not be possible until mid-November or early December.

A second racking takes place after thorough chilling, and at that time fining materials (to be discussed shortly) are also added to complete clarification.

A third is done in late winter or early spring before the coming of warm weather, separating the bright wine from its finings; by this time most wines are ready to be bottled and drunk.

If the wine is likely to profit by further storage, it is racked a fourth time the following October, to get rid of any lees that may have been thrown down during the warm weather. If held even longer, which is rarely advisable, it is racked twice a year.

Between rackings all wine containers must be topped regularly, but after the first two rackings once every two weeks instead of once a week.

Racking is best done in bright, clear weather, such as often coincides with a full moon. This is not a superstition. Clear weather usually means high atmospheric pressure and the lighter lees are then less likely to be disturbed and drawn over with the wine.

White wine, like red, is racked four times during the first year of its life. But the trend today is toward early bottling of dry white wines, for the sake of preserving their freshness and fruit. White wine may be bottled any time after fining.

As a matter of fact, the trend applies to many red wines as well, the practice being to bottle as soon after fining as they are stable and brilliant. They will continue to develop if held longer in storage before bottling, but the development is not always for the better or worth the wait.

THE FIRST RACKING. In the following discussion we assume that the vintage consists of several five-gallon bottles. The same procedure applies with qualifications to larger, or smaller, vintages. As befits a rite of purification, the first racking is a cheerful and even exhilarating occasion, to be followed by drinking and feasting. But the prospect of the feast should not be allowed to interfere with proper performance of the rite.

Rinse an empty container and the siphoning tube with hot water. Prepare a protective dose of meta. *Correct dose: 4 gm. of meta per 20 gal. dissolved in a half-cup of warm water, or 1.0 gm. per 5 gal.*

Place the empty container lower than that from which the wine is to be racked, which should be on a shelf or table. Remove the plug of cotton or bubbler from the first bottle to be racked. Insert the notched end of the siphon tube into the wine, not too far down, for that will disturb the lees. Start the flow by sucking or with a starting bulb and direct the flow into the empty container so that it will go down the inside wall of the container. This provides aeration, which is good for the wine at the first racking, though not during later ones. When the bottle is half full, pour in the correct amount of dissolved meta and distribute it by joggling or rotating the wine. Continue to fill.

When the first bottle of wine has been emptied, leaving only the lees behind, rinse it thoroughly, and it is ready to receive the racked wine from the next full container; continue in sequence giving each bottle its share of meta and filling it full. The final one will be short, so complete the filling with other sound wine or transfer to a smaller container of appropriate size. When finished, stopper all containers well but not too firmly as they must still be topped from time to time. For such small vintages in glass, wrap the cork or rubber stopper in ordinary kitchen plastic or wax paper.

CHILLING. The wine profits now by a prolonged and thorough chilling, which causes more tartrate crystals to precipitate and so keeps that from happening later after the wine has been bottled. Crystals so precipitated in bottle are commonly called "gravel." The chilling also encourages more precipitation of light suspended matter, another step in the purification. In commercial wineries the new wine is brought down as low as 25° F. and held at that temperature for several

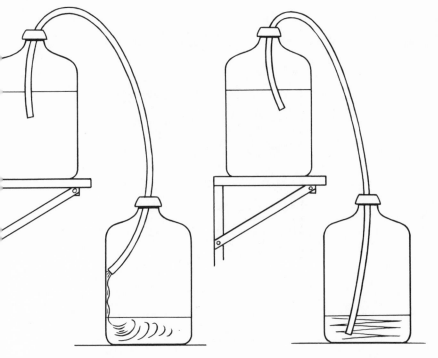

Racking, with aeration.   *Racking, without aeration.*

weeks.* Such drastic chilling is not necessary for small fermentations that will never leave home and most domestic winemakers must usually compromise; but some chilling is always desirable.

THE SECOND RACKING. This is done at convenience after chilling, when the wine is cold, normally in December. Procedure is the same, with two exceptions. First, the wine is not aerated, but is kept out of contact with the air as much as possible. This is done as shown in the illustra-

---

* Large industrial producers get around the "gravel" problem by resort to ion-exchange. The wine is passed through a column of special resins and the *potassium* ion of potassium bitartrate is exchanged for *sodium*. The sodium salt is soluble and there is no precipitate. There has been much discussion of this because sodium is not naturally present in wine in substantial quantity. Used in moderation (taking out only a part of the potassium) it is not objectionable. Wine drastically treated this way does not belong in a sodium-free diet.

Racking with bellows (Petrus de Crescentis: Liber Ruralium Commodorum, *1493). It is still done this way in some Bordeaux châteaux, but with a pump resembling a large bicycle pump.*

tion by plunging the outlet end of the siphon tube below the surface in the container being filled. Second, now is the time to add finings, their purpose being to give the wine limpid clarity free of all haze or suspended matter. This second racking requires the same dose of SO_2 dispersed in the same way. Each such dose of SO_2 has a mild antiseptic and antioxidizing effect, which protects the wine against accident and in no way harms it.

At the second racking the quantity of lees is small and compact, and with care none need be brought over.

THE THIRD RACKING. This can take place any time during the cold months once the finings have settled out and the wine is bright. It is done without aeration, and the usual dose of SO_2 (in the form of meta) is added. The finings should have made a compact layer on the bottom of the bottle, and the bright and stable wine may be bottled after this racking. If not, later rackings are carried out in the same way: SO_2 added, containers filled full and well stoppered.

Fining

A healthy wine frequently clears itself and becomes limpid spontaneously. But if it is examined critically (as by directing a beam of light across and through it from a small flashlight

Setting a cask manhole after emptying and cleaning and before refilling. The white material being squeezed out is refined tallow used for sealing.

in a darkened box or room) the pathway will reveal a slight haze. This (the so-called Tyndall effect) is caused by extremely small particles and colloidal material which are still in suspension but not ordinarily discernible. On casual inspection the wine may look brilliant, but it isn't optically clear.

Most young wines fail to achieve even that degree of clarity all by themselves. They show a distinct haze, especially young white wines, and the haze may persist though the wine itself is sound and well balanced. The object of fining is to remove this material.

A few words on the cause of these persistent suspensions may help. The heavier particles always precipitate promptly, of course; the lighter ones more slowly. For example, a yeast cell falls twenty-five times more rapidly than a bacterial organism. The very smallest cause the hazes. It so happens that most of these (tannins, pigments, yeasts, bacteria) carry a negative electrical charge; thus, they repulse each other, as do the negative poles of two magnets, and tend to remain in suspension. But if this negative charge is somehow reduced or neutralized by a positive charge these particles are no longer repelled from each other: they come together into larger particles and fall.

The function of most fining materials—if I may oversimplify shamelessly—is to bring this about. The traditional fining materials (such as skimmed milk, white of egg, blood, and isinglass) as well as their contemporary prepared equivalents (gelatins, albumins, casein) contain proteins and carry a positive or neutralizing charge. Also, they coagulate or form a coarse flocculation when dispersed in the wine. The wine's suspended matter, now sufficiently neutralized, is entrained by the flocculant and drawn to the bottom as the finings gradually settle; and so if all goes well the wine falls bright, sometimes in a matter of days, sometimes in a few weeks. Organic finings work best in cold wines (which is why fining is habitually done during the winter) and after the wine has just been aerated (which raises no problem since it is done immediately after a racking). They will not work well except in the presence of a mineral salt (which is almost always present in sufficient quantity, but which also accounts for the ancient practice of adding a bit of ordinary table salt to the finings).

PROCEDURE. Of the organic finings, gelatin is the one most commonly used for small lots. It flocculates by combination with tannin present in the wine. Since red wine has ample tannin, the fining of it consists simply of adding and stirring in the proper quantity of gelatin, which has been previously moistened and diluted with a small quantity of warm water and let stand in a warm place until it is clear. Ordinary grocery store gelatin will do, but be sure that it is the unflavored kind. No two wines require exactly the same dose for a perfect job. A safe dose for the home winemaker is 2 grams per five gallons of wine. Household gelatin comes ready-measured in quarter-ounce (7-gram) envelopes. A gram equals 15.432 grains, and a photographer's scale gives readings in grains.

As soon as the gelatin has been stirred in, the wine becomes densely cloudy. Much of this gelatin-tannin flocculation will have precipitated in twenty-four hours: the remainder falls more slowly, leaving the wine bright eventually. That is all there is to it.

White wine, unlike red, is usually deficient in tannin. So tannin must be added too, just before the gelatin. (Tannin and gelatin as well as various proprietary fining materials may be had from winemakers' shops. Pharmacists will usually obtain tannin for you too.) A dose of USP (United States Pharmacopoeia) tannic acid is dissolved in hot water and stirred in during the racking. When it is well dispersed, the gelatin follows. The precise dose of tannin is hard to determine. The old rule is to use slightly more tannin than gelatin, by weight, in the proportion of about four to five.

The one serious danger in gelatin fining is that of overfining, which is simply the use of more gelatin than there is tannin to combine with. This excess may then stay in suspension, causing a persistent haze. Overfining occurs with white wine, rarely with red. The cure is to rechill the wine, rack it in the presence of air, and then add a dose of dissolved tannin

Various types of commercial storage vessels:
glass-lined steel, white oak and redwood, and (opposite) lined fiberglass.

equal to one-half the original dose. There is another flocculation, and clearing follows.

OTHER ORGANIC FININGS. These are not likely to be used by amateurs. For the record, here are their characteristics since they are often mentioned in writings about wine:

Isinglass is fish glue,* the best of which is obtained from the sturgeon, and it does a beautiful job on delicate wines. But its preparation is difficult and tedious. It does not require tannin for flocculation.

Blood, especially fresh beef blood, is still used to some extent for white wines in the Burgundy region because it functions well in high-acid wines and has a powerful decolorizing effect. But it must be very fresh, and one can't just go out and gore an ox, can one? In France there are preparations of dried blood or blood albumen often combined with activated charcoal to reinforce the decolorizing effect. The usual dose is 2 to 3 grams per 5 gallons.

---

* The general French term for the fining of wine is *collage*, derived from the word *colle*, meaning glue. The word for an airplane take-off, *décollage*, is from the same root, the idea being that the airplane comes unstuck from the earth and is airborne.

In Burgundy the *white of egg* is still much favored for the best of the red wines, but is not used for the whites. The whites of five or six eggs are used per Burgundian *pièce*, or barrel, which comes down to slightly more than half the white of one egg per 5 gallons. It is prepared by whisking with a small quantity of water and a pinch of table salt to solubilize the globulin. Just whisk. Do not beat to a fluff because then it cannot be incorporated into the wine. Dried egg white may be used, 2.5 to 4 grams per 5 gallons in a bit of warm water.

The *caseins* do not yield as brilliant a clarification by themselves. But they have some decolorizing power which makes them useful alone or in combination in the fining of white wines which are subject to oxidation or a little too dark in color. They partly remove ferric salts as well. The traditional casein fining material is skimmed milk, ½ pint per 5 gallons. The casein salts, potassium caseinate and sodium caseinate, function in the same way, 6 grams per 5 gallons; but ordinary powdered milk obtainable in grocery stores does just as well. Be sure that it is powdered *skimmed* milk, not whole milk. This is habitually used by many small winegrowers in the Burgundy region, prepared by dissolving 10 grams per 5 gallons in a bit of water. The caseins, including ordinary powdered milk, are flocculated by the wine's acidity, not by the tannin. They have the disadvantage that they flocculate almost instantly on contact with the wine, in large curds, which fall to the bottom without accomplishing their purpose. The way to get a good dispersion is to inject them in a fine stream using a large syringe or a small plastic plunger pump with a long nozzle.

Mineral finings are clays, of which the only one commonly used today is the material called bentonite, an aluminum silicate found in nature as an impalpable powder. Like other clays of its class it swells to many times its original volume in water, and it is capable of absorbing colloids and various other materials when introduced into wine for fining. Its decolorizing action is quite strong. It does the job swiftly and effectively and is widely used in commercial winemaking especially for a fining prior to filtration. It has several disadvantages from the point of view of the small winemaker. Preparing a smooth suspension of it is quite difficult, though less so when the material is in granulated form. After precipitation it makes a much more bulky lees than other finings (thus wasting wine); and sometimes microscopic particles of it may remain in suspension, thus requiring a later light gelatin fining. *Dose:* 5 to 10 gm. per 5 gal.

One last word on fining. There is no such thing as the perfect all-purpose fining material. Each has its advantages and disadvantages. Thus, several may be combined in various proprietary formulations. For the same reason, experienced winemakers tend to develop their own pet procedures. By way of illustration, the Marquis d'Angerville, one of the best winemakers in Volnay and thereabout, customarily gives his superb white burgundies two finings: first, 100 grams per *pièce* of powdered skimmed milk and a few days later a dose of 60 to 100 grams of bentonite. Under his circumstances, experience has shown the combination to be ideal.

Filtration

Filtration is in a sense the reverse of fining. When a wine is fined a sort of veil of the fining material is drawn down through the wine, dragging all suspended matter with it. When a wine is filtered the veil, a porous wall or membrane, is fixed and the wine is forced through it, leaving the suspended material behind and emerging clear and bright.

Filtration is all but universally used today in commercial winemaking, but its common practice has come about only during the past forty years or so. The reason is that early filtration methods were defective in several ways. The material through which the wine was filtered frequently imparted off flavors or odors and unwanted substances. And since the apparatus was often constructed of inappropriate metals there was the possibility of metal pickup. The wine might be bright immediately after filtration but later develop metal haze, or *casse* (see page 250). Moreover, the wine frequently came into excessive contact with air, owing to faulty filter design, and so suffered the effects of overoxidation.

These problems have long since been solved; and the advantages of well-managed filtration are numerous. It clarifies the wine swiftly, whereas fining takes time. It yields consistent results. It eliminates only the insoluble matter in the wine and involves no chemical reaction with the wine itself. And it may be undertaken at any point in the life of the wine, even before it has finished fermentation should that prove desirable.

Since filtration is rarely used for small lots, there is no need to go very far into the question. But a few words on the principles involved are not out of place.

There are several quite different basic designs for filters. But those most commonly used, and used exclusively by small and medium-size wineries, are multiple plate-and-pad filters

A bench-size filter taking 8 × 8-inch pads.

such as the ones shown in the illustration. In these the wine to be filtered goes through one of the pads only, each pad being a separate filter, so to speak. Capacity is increased or decreased according to the number of pads (and their supporting plates) which are used, the wine being dispersed among them from an inlet channel and the filtered wine being brought together in an outlet channel. For example, a filter mounted with fifteen pads has three times the filtering surface, and filters three times as much wine at the same time, as a filter mounted with only five pads.

These prepared pads are used only once and then discarded. The materials used in their manufacture are cellulose, which has coarse fibers and a positive electrical charge, and highly refined asbestos, which has extremely fine fibers and a negative electrical charge and is inert to wine. These are mixed in various proportions to provide pads in a range of porosities from quite coarse to microscopically fine.

The two materials are used because there are two quite different mechanisms of filtration: *adsorption* and simple *screening*. In an effective filtration both mechanisms come into play.

The colloidal or gummy materials to be eliminated from the wine are eliminated by *adsorption* on the walls of the rather open pores which are characteristic of the cellulose in the pad. The particulate matter, visible as hazes, is simply *screened* out, or *blocked*, by the much finer pores characteristic of the asbestos. Thus, a pad consisting mainly of cellulose does a fine job of eliminating the gums but may let some of the particulate matter pass through. A dense pad containing a higher proportion of asbestos* yields a brilliant filtrate but is

---

* Because the breathing of asbestos fibers is known to cause serious lung disorders, the use of asbestos in filtration has inevitably been called into question, though there is an obvious difference between ingestion, that is, passing occasional stray filter fibers through the digestive tract, and inhalation. There is no evidence of physical disorder arising from ingestion. Nevertheless, the question is being investigated medically and the filtration industry is experimenting with alternative materials. To keep this question in proper perspective it is important to realize that "asbestos fibers are now ubiquitous in our environment" including the public water supply in many regions. (Cunningham and Pontefract, *Journal of the Association of Agricultural Chemists*, Vol. 56, No. 4, 1973, p. 976)

soon blocked up by the gums. The working rule is that coarse pads provide high volume but less complete filtration; the reverse is true for fine pads.

Perfected filters get around this by performing what amounts to two filtrations at a single pass. They are so designed that the wine can first be filtered through a set of coarse pads and then be passed on to a set of fine pads mounted in the same frame.

Lacking a double-pass filter, filtration is combined with fining. The wine gets a preliminary fining to eliminate the gums and most of the particulate matter. It is then given a *polish filtration* just prior to bottling.

But enough of this. Even the smallest of well-designed filters is expensive, and a poor filter is worse than none at all. The home winemaker reminds himself that good wines were being made long before filters had been perfected. A form of one-upmanship currently practiced in some small wineries is to boast that their wines are not filtered.

Testing and Blending

Not many amateurs bother with a chemical analysis of the new wine. But they will be better off if at least they know what an analysis consists of and understand its purpose. The basic tests are three: for *alcoholic content, total acidity,* and *volatile acidity.* The test for total acidity has been described on page 152. The other two tests are explained in Appendix B. We will content ourselves at this point with a discussion of their significance.

ALCOHOLIC CONTENT. This is the least important test because one knows from the original sugar content of the must what the approximate alcoholic content is going to be. A stable and well-balanced wine will show between 11 and 13 per cent by volume. It is worth noting, though, that the alcoholic content of a red wine usually turns out to be slightly less than was anticipated. The reason is that a small proportion of alcohol is entrained by the escaping CO_2 during violent fermentation; also when the peak has passed and fermentation begins to die down, another small quantity is absorbed by the skins and so goes out with the pressed pomace. If there is a real deficiency, the wine should be blended with another of higher alcoholic content—the commonest form of blending.

ACIDITY. As we have seen, the total acidity of fresh musts consists mainly of tartaric and malic acids and their salts, both of which are reduced during and shortly after a correct fermentation. What remain of these are lumped together as *fixed*, or nonvolatile, *acids*.

But the total acidity is complicated by the presence of *volatile acids* as well, which were not present in the beginning but are by-products of fermentation.* Disregarding carbonic acid (CO_2) and any SO_2 that may have been added, these are acetic acid and smaller amounts of others. In a well-fermented wine the sum of these new arrivals is very small (frequently as low as 0.030 grams per 100 milliliters)—much less than the loss of fixed acidity that has taken place, so that the net total acidity is still less than in the original must.

Small quantities of these fermentation by-products, combining with the ethyl alcohol and other constituents of the wine, contribute to aroma, bouquet, and flavor. But the presence of volatile acidity in more than a very small amount is always a sign of something wrong, of disease. A rise in volatile acidity is to wine what fever symptoms are to the human body. In aging, a small increase is to be expected. But if volatile acidity exceeds a low level the resulting vinegary and other nasty odors and the accompanying "drying out" or "hotness" of flavor make the wine undrinkable; and by then the wine is beyond rescue. In all winegrowing areas there are established maximal levels of volatile acidity beyond which a wine is declared unsaleable. The allowable maximum in California

* Lactic acid is slightly volatile but not so considered in this context.

is 0.110 grams per 100 milliliters for white wines and 0.120 for red.

Any suspicion that the volatile acidity may be rising calls for prompt measures. For the home winemaker these measures are to rack and fine immediately with a doubled dose of meta to which has been added an activated charcoal such as Nu-Char, 1 gram per gallon, and to rack again as soon as this fining is completed. The object is of course to get rid of the spoilage organisms as swiftly and completely as possible. Such wine should under no circumstances be blended with other wine; and it should not be bottled for aging but used up before the chance of any recurrence. Commercial wineries will sometimes resort to pasteurization when excessive volatile acidity is a problem, and then "lose" the wine in cheap pop wine or something of the sort.

BLENDING. Let us assume that we know the approximate alcoholic content of the new wine. We know what the total acidity is by either test or tasting. The wine has a clean, vinous odor, and we assume a healthy fermentation without any suspicious excess of volatile acidity. We also assume that the malolactic fermentation has run its course. From here on the small-scale winemaker uses his nose, his taste buds and his eyes as his laboratory instruments and as guides in any blending he may want to do.

Some blending may have been done prior to fermentation, if several grape varieties were crushed and fermented together. If not, any blending should be done using new wines, prior to fining. This is not an absolute rule. But when finished wines are blended there may develop unexpected hazes and precipitations since the balance of composition is somewhat altered. It is better that this happen before fining. Beyond that, blending is very much a subjective matter. But a few elementary rules may be kept in mind.

1. The importance of "varietal" wines has been exaggerated. Wine of a single variety does indicate the potential of a given grape, and some few varieties yield perfectly bal-

anced wines all by themselves. But generally speaking, a blend is a more "complete" wine, whose components tend to complement each other.

2. An exception is never to blend wines of the *labrusca* grapes (such as Concord or Catawba) with non-foxy wines made from *vinifera* or from the French hybrids.

3. A low-alcohol wine is improved by blending with a wine of higher alcohol.

4. A persistently high-acid wine is brought into balance by blending with a low-acid wine. The low-acid wines made from concentrates are useful for this purpose when the goal is ordinary domestic consumption.

5. A deficiency of color is corrected by adding a small proportion of deep-colored wine—what the French call a *vin médecin* or *teinturier*.

6. Whatever the reason for blending, do it on a small scale first, in a graduated glass. Then make the larger blend proportionately.

7. The wines entering into a blend should all be absolutely sound. The outcome of a blend of sound wine with an unsound wine is always disastrous.

8. Eastern-grown wines, which as a rule are rather low in alcohol and high in acidity, will blend well with wines from California grapes, with their opposite characteristics. This is regularly done in many Eastern wineries.

9. The wines to be blended should, if possible, be of approximately the same age, for the reason mentioned above.

10. Never blend a sweet wine with a dry wine.

With time, the winemaker develops know-how in making blends. There is no substitute for practice.

Bottling

There is a satisfying finality about bottling. The wine has been brought safely through the crisis of birth and the dangers of its youth, and the principal hazards to which wines are exposed are left behind as the cork is driven home.

The precise moment to bottle depends partly on the whim of the winemaker, partly on the time at his disposal, and also on the character of the wine. But certain fundamental conditions must be met before bottling is undertaken. *First*, the secondary or malolactic fermentation must have been completed. *Second*, the wine should be brilliant before it goes into bottle. If not, the wine will either remain persistently hazy or form more sediment in bottle than a good wine should. *Third*, the aroma should be perfectly clean—free, for example, from any H_2S, or rotten-egg, odor. This can be eliminated earlier but will not go away once the wine is in bottle. *Fourth*, the wine should have been well chilled, especially white wine, in order to make sure that all excess tartrates have been eliminated. Otherwise some may form in the bottle as "gravel" or the wine may cloud up on being chilled before drinking.

These are the essential conditions. The time for bottling also varies depending on whether the wine is white or red, or whether a fruity young wine or what the French call a *vin de garde* is the objective.

Most *white wines* benefit by an early bottling, since prolonged aging with its inevitable exposure to oxygen tends to darken it, sometimes to give it a woody taste, and to destroy the freshness which should be one of its charms. Certain "big" white wines, such as the white Burgundies and the white Bordeaux wines, are not usually bottled until they have gone through one summer in cooperage. Most white wines, however, are ready to bottle as soon as they are bright and stable, which may be as early as December and in any case should be before June. It may be interesting to bottle part of a vintage early and the rest a year later, to see how different they can be.

Red wines, some of them, do undoubtedly benefit by a year or eighteen months of aging in good cooperage. Several rackings, with their mild oxidation, eliminate the "newness" and encourage those reactions within the wine which help to give it roundness and good balance and contribute to bouquet; and the less stable pigments and other colloidal materials gradually fall. The purple-red of young wines gives way to the yellow-red of the more stable pigments. And if there is enough wine, really good oak cooperage contributes its bit to bouquet and flavor. The wine evolves.

The evolution continues in bottle; and this is the time to mention the pros and cons of bottle aging, which is essentially different from aging in bulk. The latter provides mild oxidation. But once the wine is in bottle, access to oxygen is denied and subsequent changes in the wine are *reducing* reactions. There ensues a reverse process, subtle in nature and extremely complicated, whereby the natural fruitiness of the wine is gradually lost, and if the grapes are the right ones and all goes well some bouquet begins to develop and the wine undergoes a general softening and refinement.

But the importance of bottle age is often exaggerated. Improvement does not go on indefinitely: beyond a certain point the wine passes its peak and a process of decline sets in. This evolution ends in the death of the wine. Most red wines capable of being improved by bottle aging may be said to have reached their maximum of quality after three or four years in bottle, and there is no point in keeping them any longer. In the case of most wines kept for a long period in bottle, say fifteen or twenty years, the marvel is that they are drinkable at all.

Moreover, evolution in bottle, though it always takes place, is not always for the better. The fruitiness of youth is lost, and depending on the particular wine, what takes its place may not be worth waiting for. There is virtue in young red wines, and many prefer them. Most of the world's wine is drunk within the year; and what is true of ordinary wines is equally true of many wines entitled to be called superior or demi-fine. A case in point is Beaujolais. Such wines are never better than when bottled young and drunk at from four to twelve months. The only proviso is that they be fully stable before bottling.

BOTTLES. Always use wine bottles if possible, with correct traditional color and shape. This may seem a small point, but wine does seem to taste better when poured from a wine bottle than when poured from a pop bottle. Green glass is usual for red wines, and also for many white wines and rosés: a green that tends toward the yellow is somehow more attractive than ginger-ale green. Some Rhine-wine bottles are brown, whereas the Moselles are usually green. (Many a "connoisseur" has dazzled others at the table by distinguishing between a Moselle and a Rhine merely by noting the

A fiberglass bottling tank and a gravity bottle filler.

color of the bottle.) The white Bordeaux such as Sauternes are usually bottled in flint glass.

Wine bottles may be bought from winemakers' supply houses, but are expensive. A good idea for small-scale wine-makers is to make a connection with a club or restaurant for used bottles. Once a supply is gathered, they may be reused indefinitely. Cork-finish bottles are more pleasing than screw-cap or crown-cork bottles.

CORKS. These should be first-quality No. 9 1¼ to 1¾ straight wine corks. Corks may be reused after rinsing and then boiling briefly and allowing to cool—provided they have not been punctured all the way through by a corkscrew.

BOTTLE FILLER. Small lots of wine may be bottled with the same siphon hose or tube used in racking. There are small stop-start devices that fit into the filling end of the tube and make accurate filling easier by holding the suction between bottles.

CORKER. Two small types are illustrated on page 200.

PROCEDURE. Place the wine to be bottled at an appropriate height. If it must be moved first, do it the night before so that any lees that may be disturbed will have time to settle. Begin by racking the wine with great care for the final time, stopping a bit short of the lees so as not to pick up any. During this final racking a last protective dose of meta (2 grams per 20 gallons) should be added to counteract oxidation and provide insurance against misbehavior after the wine is bottled.

Raise the racked wine, perfectly clear, to a proper height. Prepare the bottles. If they are new, rinse with hot water and set upside down in a rack to drain. If previously used, soak in a tub for several hours in a weak solution of washing soda, wash with a bottle brush, rinse thoroughly, and set to drain. Small bottle rinsers are available that screw onto a

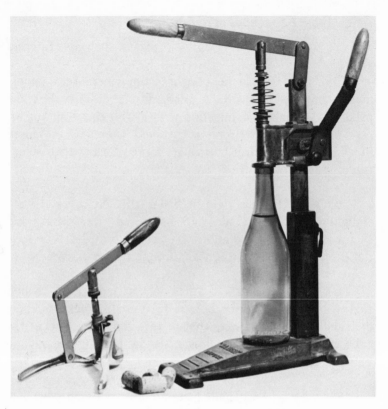

Hand corkers for straight corks, two of many styles.

water faucet, direct a stream of water up into the bottle, and speed up the rinsing process.

New corks are first soaked for an hour or two, then rinsed several times in warm water. The process softens them somewhat and rids them of cork dust. A pinch of meta may be added to the final rinsing water. Used corks should be soaked, brought to a low boil, then given several hot-water rinsings. This will soften them too much for driving evenly, so give a final cold-water rinsing, and allow them to harden again a bit.

When the bottles are drained, line them up conveniently on the floor or bench and fill one after another, just into the neck. All of the wine in a container should be bottled at one time. Corking follows immediately. Leave a small air space (about one-third inch) in the bottle neck, as wine is usually quite cool when bottled and this air space allows the wine to expand without pushing up the cork, should it be stored in a warmer place. After corking, let the bottles stand upright overnight to equalize the air pressure under the cork with outside air pressure and to let the corks harden. As a precaution against deterioration of the corks, or for aesthetic reasons, they may be sealed or else dressed with lead foil or plastic caps. For a traditional wax seal, mix one part of beeswax to four parts of rosin, melt these together in a tin can, and dip the corked mouth of the bottle. Or the material may be bought ready prepared. Some like to imprint the top with a seal of their own devising, a pretty touch.

With bottling, the task of winemaking is finished. Bin the bottles on their sides so that the interior surface of the cork is kept constantly moist and the air bubble is in the middle of the bottle. The storage place should have moderate temperature, say around 60° to 65° F. The precise temperature is less important than avoidance of extreme fluctuations.

Rosé Wine and Other Special Fermentations

 CONSIDER THE EGG: how different a hard-boiled egg is from a soft-boiled, or a fried, or a scrambled, or a poached egg, or an omelet. So likewise a winemaker can do many different things with the same raw material. A few of these possibilities will be briefly considered in this chapter before we move on to others dealing with concentrate wines, sparkling wines, and sweet wines.

Rosé

Rosé wine is intermediate between white wine and red, partaking of both in some degree. It is admired for its gay color. It is drunk cool, or even chilled, which is the way many Americans prefer their table wine. At the table it gracefully replaces either white or red. But it eludes exact definition because rosés can be so different. At one extreme they approach the character of a light red wine; at the other they are essentially white wine that carries a bit of color. There are two traditional ways of making rosé.

ROSÉ BY MACERATION. To make it this way, red-wine grapes are crushed into a fermenter as though for red wine. A period of maceration follows, during which the must begins to pick up some of the pigments, or anthocyanins, from the skins. The period may be twenty-four hours or more at the beginning of the season or in the case of lightly pigmented grapes. Later in the season, when nearby fermentations are going full blast, sufficient pigment may be picked up in a matter of hours.

After this wait, a portion of the still-sweet free run must is drawn off and fermented separately, white-wine fashion. This is the method known as *saignée*, or bleeding. The skins and the remainder of the must are kept in the fermenter to ferment out conventionally into red wine, which is heavier bodied than it would be otherwise because the proportion of skins to must has been increased. The same batch of grapes thus yields both rosé and red wine: the proportion drawn off for rosé is usually about one-third.

An alternative is to draw off the free run, then press the remainder of the mass immediately afterward before it has begun to ferment and add this to the free run. This gives a wine that has more body and is somewhat more deeply colored than the free run alone. Depending on the amount of maceration, such wines as these are also known in France as *clairets*, *vins de café*, *vins souples*, and *vins d'une nuit*. They begin to approach red wine in character, yet are different. They attain all their quality quickly and are best drunk young —carafe wines. As I remarked on page 7, the reputation of the wines of the French Burgundy district was originally based on wines of this sort and not on full-bodied red wines of the kind now associated with the district. The grapes were crushed in tubs by footpower in order to obtain some extraction of color, the must then being pressed and drained off and fermented in the absence of the skins. This explains why a true fermenting vat is not depicted in the famous Cluny tapestry that illustrates the entire annual winegrowing cycle in that district. See also the reproduction of an old woodcut on page 100.

ROSÉ WITHOUT MACERATION. To make it this way, crush red-wine grapes, but then press them immediately and ferment the juice white-wine fashion. In the course of crushing and pressing there will be some leakage of pigment from the ruptured skins, but not nearly so much as when the grapes have a period of maceration. The degree of color depends on the variety of grapes used. Heavily pigmented varieties may contribute quite a bit: lightly pigmented ones, much less. In France those that carry hardly more than a hint of color are known as *vins gris*, and in some regions (for instance Lorraine around the city of Nancy) they are a specialty. In any case, rosés without maceration are strictly akin to white wines. They are sometimes cross-blended later with rosés obtained by maceration in order to adjust color to a predetermined standard. This method is also used a great deal in the cooperatives of southern France as a way of handling the coarser and rougher red-wine grapes, and the wines are later used by the negotiants of the region to soften and give more finesse to red wines.

Blanc de Noirs

One occasionally encounters a wine, usually dressed up in a fancy package, that is labeled *Blanc de Blancs*. The term is impressive, and meant to be. But it means nothing more than that the white wine in the bottle was made from white grapes. Since 99 per cent of the world's white wine is made from white grapes, the expression is next to meaningless.

It is otherwise with *Blanc de Noirs*, which signifies white wine made from black, or red-wine, grapes. Since the pigment of most red-wine grapes is contained entirely in the skins, white wine may be made from them, provided the juice of such grapes can be extracted without picking up any pigment. Thus, in the French Champagne district the *grandes marques* are made from a blend of some white wine from the white Chardonnay and much more white wine made from a careful pressing of the black Pinot Noir. The latter is obtained by using the colorless free run drawn off immediately after crushing, plus the yield of the first gentle pressing.* Such trifling amounts of pigment as may be present tend to be lost in the course of fermentation. If any remains, it is eliminated by appropriate treatment, mainly with activated charcoal. The *blanc de noirs* thus obtained has a characteristic aroma and a deeper golden color and more body than the *blanc de blancs* from Chardonnay. The two types, from various parts of the district, are then blended together in various proportions to obtain the characteristics traditionally associated with a given *marque*, or brand.

Trying one's hand at a *blanc de noirs* can be fun, but unless great care is lavished on it, the result is usually a *vin gris*.

Blanc sur Lie

This is white wine that has undergone the least possible manipulation. It is fermented in the normal way. When the primary fermentation is finished, the fermenter is filled *full* and becomes a storage vessel, the wine still resting on its original lees. The wine undergoes the malolactic fermentation and is chilled, still without racking. When it has fallen bright, or almost bright, it is bottled direct from the lees without fining or filtration and with a minimum dose of SO_2, usually in midwinter. These wines preserve the maximum fruitiness of the grapes, plus a characteristic aroma contributed by some autolysis of the yeast; and a bit of dissolved CO_2 adds an agreeable tingle to the flavor. The best known of these are produced in the Muscadet region of the lower Loire around Nantes. Since wine falls bright most readily in small containers, and the process can be easily observed in five-gallon bottles, *blanc sur lie* is a natural for the home winemaker.

---

* The yield of later pressings, containing a fair bit of pigment, is used for the pale orange-pink champagne known as *oeil de perdrix*, or partridge eye, no relation to Cold Duck.

Hot-Press Wine and Its Variants

Although the pigment of a red wine is usually picked up from the skins during fermentation, it may also be extracted by heating. Ordinary commercial grape juice gets its color this way: by crushing, heating the crushed grapes either in batches or by a continuous process, pressing out the deeply colored juice, and then preventing fermentation by one or another of several methods.

The traditional New York State red wines, based on Concords, are made by a hot-press method, and during fermentation there is no contact with the skins. The heating has the advantage of eliminating some of the foxy aroma and coarse flavor of the *labrusca* grapes; also nearly 100 per cent of color is extracted, as against about 60 per cent the conventional way. The hot-press method has the disadvantage that it may contribute a somewhat "cooked" flavor and a brownish cast to the color if grapes other than the *labruscas* are used.

Over the years innumerable variants of the heating method of extracting color have been devised and applied in various parts of the world. The object in most cases has been to substitute the efficiency and uniformity of continuous processing for traditional batch processing in the mass production of ordinary wines.

But preliminary heating is also used in some fine-wine regions where the vintage is likely to come late in cold weather, such as the Burgundy region. The danger lies in overheating, of course. But if done with moderation, it improves color extraction and assures a prompt start of fermentation without damage to quality. For example, the Marquis d'Angerville (whom I have already mentioned in connection with fining) customarily heats about one-fourth of his stemmed red-wine grapes to 60° C. (140° F.), then adds them to the rest; and his Clos des Ducs is a Burgundy of the highest quality. The Burgundy wines of Louis Latour and other fine growers are also handled in this way.

Carbonic Maceration

This is a method of making red wine that surely goes back to neolithic times and that seems to contradict much of the conventional practice already set forth in this book. It is still used here and there where winemaking is primitive and rigidly traditional; and as often happens, there turns out to be some virtue in tradition. Since the method has been closely studied in recent years, there is now a better understanding of what happens. Though it is the subject of much dispute, it has been restored to favor in certain places, notably in the Beaujolais and some large establishments of the south of France.

The grapes are emptied into a fermenter without being either crushed or stemmed. The fermenter is closed, except for a gas trap. Under a blanket of carbon dioxide that develops spontaneously and without any access to air whatever, the intact grapes submit to complex modifications. There is fermentation within the cells of the berries, which produces a small quantity of alcohol and CO_2 and also a bit of glycerol, succinic acid, and various other secondary products of sugar fermentation. The combined effect of the alcohol and asphyxiation kills the cells of the grape berries, which thereupon yield their pigment, mineral matter, aromatic substances, and so on. The pectins are hydrolized, and much of the malic acid undergoes a transformation into lactic.

The grapes are maintained this way for a period of ten days to three weeks. They are then pressed, and the resulting partly finished wine completes its fermentation very swiftly in the usual way. If all goes well, the resulting wine is normal so far as alcoholic content is concerned, the total acidity is less than that of a conventionally made "control," volatile acidity is normal or only slightly increased, color is more nearly that of a mature wine, and it is endowed with a special and agreeable aroma.* The quality is excellent. It is even claimed that the foxiness of *labrusca* grapes may be reduced by this method (though I have not had the pleasure of tasting the proof). On the other hand, results of experiments in California have been consistently negative, with unacceptable development of volatile acidity. The chief objection to its use as a commercial winemaking method is that the prolonged carbonic maceration ties up too much fermenting capacity. In view of the hazards, the method is at this point for the experimentally inclined only.

Vin Jaune

This is a white-wine specialty of the Jura region of France, produced around the town of Arbois, and again the making of it seems to contradict accepted winemaking methods. It is made by fermenting certain high-sugar grapes to complete dryness and unusually high alcoholic content (14.5 to 15.5 per cent by volume). From this point on, however, the wines are not topped. An air space is allowed to develop in the cask, and the casks are left in this condition for years. In the mean-time, one or more special strains of *Saccharomyces* yeasts called *flor* yeasts develop a film on the surface, thin in the beginning and gradually growing thicker, which protects the wine beneath from exposure to air. The phenomenon resem-bles that in the production of sherry (which will be described later): a pronounced development of aldehydes unaccom-panied by an increase of volatile acidity. The result is a wine much darker in color than normal white wines and with a pronounced sherry-like odor and flavor—the flavor one calls "oxidized" when it occurs by mistake in making conventional white wine. The method does not succeed unless the base

---

* For a description of controlled experiments with the method, including flushing with CO_2 gas every two days to maintain anaerobic conditions, see Beelman, "The Influence of Macération Carbonique," *Proceedings of the Sixth Pennsylvania Wine Conference*, Pennsylvania State University, 1973.

material is of unusually high natural alcoholic content, but instead yields a wine that is merely spoiled, with high volatile acidity and a nasty taste and smell. At its best, *vin jaune* is an acquired taste, like *retsina*, that Greek granddaddy of all pop wines.

Wine From Concentrates or Sugar

 FRUIT CONCENTRATES are an old story in the food industry. Practically all commercial jellies and preserves are made from them. Most breakfast "juices," such as orange juice, are concentrates diluted back to their original volume. And concentrates are important ingredients in ice cream, candy, soda pop, baked goods, and all sorts of other things. A great deal of grape concentrate is also used in commercial winemaking for producing, ameliorating, and sweetening the cheaper wines.

Concentrate Wine

More to our point, home winemakers learned to use grape concentrate during prohibition, and its use for this purpose has lately come back into vogue in a large way. Where suitable grapes are not available, or their use is impractical, as on the twentieth floor of a skyscraper, tidy cans of concentrate may provide a tolerable substitute for the real thing, a substitute that is indeed often better than tolerable. A well-made concentrate wine, from superior concentrate, is better than a badly made natural wine. Concentrates are easily available, too, their sale being the chief business of the present generation of winemakers' shops.

In the world of concentrate wine, we begin with high technology and end with low, which is to say that the production of high-grade concentrate is a complicated industrial process, whereas its conversion into domestic wine requires no more competence than the ability to follow a recipe in a cookbook. The key to success is to begin with a concentrate of the best quality.

Let us see what we mean by "best." As always, the grapes come first. It must be obvious that grapes capable of making the best wine are not used for concentrate. Why should the proprietors of Romanée Conti or Château Margaux send their precious fruit to the concentrator? The concentrator couldn't afford their prices anyway. The going price for first-quality grapes in the French Champagne district in 1974 was $1,600 a ton (at the prevailing rate of exchange); on the other hand, sound Thompson Seedless could be had that same year in the Central Valley of California for $60 or $70 a ton. The conclusion is clear. Grapes used for concentrate are mainly the bulk varieties of ordinary quality, no matter whether the label on the can says burgundy, claret, sauternes, or chablis (though some "varietal" concentrate from the next-best grapes is sometimes available nowadays). Such labeling is not to be held against the producers of concentrates so long as the customer understands.

But concentrate quality involves more than the raw material. Its preparation is of equal importance. Concentrates are made in California, Spain, Italy, Yugoslavia, France, and many other places. Methods of manufacture range from the quite primitive to the highly sophisticated.

Concentrate is essentially boiled-down grape juice—but boiled down in a very special way. The object is to preserve as much as possible of the character of the fresh grapes, which of course is sacrificed somewhat to the heat of simple boiling as in home jelly-making. The technique is to "boil" under a vacuum. We all know that at sea level water boils at a temperature of 212° F., but at a lower temperature than that on top of Pikes Peak, where the atmospheric pressure is lower. Reduce the atmosphere to negative pressure (in other words, create a vacuum), and the boiling point falls even lower. The higher the vacuum, the lower the boiling point. Vacuum concentraters that boil grape juice at 132° F. are common; those doing this at 92° F., less so. The most advanced equipment, which is also the most complicated and expensive, will do it at 69° to 71° F. or even lower. Cooking effects are avoided and the freshness of the grape remains intact—except that the volatile or odorous constituents of the grape juice are evaporated and thrown off along with the water vapor. The trick here is to recapture the odor as it is given off, by condensation, and put it back afterward. There are other difficulties. As the sugar content is concentrated, so is the acidity, much of it in ways that are not reversible when the concentrate is diluted back to grape juice consistency. And if red-wine concentrate is the objective, the color must be extracted from the skins by heating prior to concentration. On the other hand white-juice concentrate tends to darken and caramelize.

Such technical problems have been pretty well conquered. Acidity can be adjusted. Odor and flavor can be put back (and not infrequently strengthened by synthetics). The same is true of color. But the concentrate available in cans to the home winemaker is always to some extent an artificial product when it has been reconstituted by dilution, not quite the same as natural grape juice. There is a slightly disappointing difference, just as there is a difference between diluted orange juice concentrate and natural orange juice.

Then there is the important question of the degree of concentration. In the food industry, where concentrates are used quite promptly, it is usually concentrated to about 68° Balling, as compared to the normal 20° to 21° Balling of single-strength juice before concentration. At this concentration, it is a heavy goo, but still pourable. If it is to be stored for any length of time, it is concentrated to about 74° Balling to discourage any fermentation, which would be disastrous in a canned retail product. But at that concentration the grape sugar tends to crystallize and solidify. And no matter what the concentration, undesirable color changes may take place with storage above 85° F.

So buying concentrate at retail is always a chancy business. The retail source is important; the original source, even more so. There is no alternative to trial and error. Look for a dealer who as a matter of routine makes a sample fermentation before putting a new concentrate on sale.

PROCEDURE.   The first step is to bring together the necessary equipment. Beware of miniature one-gallon plastic kits. The most satisfactory home fermenting unit, as for natural wine, is again the five-gallon bottle. Neither crusher nor press is necessary, of course.

The first step is to dilute the concentrate to the proper consistency of about 21° Balling with water of good quality (most tap water these days is of excellent quality). Instructions for dilution are usually printed on the can, or in an accompanying leaflet—as, for instance, three cans of water to one can of concentrate. The diluted concentrate is brought to the correct Balling degree by adding sugar, if necessary, and then checking by means of a saccharometer. What you have after dilution is reconstituted grape juice; and it is handled like natural grape must.

Instructions on the can or in the leaflet describe the next steps. Always use a yeast starter when working with concentrate. Thorough aeration is important, and it may be prudent to add a bit of one of the proprietary yeast foods to be had from most winemakers' shops. Once fermentation is under way, the rest of the procedure is the same as that described in Chapter 9, "Making White Wine," whether the diluted concentrate is red or white, and in Chapter 11, "From Fermentation to Bottling." Do not strive for the malolactic fermentation and keep in mind that concentrate wines almost always settle and clear more rapidly than natural wines, rarely need fining, and are ready to bottle and drink soon afterward. These wines should have the usual dose of so₂ on racking, either as meta or in the form of the widely used compressed Campden tablets.

Winemakers' shops stock an array of adjuvants such as special yeasts, yeast foods, acid blends, and materials for arresting fermentation or simulating various sorts of wine. Some of these are useful; some are catch-penny merchandise.

CONCENTRATE PLUS GRAPES. Although so much technology is lavished on the manufacture of concentrate, the resulting wine is rarely equal to a well-made natural wine in quality. Winemakers who have the space will achieve better results by combining concentrate (properly diluted) with a proportion of good grapes, even a small proportion, if a source of the latter is available. Good concentrate also provides a ready means of reducing the acidity or increasing the sugar content of grapes that are not in good sugar/acid balance. There is no need to labor these possibilities: they are many.

CONCENTRATE PLUS OTHER THINGS. For those who are not content with simple concentrate wine, and have no access to suitable grapes, it is possible to fabricate wine-like beverages out of a vast and miscellaneous array of fermentable materials. As I wrote at the beginning, such fabrications are not within the compass of this book. But by way of illustration one recipe typical of these *boissons de fantaisie* is offered without prejudice:*

BUAL OR MALMSEY MADEIRA
3 qts. white grape concentrate
76 oz. fig concentrate
24 oz. dried bananas

* This recipe appears in S. F. Anderson and Raymond Hull, *The Art of Making Wine*. New York: Hawthorn, 1970.

    11 gallons hot water
    10 Campden tablets [a form of meta]
    4 oz. acid blend
    3 tsp. yeast energizer
    3 tsp. yeast nutrient
    80 oz. Madeira or sherry wine yeast starter
    Sugar syrup

This recipe is for twelve gallons of finished product. The sugar syrup is added by degrees as the mixture ferments: it is then "baked" for three or four months at 130° F. in an estufa, or hot box, consisting of an insulated wooden crate containing a light bulb as a heat source. Then it is fined, 1 or 2 ounces of brandy per bottle are added, and it is aged one or two years. The authors are keen about this recipe. I have never tried it.

Fresh-Bought Must

For the home winemaker whose space is limited, who does not find concentrate wine to his taste, and who lacks a source of good grapes, there is another choice. This is to buy ready-pressed must and bring it home in bottles or plastic tanks for fermenting, much as people used to take jugs and kegs to a nearby cider mill in the old days. This eliminates all the labor and mess of crushing and pressing. Sometimes the fresh-pressed must is already corrected for acidity and sugar content at the time of purchase, and there is nothing to do but add a yeast starter and let the fermentation proceed. Or the juice may be just as it comes from the press. Custom retailers of fresh must are still fairly scarce,* but their numbers have begun to increase as growers of wine grapes and proprietors of roadside stands who grow their own fruit have discovered the existence of a substantial market. For the most part, these

---

* One of the earliest and most successful innovators in this field is Presque Island Wine Cellars of North East, Pennsylvania.

fresh-pressed musts are blends. Sometimes they are from grapes of a single variety, which is to say varietals. Since different grapes ripen at different times and the juice is fresh-pressed, advance arrangements for prompt pickup have to be made. And since this is such a personal, retail sort of thing, prices are fairly high.

Piquette and Sugar Wines

No matter how thoroughly red-wine pomace is pressed, it still contains considerable quantities of coloring matter, alcohol, acid, and still-unfermented sugar. From time immemorial it has been the custom in winemaking countries to extract these desirable constituents by adding a quantity of water to the red pomace after it has been pressed, stirring water and pomace together, and pressing again after several days of maceration. The liquid thus obtained is of course extremely low in alcoholic content (3 or 4 per cent at most) and only lightly colored, but tart and fresh. It clears rapidly and is used during the months immediately following the vintage. A taste for *piquette* must be acquired, but it is thirst-quenching and better than water of poor quality. The use of it in European rural life goes back to the time of the Romans, and even before.

SUGAR WINE. This is a sort of fancified *piquette*, which also makes use of the pomace but produces a beverage more closely resembling real wine. The pomace, after being pressed, is thrown back into the fermenter and broken up. A sugar solution equal in quantity to somewhat less than the wine that has been pressed off (no more than one-half if a plausible product is desired) is then added to the pomace. The sugar solution should be about 21° Balling, or approximately the sugar content of the normal must—1.7 pounds per gallon dissolved in tap water assuming that the quality of the water is good. A small dose of tartaric acid (3 grams per gallon, dissolved in a bit of warm water) is added to keep the concoction from being too insipid. The pomace is of course full of active yeast, and when the sugar solution is added, this yeast immediately undertakes, once again, its function of helping sugar to become alcohol. It will be encouraged in this endeavor by the addition of some patent yeast food. A new fermentation is soon under way, and procedure from then on is the same as for real wine.

Sugar wine is of course much lighter in color and body than real wine, but it can be agreeable and will help the amateur to eke out his supply if he is short of grapes. But when the price of sugar is high, as it was in 1974, it is no bargain. The story is different when sugar is cheap. Such concoctions of water, sugar, tartaric acid, and tired grape skins, with perhaps some artificial flavor and color and a bit of glycerin for body, were resorted to on a massive scale in Europe during the phylloxera epidemic of the nineteenth century. What was learned then has not been forgotten. Sugar wines are still the basis of many of the wine scandals that occasionally pop up in the press. Their manufacture and sale as wine is illegal for commercial wineries the world over. It is neither illegal nor sinful to play around with them at home.

Sparkling Wines

 SPARKLING WINE and champagne are not quite the same thing although in American usage they are considered to be synonymous. Under French law and regulations champagne is produced only in the *département* of the Marne and parts of the neighboring *départements* of Aube and Aisne. It is produced only from the three *cépages* Pinot Noir, Pinot Meunier, and Pinot Chardonnay. It is made to sparkle only by the traditional process known as the *méthode champenoise*.

So champagne is a sparkling wine, but most sparkling wine is not champagne. The others fail to qualify as champagne by reason of the grapes from which they are made, the region where they are made, or their method of manufacture. Yet quite a few of these are famous in their own right, such as sparkling Saumur, sparkling Vouvray, certain sparkling wines from Savoie, Asti Spumante, and the best so-called American champagnes. They should be judged on their own merits.

Méthode Champenoise

This calls for more work than the making of still wines, and some special equipment. But the elements are simple and the necessary manipulations are not difficult. One nice thing about it is that the method does as well for small-scale wine-making as for large.

First, a synopsis of the method. A white wine is fermented out absolutely dry as though to make still table wine. It is racked, chilled, fined, and racked again. When it is stable and bright, say in midwinter, a measured quantity of sugar is dissolved in the wine, a yeast starter is stirred in, it is bottled, and the bottles are capped or else corked with oversize corks that are tied or wired down. The bottles are laid on their sides, and the added sugar proceeds to ferment. But the gas, instead of being allowed to escape, is held in by the cap or cork and hence builds up pressure, which provides the bubbles, or *mousse*, that distinguishes champagne from still wines.

A sediment of yeast cells is formed during this bottle fermentation. When that is finished and the wine clears, the yeast gathers in a streak along the side of the bottle on which it is lying. With the return of cold weather the next winter, the bottles are placed in a frame, sloped but with the necks pointed down. By a series of slight shakings and turnings the yeast is persuaded to slip down until it settles compactly on the inside end of the cork. When this has been accomplished, the bottle is chilled and carefully disgorged in such fashion that all sediment is blown out along with the cork, but without blowing out the wine. A dose of liqueur consisting of sugar syrup plus a bit of wine or brandy is added to the bottle to replace any wine which may have escaped, and the bottle is swiftly recorked, rewired, and laid away, finished and ready.

The synopsis really tells the story. But I will now discuss the steps one by one. Though scaled to mini-production, the description differs in no important way from the classic *méthode champenoise*.

BASE WINE.   The wine to be rendered sparkling must be absolutely sound. It should also meet certain other requirements:

1. The wine should be light in body and completely dry, with an alcoholic content between 10 and 11 per cent. Wine

with less alcohol does not absorb the carbon dioxide readily. Wine with more may not re-ferment satisfactorily.

2. It should have a total acidity of about 0.8 expressed as tartaric, to assure a sound re-fermentation and to give vivacity to the finished product.

3. It should contain tannin as an aid to clearing. Give it a tannin dose of 5 to 6 grams per hectoliter (1 gram per 5-gallon bottle) prior to its original fermentation.

4. It should be brilliant and stable, well chilled to eliminate tartrates, and well fined. Once in bottle it is beyond reach of treatment.

In the Champagne district, the base wine is prepared by blending together wines from several parts of the region, together with not more than one-fourth of an older wine—what the French call *vin de réserve*. The proportions of this blend account for the difference between one famous *marque* and another; the *vin de réserve* improves the bouquet and provides consistency from year to year. The result is called the *cuvée*. True vintage champagnes are more variable than the nonvintage champagne of the same maker. Only the most experienced American amateurs play around with such blending.

BOTTLE FERMENTATION. What we have, then, is a finished still wine. Do not add the usual protective dose of so₂ when the wine to be sparkled is given its final racking. That may inhibit the fermentation in bottles. But this is the time for a final analysis (if one is going to be meticulous) to determine whether the alcoholic content and total acidity are within the limits prescribed above and also to confirm the absence of residual sugar.

The next step is to prepare the sugar dose, or *liqueur de tirage*, which will be the source of the bottle fermentation and hence of the bubbles, or *mousse*. The dose must be exact. If too small, there won't be enough sparkle; if too large, excessive pressure will be generated and the bottle will explode. Many an inaccurate amateur has been startled, and sometimes wounded, by a barrage of exploding bottles. The average champagne is fermented to a pressure of between 4 and 5 atmospheres, or about 60 pounds pressure. The champagnes called *crémant* (creamy) are less bumptious; their pressure is usually about 2 atmospheres. Beginners do well to aim for a *crémant*.

Vineyards outside Cramant, in the Champagne district.

In calculating the amount of sugar to add, the rule of thumb is that *4 grams of sugar per liter of wine yield 1 atmosphere of pressure after fermentation*. Application of the rule requires only a bit of elementary arithmetic.

> EXAMPLE: *The quantity of wine to be sparkled is 20 gallons (75.7 liters). The wanted pressure is 4 atmospheres. Then 75.7 (liters) times 4 (grams per atmosphere) times 4 (atmospheres) equals 1211.2 grams of sugar, or 43.7 ounces. A good use for your new pocket calculator. A metric conversion table is provided on page 297.*

Prepare the *dosage* syrup by dissolving the appropriate quantity of granulated sugar in some of the wine, say three gallons of it. Dissolve it completely, but without warming the wine-sugar solution. When the solution is clear, prepare the yeast starter by rehydrating a standard 5-gram packet of dehydrated wine yeast with a bit of warm water and then a bit of the wine to the consistency of thin cream. If available, a culture of *S. oviformis*, the "finishing" yeast (see page 115), may be used. Add this yeast starter to the sugar syrup and see that it is well stirred in.

BOTTLES AND CLOSURES. Ordinary wine bottles will not do for sparkling wines. Use only champagne bottles, which are designed to withstand pressures up to 8 atmospheres, though they should never be made to. Used champagne bottles are satisfactory. Wash them scrupulously and rinse with great care just before the bottling.

The standard champagne cork, capable of withstanding pressure, is of such large diameter that it looks as though it could never be crammed into the neck of the bottle. Indeed it cannot be with the corking devices available for amateurs. But during the past several decades a new kind of champagne bottle has come into general use. It has a lip resembling that of a pop or beer bottle, and takes crown caps. These bottles, together with crown caps, are now almost universally used during the bottle fermentation and are more satisfactory on all counts. In commercial production the cap is abandoned at the time of disgorging and a conventional champagne cork with a wire hood to hold it in place is used for the final closure. For the cheaper grades a preformed plastic cork that simulates the mushroomed shape of a classic champagne cork is used.

Thus, the closure problem has been solved for the amateur. He simply scouts around for the newer type of bottle and a supply of crown caps and obtains an inexpensive hand capper; he uses preformed plastic corks for final closure, or if he doesn't mind their appearance, fresh crown caps.

TIME FOR THE TIRAGE. Bottles and caps are ready. The sugar syrup with its added yeast culture is ready. Mix this thoroughly with the base wine by stirring and shaking. The shaking lets the wine absorb the oxygen necessary for the growth of yeast in the wine. This is the wine's last chance to get oxygen. Fill the bottles by siphon tube to about 1 inch from the mouth. During this actual bottling stir the wine occasionally to keep the yeast in suspension. Then carefully crimp on the caps.

As soon as they have been capped, the bottles are stacked on their sides. In the Champagne district they are ordinarily stacked twenty tiers high, the first tier being placed on a solid wooden base in which notches to receive the necks and bases of the bottles have been cut. The next tier is stacked in the opposite direction, with a lath placed along the base of the bottom tier of bottles to support the necks of the next. In this way each tier is made as solid as the bottom one. In champagne cellars the end bottles are held in place, making vertical-sided piles feasible, by an arrangement of laths and wedges that defies description. An amateur stacks between the walls of a closet or the sides of a packing box. As each bottle is laid in place, it is marked with damp chalk or thick whitewash directly over the air bubble. When bottles are restacked they are always laid with this mark up; the yeast sediment thus resettles in the same place, which experience has shown to be desirable.

The speed of bottle fermentation is governed by tempera-

A pupitre, *or clearing rack, showing how bottles
are gradually brought to their points. Used also
for draining washed wine bottles of any sort.*

ture. The higher the cellar temperature, the faster the fermentation. At 77° F. the bottle fermentation takes about three weeks; at 60° F. it may poke along for several months. Conclusion of fermentation is indicated when the yeast in the bottle begins to settle down, forming a streak, and the wine becomes clear again. In addition to providing gas for bubbles, bottle fermentation adds 1 to 1.5 per cent of alcohol to the wine, bringing it to roughly 12 per cent.

At this point, the bottles are thoroughly shaken one by one, in order to stir the yeast cells for a final cleanup of sugar, and are then restacked, mark up, for clearing and ripening. The period of ripening is important in producing champagne of the best quality. It is during this time that autolysis, or breakdown of the dead yeast cells, occurs, which contributes importantly to the bouquet of the finished wine. The best qualities may be held for years, with periodic shaking and restacking. But this is too much for the patience of most amateurs. Six months to a year should be allowed for ripening nevertheless, with, if possible, a good chilling during the period.

REMUAGE. After the wine has been ripened and is bright in bottle (with a compact streak of yeast sediment along the under inside of the bottle) it is time for the *remuage* (literally twirling or stirring), or in English, "riddling." The bottles are placed in a frame such as that shown in the illustration, or some homemade equivalent, with the neck of the bottle barely thrust into the hole, so that it is at an angle just above the horizontal. As this is done, each bottle is thoroughly shaken for the last time, so that no sediment clings to its inner wall. Occasionally some of the sediment sticks to the bottle and forms a "mask." The answer in that case is more shaking, wearing gloves and goggles. But such sticking rarely occurs if the base wine was given its preliminary dose of tannin and was well fined.

Once the shaken bottles are placed in the rack, they are allowed to rest until clear again. Then the actual *remuage* begins. Mark each bottle with damp chalk once more, but in a different place: on its base at the point which would be twelve o'clock if the base were a clock. Grasp a bottle by its base, draw it out of its hole an inch or two, rock gently, turning it clockwise one-sixth of a turn (to two o'clock), and drop it back into the hole with a gentle jar. Each bottle is given the same amount of turn.

In two or three days do this again, bringing the mark on each bottle to four o'clock. Repeat every few days until the mark on each bottle has traveled all the way around to twelve o'clock again. By then the yeast sediment will have slipped well down toward the inner end of the cork, without floating off into the wine.

The *pupitres*, or racks, in the great champagne cellars normally hold sixty bottles on each side, in ten rows of six bottles each. The *remueur*, doing two bottles at a time, one with each hand, can give as many as 25,000 bottles their fractional turn each day; and the sound of this work is like the ticking of a clock. The job is inexpressibly tedious, competent *remueurs* are increasingly hard to find, and in many cellars mechanical systems of riddling have been devised to get around this.

Having gone all the way around the clock, start over again. The second time around, the angle of each bottle is raised slightly when it is returned to its hole, encouraging the yeast to slip down more rapidly. The third time around, with the bottles approaching the vertical, the bottles can safely be given a full quarter turn: to three o'clock, six o'clock, nine o'clock, and back to twelve o'clock. With that, the job is usually done. The bottles may be left in their racks until time for disgorging, or carefully removed and stacked vertically, necks down. The longer they are left on their points, the more

The clearing room for sparkling wine
in a large California winery.

compact the sediment becomes and the more successful the later disgorging. In commercial cellars they may stand that way for years, depending on demand.

DISGORGING AND FINAL DOSAGE. Final treatment consists of removing the sediment, known as disgorging, adding the final sweetening *dosage*, and corking.

The matter of this final dosage requires a bit of explanation. Commercial champagnes are usually labeled *brut*, *sec*, or *demi-sec*. Literally, a *brut* champagne is a bottle to which nothing has been added but enough of the same wine to make up for any lost during disgorging. It is completely dry, with an added tingle or prickly taste provided by the *mousse*, or gas bubbles. To counteract this tingle or roughness, commercial sparkling wines are almost always dosed in the finishing process with a liqueur composed of cane sugar and wine or brandy, the quantity of sugar per bottle being approximately: for *brut*, 6 to 10 grams per liter; for *sec*, 20 grams per liter; and for *demi-sec*, 40 to 50 grams per liter. The amount of such dosage is determined by the market. There is a growing preference in this country and in England for wine that is literally *brut*. On the other hand, the Russians like their champagne almost cloyingly sweet, and the French like it just perceptibly sweet. To find out how sweet most champagne really is, just stir out all the bubbles and then taste it: you will be surprised. Obviously, it is simpler to finish sparkling wine without any dosage at all.

Disgorging is the most ticklish of all the steps in making sparkling wines since the problem is to remove the cork or cap and with it all sediment while losing a minimum of wine and pressure. This operation is best done by two people to avoid the loss of too much pressure. One does the actual disgorging. The other adds the dosage or replaces any lost wine and also does the final corking.

Well in advance of disgorging, the bottles are placed outdoors point down to be chilled, or else in a freezer. The colder the wine, the more carbon dioxide will be held in solution and the less pressure will be lost. When the bottles are as cold as they are going to be, a brine of chipped ice or snow and coarse salt is prepared. A washtub will do for the brine. A way is devised for inserting the chilled bottles, neck down, to a depth of about 2 inches. A bit of the wine next to the inside end of the cork or crown cap, including the sediment deposited there during *remuage*, freezes into a solid plug of ice. This requires from half an hour to an hour, depending on the strength of the brine and the degree of preliminary chilling. In commercial practice a shallow bath of chilled glycol, the material of antifreeze, is used instead of brine.

If dosage is to be used, prepare the concentrated sugar syrup well before the actual disgorging, using some of the same wine. A quart of wine will dissolve 24 ounces of sugar at room temperature. The addition of brandy is a matter of choice. The amount of dosage to add is calculated on the basis of sugar content, not total volume. The sweetening provided by the dosage will not give rise to another bottle fermentation because few if any yeast cells remain in the bottle after disgorging and those still present are enfeebled by lack of oxygen and nutrients and because the fermentation in bottle will have raised the alcohol content high enough to discourage further fermentation.

We will assume that crown caps have been used. Have ready a sturdy cap remover and wear an apron and gloves. Take one of the bottles from the brine and dip the neck in a pot of hot water. This will rinse the neck and loosen the ice plug. Hold the bottle by the neck with the left hand, couching it in the crook of your elbow. Position the bottle at an upward and outward slant. It must be aimed into a box or large can, which has been placed fairly high for the purpose. Remove the crown cap with the right hand, and the loosened ice plug containing the sediment will blow out along with a bit of the wine. It is mandatory to hold the bottle at a slant. If it is held upright, most of the wine will gush out like a geyser.

Hand the opened bottle, always slanting, to your assistant. If dosage is to be added, he should have the correct quantity ready in a small ladle or pitcher and add it immediately. The wine will have a tendency to foam as the dose is poured in. The foaming is reduced if the liqueur is cold and if the bottle is rotated gently as it is poured in. He fills any remaining space from a bottle of the same sparkling wine, already opened for the purpose. He then inserts the cork, which we will assume to be the preformed plastic kind, drives it home with a rubber mallet, and ties it down with one of the ready-made wire hoods to be had from any winemakers' shop. He next shakes the bottle lightly to distribute the dosage, and the job is done. There may be a false start or two, but the routine is soon mastered. The key operation is to loosen the ice plug just sufficiently in the hot water, so that it will blow without urging.

One more point. If you like truly *brut* sparkling wine and have steady nerves, disgorging can be delayed right up to the moment of serving. Chill the bottle, point down, in the refrigerator. When the time for serving the champagne arrives, disappear into the kitchen, take the bottle out of the refrigerator, still keeping the point down, and retire to back porch, balcony, or bathroom (if there is a shower), carrying the bottle point down in one hand and a bottle uncapper in the other. Then with one deft motion remove the cap while swinging the neck of the bottle upward, blow out the sediment, and place your thumb over the mouth before much wine escapes. Return to the dining room with your thumb still serving as a closure, and serve.

Other Techniques

In the commercial production of sparkling wine there are two important variants of the classic *méthode champenoise*. Both the transfer method and the bulk process method are inspired by the high cost of hand work. Both involve expensive equipment and so are not available to the amateur.

TRANSFER METHOD. This process was devised by the Germans for the production of *Sekt,* their name for sparkling wine. The wine is fermented in bottle after the traditional fashion. But when bottle fermentation is finished, the bottles are rinsed and fed into a machine which automatically opens them and dumps the wine into a tank under a pressure of nitrogen gas, sediment and all. The dosage is added to the tank; the mixture is refrigerated. It is then filtered and bottled cold, always under isobarometric pressure and without loss of the fermentation gas. In the meantime the emptied bottles, riding on a conveyor, are automatically washed and chilled and emerge to receive the filtered wine at the other end. Such wine is truly "bottle fermented," but it doesn't wind up in the same bottle. Small print on the label tells the story. If the label says "Fermented in Bottle," it was probably produced by the transfer process. If it says "Fermented in *This* Bottle," it was made by the *méthode champenoise*.

BULK PROCESS. In this case a large pressure vessel equipped with assorted controls is substituted for bottle fermentation. It is in effect a very big bottle. There are many variants. Usually these pressure tanks are jacketed so that the fermenting temperature may be controlled exactly, to be followed by refrigeration to exactly the point desired and for exactly the length of time specified. In some installations provision is made for the addition of dosage; in others the equivalent of dosage is provided by stopping the fermentation while the wine still contains the desired residue of unfermented sugar. After a suitable period of chilling and repose, the wine is filtered and bottled under pressure. The weakness of this process is that the expensive equipment must be kept producing batches in steady succession in order to pay for itself: hence, a batch cannot be held for the prolonged period of ripening prior to bottling, with yeast autolysis, which is an important part of the *méthode champenoise*. Wines made this way must say so on the label. The usual American term is "Bulk Process." The usual French term is *"En Cuve Close."*

CARBONATION. By this method a still wine, with or without its dosage already mixed in, is impregnated with CO_2

gas to the desired pressure, with equipment not greatly different from that used in making soda pop, then filtered and bottled under pressure. It must be described as carbonated on the label, which considerably reduces its glamour. Such wine is subject to a lower tax than the naturally fermented sparkling wines, $2.40 per gallon as against $3.40.

A point to remember is that except for the contribution of yeast autolysis sparkling wines made by these various methods are more dependent on the quality of the original base wine than on the method itself. A blunt way of putting it is that a carbonated sparkling wine made from first-class base material is far better than a sparkling wine laboriously made by the *méthode champenoise* out of inferior material.

Sparkling Burgundy

This has become the generic term, in this country at least, for red sparkling wines. There is such demand for the fine still burgundies that there is no incentive to make them sparkle; so in France secondary wines are used in the fabrication of sparkling red wine. As is clear by now from the previous chapters, a characteristic of all red wines is their persistent tendency to precipitate some part of their coloring matter. In making sparkling burgundy, therefore, usually only lightly pigmented red wines, or rosés, are used for the base material. Then a deeply pigmented red wine is used in making the final sweetening liqueur, with a bit of citric acid added to help keep the coloring matter in solution.

Vins Pétillants

Many wines not properly classified as sparkling contain small quantities of carbon dioxide in solution, so that when they are uncorked they tend to bubble a bit, very gently and prettily, in the glass. Or they may do no more than form a few bubbles that cling to the side of the glass. Or if the quantity of gas is very small and the wine cool, it may do no more than give a bit of extra freshness of flavor to the wine. The source may be a bit of residual fermentation gas held in solution if the wine is stored cool and bottled early. It may be the by-product of malolactic fermentation, again in wine bottled early. Or a small amount of carbon dioxide may be deliberately added. Thus, it has long been a Swiss practice to attach a CO_2 trickler to the output end of the filter. Addition of the gas by this or other methods is a now-legal practice in California, too, injecting a much-needed freshness to some of the low-acid wines of the Central Valley and giving a bit of zip to some of the flavored pop wines and light, sweet muscats. The law was amended not long ago to make way for this sensible practice without subjecting the wine to the excessive tax on sparkling wines.

Sweet Wines:
The Two Categories

 ONCE UPON A TIME sweet wines were accounted a great luxury, the reason being that the human craving for sweet things was rarely satisfied. Sugar itself was sparingly used and something of a luxury into the nineteenth century, and except for honey and ripe or dried fruit or boiled-down fruit syrups—and sweet wine— there was very little to satisfy the human sweet tooth. The history of sugar as an everyday commodity doesn't go back very far. Today our diet is saturated with sweetness.

A very few sweet wines are still accounted great luxuries, but from another point of view: as works of art. Call them minor works of art if you will, but still that is what they are. People don't crave sweet wines any more. But these do give pleasure on occasion, and certain types continue to be used and enjoyed in very substantial quantities. Let us see what they are.

Basically, sweet wines fall into two groups. There are the unfortified or natural sweet wines, which derive their alcohol entirely by fermentation and in which a portion of the sugar of the must remains unfermented. Their alcohol usually falls between 12 and 14 per cent. And then there are the fortified sweet wines, which are called dessert wines in the California trade because the word fortified seems somehow to sound the wrong note. These derive their alcoholic content partly by fermentation and partly by the addition of spirit, and they usually contain notable amounts of sugar. Their precise alcoholic content is determined by the quantity of spirit poured into them by the winemaker and in practice ranges from 18 to 20 per cent.

Natural Sweet Wines

We have seen that in a normal fermentation of white wine the work of the yeasts slows down as the alcohol increases. In most cases the yeasts are inactivated (but not necessarily killed) before the alcoholic content reaches 14 per cent, even though there is still sugar in the must. The result is a sweet wine. A natural sweet wine is produced, therefore, under one or the other of two conditions: either the must contains more sugar than the yeasts are able to convert, or the yeasts are called off by one means or another before they have finished their work.

Even where they are able to ripen fully, not many grape varieties normally develop so much sugar that the yeasts cannot ferment it all. A few do, regularly, and this is most conspicuously true of the Muscat subgroup, though there are others such as Grenache, Maccabeo, and Mission. Still others, if allowed to overripen (on the vine in hot, dry climates, or elsewhere picked and laid out on straw for a partial evaporation), produce truly natural sweet wines superior to the Muscats.

The most admired of all are wines made from grapes that have been allowed to grow overripe under very special conditions—from grapes that, to be blunt about it, have been allowed to rot a little. These are especially the great Sauternes of France, with Château d'Yquem at the head, the Trockenbeeren Auslese wines of the Rhine and Moselle valleys of Germany, and the Hungarian Tokay. What happens in the case of these wines is that in late autumn the gray mold *Botrytis cinerea* attacks the grapes, which still hang slowly ripening. This *pourriture noble*, or noble rot, feeds on the moisture of the grapes and thus concentrates their sugar; it also reduces the grapes' acidity and contributes flavor elements of its own. When the botrytis is well advanced, the vintage

Grapes in the "pourriture noble" condition.

The vineyards of Château d'Yquem, Sauternes.

begins, the workers harvesting *only* the moldy grapes. Such partial harvestings are repeated. The botrytis action reduces the yield greatly and increases harvesting costs, and that is why these wines are so scarce and expensive: only in exceptional years can they be made at all. The noble rot rarely occurs in California because the climate is so dry—though it has been induced experimentally and such wines have been made in small lots at great expense. In the East botrytis is just another fungus disease that some of us call the "ignoble rot" and that causes considerable damage in wet years. It has been nursed along occasionally on some of the scarce plantings of Rieslings, but such ventures are the stuff of dreams and nothing to build expectations on.

The vinification of natural sweet wines resembles that of dry wines in its early stages. The steps are crushing, pressing, mingling the free-run must with the pressed must, addition of a small dose of meta—2 grams per 5 gallons, addition of a yeast starter, slow fermentation at moderate temperature.

A difference is that sugar content prior to fermentation should be at least 26 per cent and, if deficient, should be adjusted to that level rather than to the 21° Balling, which is the normal level for dry wine.

When the fermentation slackens noticeably or comes to a stop, the wine is racked immediately and given three times the normal dose of SO_2 (3 grams of meta per 5 gallons). This has a triple object. It stops further fermentation, kills some of the yeasts and immobilizes the rest, and protects the fermentation from bacterial spoilage.

The wine is racked again a few days later after it has settled, with another addition of meta in the same amount. The purpose is to separate the wine from the fallen yeast cells and bacteria as soon as possible. There is no question here of inducing or even tolerating the malolactic bacteria. These are only too eager to cause spoilage by attacking the residual sugar. Besides spoilage, there is the risk of later re-fermentation in bottle. The usual rackings follow, with more moderate addition of meta and with chilling and fining as soon as practicable. Since the SO_2 that is introduced into wine is converted progressively by oxidation from its "free," or effective, form to its ineffective "combined" form (as sulfur salts), the addition of a moderate protective dose of meta with each handling, right up to bottling, must never be neglected. The level of free SO_2 must be continually renewed.

The sugar content of a natural sweet wine varies according to the original sweetness of the grapes and the point at which fermentation stops or is stopped. It may be anywhere between 3 and 10 per cent. At the lower point the French call it *demi-sec* or *moelleux*; at the higher levels, *doux* or *liqueureux*. At the lower end the impression is likely to be that of a wine which started out to be dry but couldn't quite make it. This is especially the case with many German wines of quite high natural acidity which are deliberately finished with a slight residual sweetness and give a disconcerting sweet-sour effect.

Natural sweet red wines may be made this way too, especially from Grenache and Mission grapes, and they may eventually develop the port-like odor and flavor known as *rancio.* Red wines of this sort, more or less, are known in France as *vins doux naturels*.

SUGARED WINES. Another way of making sweet wines is to build up the sugar in advance, ferment as above, and then make lavish additions of sugar or concentrate afterward. The so-called kosher wines, with a base of Concord, either juice and concentrate, are of this kind.* To distinguish them from normal wines they are required to be labeled "special natural wine." Much old-fashioned "homemade" wine is of this type, sweet and sticky and often agreeable if treated as liquid candy rather than a beverage.

Then there is the California practice, mentioned briefly in the opening chapter, of sweetening table wines of the humbler grades, very slightly, after fermentation but before finishing in order to "smooth" them. This is done with grape concentrate, the addition is hardly more than 1.0 per cent, and in the Central Valley this treatment of the so-called dry wines is so nearly universal that plain, rough, untreated table wines are rarely encountered. If the addition is high enough to make the wines perceptibly sweet, they are likely to carry such label designations as "mellow" or "*vino di famiglia.*"

Such sweetening is also practiced in some Eastern wineries, but with less justification.

Fortified Sweet Wines

The fortified wines differ from those just described in that a part (it may be much or little) of their alcohol was added in the form of spirits, usually high-proof alcohol distilled at the winery from the cheaper grades of wine or from pomace. The two most important of these are port and sherry.†

---

* Of course many other wines, even some domestic champagnes, are made kosher by the intervention of a rabbi.

† Since spirits are essential to sherry production, it is no accident that the big Spanish sherry houses also produce beverage brandy, such as the Fundador of the house of Pedro Domecq.

SHERRY. There exist in English many expert accounts of the sherry-making process and its end products. Here it is enough to put down the rudiments only—so that the reader will have some idea what he is tasting when he picks up a glass of sherry, why a few California sherries strongly resemble Spanish sherry but many do not, and how to proceed with sherry-making experiments if he is so minded.

Sherry is made in the region around Jerez de la Frontera, lying between Seville and Cádiz in southern Spain. The principal grapes are Palomino and Pedro Ximenes (there is a great deal of Palomino grown in California but very little Pedro Ximenes). It is a much manipulated wine, which is finished in a considerable range of styles. The principal ones are Fino, which is pale, delicate, and almost dry; Manzanilla, also pale and dry but less fine; Amontillado, the general-purpose grade, noticeably sweet, darker in color, with a coarser bouquet and flavor; Oloroso, also known as brown or cream sherry or christened with more fanciful names, which is sweet and syrupy, heavy-bodied, dark. The sweetening of these wines is done with *arropa*, an aged grape syrup made from the Pedro Ximenes grape.

After picking, the grapes are laid out on straw for partial drying, then crushed and lightly pressed, the must going into butts, or *botas*, of about 130 gallons for fermentation. The sugar content is usually 26° to 28° by volume and, of course, acidity is low. Traditionally, a small quantity of gypsum (which is crude calcium sulfate, or plaster of Paris) was added. This had the effect of increasing the total acidity and so protecting against spoilage during fermentation: the practice today is to use tartaric acid for the purpose. The local yeast flora are usually counted on for fermentation, rather than a pure yeast starter. The alcoholic fermentation ordinarily reaches 15 per cent in these conditions.

When fermentation is concluded, the *botas* are left out in the open, and they are not filled. Anyone familiar with the extraordinary care given to other young wines is apt to be dismayed by the apparently careless treatment that sherry receives during its early stages. The casks lie around every-where, in sheds and gardens, out in walled fields with no pro-tection, exposed to heat of noon and chill of evening. Some-times the casks even lack bungs. But there is method in this carelessness. The winemakers are watching over the new wine and waiting for the *flor* yeast to develop.

This begins to happen ten days to two weeks after fer-mentation, appearing as a thin film on the surface of the wine in the partly filled *botas*. A number of different yeasts have this *flor*, or film-forming characteristic, in the presence of air, and all winemakers are familiar with its appearance in wine vessels that have been left not quite full. Most of us take it to be punishment for carelessness and make haste to avoid spoilage by filling the container and so getting rid of the film. But here its growth is encouraged, since it is the *flor* growing on the surface of these relatively high-alcohol wines that ac-counts for the flavor and bouquet of sherry. The film grad-ually thickens, and the wine is left beneath it for a year or more. During this time the wine's content of aldehydes and other materials affecting color and flavor is increased; but, wonder of wonders, the volatile acidity is not. The wines are repeatedly classified and reclassified, with cryptic identifying symbols on the *botas*, to determine their destination in the various blends. Ultimately they go into the *bodegas* to be fortified and sweetened and take their place in the peculiar style of blending known as the *solera* system, which is a way of ensuring consistency and which eventually produces the rec-ognized commercial types. A *solera* consists of several rows of barrels piled on top of each other and is a method of fractional blending. A portion of the oldest wine (in the bot-tom row) is withdrawn for bottling. It is replaced by younger wine from the row above, which is replaced by still younger wine from above; the top row is replenished with new wine. Thus, consistency is maintained. A California iconoclast has demonstrated that a *solera* may be established with a single barrel, drawing off sherry as needed and always replacing it with new—the same result is achieved, but less picturesquely.

Early and late stages of Sherry film growth.

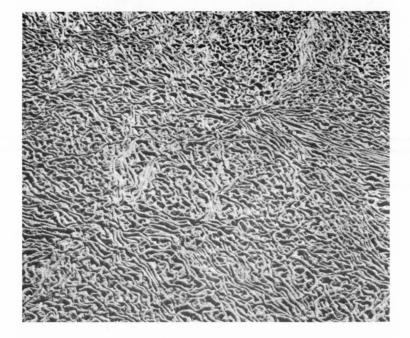

Today some *flor* sherries are being produced in California, using Palomino grapes and various adaptations of the traditional Spanish process. The best of them are quite comparable to Spanish sherries. And it is possible for an amateur to experiment with *flor* sherry-making if a culture of *flor*-producing yeast can be obtained. The other requisites are a neutral white wine that has been coddled up to an alcoholic content of 15 per cent and a storage space such as an attic or furnace room where heat and coolness fluctuate. Most often, though, the amateur will wind up with a caricature: a wine of high volatile acidity that is just badly oxidized.

California sherries other than those made by the *flor* process (and this means most of them) resemble true sherry in a loose way only, because they are not made as sherries are made. There is no *flor* effect, the grapes are likely to be whatever is lying around. The *solera* system of blending is not used. A superficial sherry-like aroma and flavor are imparted by "baking," which is accomplished either by aging the wine several months in a special hot room or by introducing heating elements into the wine. A variant is to trickle oxygen through the wine in the course of the heating. The characteristic aroma and flavor are then a result of oxidation and some caramelization. The run of California sherry is in fact closer to Marsala and Madeira, both of which are "baked" wines. Similar sherries are also produced successfully from Eastern-grown grapes, the point being that the baked aroma and flavor predominate over all other characteristics. An amateur may approximate the baked effect by storing a suitable fortified and sweetened five-gallon bottle of white wine in a hot attic or next to a furnace.

PORT. This comes from the terraced vineyards of the wildly beautiful valley of the Douro River and its tributaries in northern Portugal. But its name comes from the town of Oporto, where the Douro meets the Atlantic and where all the great port shippers have their lodges.* The wine is fer-

* Actually their lodges are located across the river in Vila Nova de Gaia.

mented up-river at the *quintas*, or vineyard farms, then shipped downstream for aging, blending, and finishing. It is sweet, fortified, and usually red. Small quantities of white port are made and must be counted among the best apéritif wines of the world.

In California, Australia, South Africa, Spain, Italy, France, Canada, New York State, and indeed Soviet Russia red, sweet fortified wines are made in the style of port, and port is what they are called. The winemakers are not trying to be deceptive, nor is the public deceived. Port has simply become a generic name for wines that are red, sweet, and fortified, no matter how else they may differ from one another. Qualified by the name of the place of origin, the term serves well enough, and to abandon its use for all these non-port ports would only cause confusion.

Several dozen local grape varieties are grown in the Douro Valley, including among others Alvarelhao, Bastardo (deemed by some to be identical with Trousseau of the French Juras, though the Portuguese refuse to accept this), Donzellinho, Touriga, Tinta Francisca, Mourisco Tinto, and Tinta Cão. The Portuguese are little touched by the rage for standardization and the singling out of special clones that prevails in most viticultural parts of the world. With few exceptions, the growers plant these grapes indiscriminately and indeed find virtue in the confusion. When it comes to port production, California resembles Portugal in this one respect: California port is made from any and all of the standard red-wine grapes of the Central Valley (with the notable exception of the Ficklin vineyard and winery near Madera, which uses only classic Douro Valley varieties).

Let us see how port is made. The grapes are crushed in shallow stone tanks, less and less by the traditional foot treading, which involved prancing about all night to the accompaniment of an accordion and with frequent refreshment. The must is fermented on the skins for several days with frequent stirring. When the sugar content has been reduced by fermentation to 8 to 10 per cent, the must is drawn off and goes into *pipes* (casks) into which a predetermined quantity of brandy has already been poured. The quantity of brandy is sufficient to put a halt to yeast growth, and fermentation decelerates and comes to a stop in the course of the next twelve hours or so. A wine fortified in full fermentation will keep fermenting long enough to reduce the sugar by another 2 per cent (and increase the alcohol accordingly), which is anticipated by the winemaker. The quantity of spirits added is sufficient to yield a wine of 18 to 22 per cent of alcohol and between 7 and 8 per cent of residual sugar.

The big difference between sherry-making and port-making, then, is that sherry is fortified and sweetened (if desired) *after* fermentation, but port is fortified and left sweet *at the height of* fermentation.

As soon as the new port has quieted down and begun to drop its lees, there is the usual routine of racking into clean pipes, which have approximately the same capacity as sherry butts but are of slightly different dimensions. These are kept constantly topped, and in the spring the wine goes down to the lodges of Vila Nova de Gaia for aging, blending, the slow development of the typical port nose and flavor, and all that. The usual types are vintage port—the best, which with age throws a heavy sediment, or "crust," in the bottle and is expected to—and ruby port and tawny port, which may be blends of wine from numerous vintages and vineyards and are ready to be drunk as soon as they reach the market.

For the amateur winemaker's purpose, the important point is that the method of fortifying in midfermentation while the must still contains a great deal of its own sugar may be applied to any grapes, grown anywhere, often with interesting results and especially if the wine so produced is aged, with racking, for several years. But the fortification must be done accurately, at the correct moment, and using the correct proportion of spirit of a given strength. The main problem for amateurs is that they must use tax-paid spirits for fortification, which are very expensive. Commercial winemakers may use bonded (untaxed) spirits, which are cheap.

Putting together all the variables involved in fortification would be a branch of the higher mathematics were it not for an old, old formula named after someone called Pearson that turns the exercise into something like a crossword puzzle, but easier. The best way to demonstrate this formula is by way of a practical example.

Example. The winemaker begins with a must of 24 per cent sugar. He wishes to produce a port of 18 per cent alcohol and 10 per cent sugar and has on hand a supply of fortifying brandy with an alcoholic content of 70 per cent.

By fermentation the sugar content is brought down to 10 per cent (the point at which the alcoholic content has reached 7 per cent by volume). At this point he arranges three figures in a triangle:

Alcoholic strength of brandy 70%		Alcoholic strength of must 7%
	Desired fortification point 18%	

He then subtracts the 18 from the 70 diagonally in one direction, and the 7 from the 18 in the other direction and arranges the results as follows:

$$70 \qquad\qquad 7$$
$$18$$
$$11 \qquad\qquad 52$$
$$\text{(gal. brandy)} \quad \text{(gal. must)}$$

This means that by adding 11 gallons of 70 per cent brandy to 52 gallons of 7 per cent must, he will obtain 63 gallons (52 gallons plus 11) of port containing 18 per cent of alcohol by volume and 10 per cent of sugar. In using the formula the winemaker works in percentages by volume or percentages by weight but cannot mix the two. The formula may be applied to any given combination of sugar and alcohol in the must, alcoholic degree of fortifying spirit, and desired fortification point.

CHAPTER 16

What Can Go Wrong

 LIKE OTHER living things, wine is vulnerable. It may have a sturdy or a fragile constitution. From its birth onward, it is liable to infection of various sorts. It may also be injured accidentally. With age it goes into decline and eventually dies.

As to the infirmities of old age, they can easily be avoided if the wine is used and enjoyed before it reaches that point. Altogether too much is said and written about the virtue of old wines. They are but faded memories, and ancient bottles should be kept intact and dusted occasionally, like museum pieces.

A wine that shows conspicuous symptoms of illness or accidental damage during the span when it should be drinkable is usually so far gone that it is not worth rescuing: it can rarely be restored to health. One cannot emphasize too strongly that the way to be sure of good wine, as is true of preserving human health, is by hygiene and prophylaxis: cleanliness in the making, a sound and vigorous fermentation, and the elementary protections ever after against infection and accident.

A winemaker should be able to recognize the ailments that do develop from time to time, if only to guard against them in subsequent vintages. These fall into three general categories: microbial ailments, physico-chemical ailments, and accidents. We will consider them briefly in that order:

Microbial Ailments

FLOWERS. This disease is caused by the class of microorganisms that in sherry-making are actually encouraged. Under the microscope they look like the ordinary elliptical yeasts. Without entering into the endless arguments about classification and nomenclature, let us just call them film-forming yeasts and give them their traditional name of *Mycoderma vini*. They are aerobic, which is to say they require air for their growth. If air space is left in a container of wine, they promptly form a film on the surface, called *flowers* in English, *flor* in Spanish, *fleur* in French, and *flora* in the Latin of Cato the Elder. If allowed to increase, these yeasts damage wines of ordinary alcoholic degree: they feed on the alcohol and the organic acids and impart a disagreeable flavor. But the damage need not be serious if the flowers are promptly disposed of. What one does is to eliminate their access to air by filling up that space and keeping it filled, thus asphyxiating them.

ACETIC FERMENTATION. This is caused by a class of bacteria always present in wine called *Acetobacter*, or in the old terminology *Mycoderma aceti*. These likewise are aerobic, meaning that they must have air to develop, and form a veil or film on the surface of young wine, but finer and less noticeable than that of the film-forming yeasts. Eventually, they fall back into the wine and form a gummy mass, what is called "mother of vinegar" when it happens in apple cider. But long before that occurs, the wine is irremediably spoiled. The mechanism is an oxidation of the alcohol of the wine into acetic acid, ethanal, and ethyl acetate. This can sometimes take place during a badly conducted fermentation as well as in the new wine. The result is the odor and flavor of vinegar, called *piqûre*. (If served a bottle that is *piqué* in France, all you have to do is ask the waiter to smell it. He will blush, and bring you another bottle. If served such a bottle in this country you will probably have to make your point more explicitly and firmly; but stand your ground. A wine that is *piqué* exceeds the legal limit for volatile acidity and is not saleable.) A controlled fermentation of this type is in fact the process by which vinegar is made. By the time the smell and taste of vinegar are evident in wine, the wine is spoiled. The earlier signals of acetic fermentation are a diminution of the alcoholic degree and, especially, a rapid increase in the wine's volatile acidity, which is why practiced winemakers follow volatile acidity and call it the "pulse" or "fever thermometer" of wine. If the rise of volatile acidity is spotted before the odor and flavor are evident, the wine can sometimes be rescued.

In practice, the only treatment is preventive. Since the acetic bacteria must have air, they are kept at bay, as are the film-forming yeasts, by keeping the wine container filled full. This is the main reason for the routine topping of all new wines. The other preventives are the moderate but regular use of SO_2, with racking and fining; and pasteurization, which kills the bacteria but is hard on wine quality.

ANAEROBIC BACTERIA. As distinct from the microorganisms that cause flowers and acetic fermentation, which require air for their growth, these grow and do their damage in the absence of air. Hence the term "anaerobic." For this reason, they are peculiarly insidious; the more so because the effects of some of them are benign and much sought after, as we have seen in the discussion of malolactic fermentation.

They attack any residual sugar that may remain in the wine, certain fermentation by-products such as glycerol, and the wine's organic acids. On the basis of this latter trait they are ordinarily divided into the two groups mentioned on pages 175–6: those which attack the tartaric acid, causing a large increase in damaging volatile acidity; and those which attack only the malic acid, degrading it to lactic acid and CO_2, with only a slight and unimportant production of volatile acidity.

Anaerobic bacteria of the first group are the menacing ones. They are the cause of the dreaded symptoms (or resulting conditions) known as *tourné, poussé,* bitter disease, and mousiness. The wines thus affected are gassy, cloudy, with nasty odors and the sickish sweet-bitter taste which comes from the production of mannitol and is known in California as "mousiness" (and in the low-acid wines of the French Midi as *"goût de souris"*). The wine may develop a curious oily consistency and, when a bottle is shaken, shows a kind of sinuous silky sheen, the immense accumulations of bacteria becoming in this way visible. Conditions most favorable to the development of anaerobic bacteria are high temperatures, low total acidity, and the presence of residual sugar. These organisms caused appalling spoilage in California in the years immediately following repeal, before sound winemaking techniques had been re-established, and they are always a threat in hot countries where grapes tend to overripeness. Again treatment is essentially preventive: meaning sufficient total acidity of the must, the use of SO_2, and control of fermentation and storage temperatures.

The second group of anaerobic bacteria, the ones that attack the malic rather than the tartaric acidity, have been sufficiently discussed in connection with the malolactic fermentation. But it should be noted that the bacteria of *both* groups will attack any residual sugar that may be present, with damaging results, the more eagerly if total acidity is low. This is the reason why malolactic fermentation is never encouraged in the making and finishing of natural sweet wines.

HYDROGEN SULFIDE. From time to time a new wine may give off a highly disagreeable and disconcerting rotten-egg smell, especially if California grapes were used.

The usual cause is the reduction of elemental sulfur into H_2S by some strains of yeast. The amount perceptible to the nose is very small indeed, no more than a few parts per billion. The sources of the sulfur are two: sulfur dust that was used in the vineyard as a fungicide against powdery mildew (also called oidium); and the dripping or sublimation of sulfur when sulfur wicks were burned to produce SO_2. Sulfur compounds naturally present in wine in small quantities may also be a source. So far the subject has not been fully studied. The small quantity involved is easily eliminated by a prompt racking with abundant aeration, followed by a dose of meta (2 grams per 5 gallons). If this doesn't destroy the odor, rack the wine again, letting it flow over a piece of polished copper such as is used for roof flashings. The H_2S reacts with the copper to form insoluble copper sulfide. For small quantities of hydrogen sulfide, another old-fashioned remedy (best used when the lady of the house isn't looking) is to suspend a piece of the best table silver in the wine. The H_2S is picked up by the silver as tarnish; that is, it reacts with the silver to form insoluble silver sulfide. Withdraw the family heirloom, clean off the tarnish with silver polish, and return to sideboard or silver chest before being discovered. If the H_2S is not removed promptly from the new wine it may be converted to mercaptan and the situation becomes hopeless since the odor of mercaptan is intolerable and it can't be removed. One of the reasons why California winemakers rack immediately after fermentation is to guard against H_2S, since all well-kept California vineyards get regular sulfur dusting.

Chemical Ailments

METAL CONTAMINATION. The most common chemical ailments are caused by metal contamination, the offending metals being iron and copper.

The point is that must and wine are mildly acid solutions. The acids react with the metals to form metallic compounds or salts. These salts may behave in ways that adversely affect wine quality, even though present in very small concentrations. They give rise to a persistent haze or cloudiness which spoils appearance and imparts a metallic bitterness. The ailments are known as *iron casse* and *copper casse,** depending on which metal is involved.

Ironically, these ailments are by-products of progress. They were practically unknown when grapes were crushed by human feet or wooden rollers, handled in wooden tubs, pressed in wooden presses, stored in wooden casks, and so on. Casse showed up as a severe problem with metal processing machinery. Experience in California's industrial winemaking illustrates this in a curious way. After World War II, much of the iron and steel equipment used in the mass handling of must and wine was replaced, the object being to deal with iron casse. Iron casse was eliminated, sure enough, but the copper casse problem promptly emerged, since most of the changeover had been to copper, brass, and bronze equipment. This has in turn been resolved (or, rather, is in process of being resolved) by resort to less troublesome metals and alloys such as stainless steel, as well as to glass and inert protective coatings and plastics.

Iron and copper as well as other metals do occur naturally in wine, but in very small quantities that offer no danger. The danger comes when the normal concentrations are substantially exceeded. The chemistry of the two metal casses is too complicated to be fully explained here, and is not completely elucidated in any case. Suffice it to say that iron casse is an oxidative reaction, whereas copper casse is a reducing reaction. This means that iron casse occurs during the oxidative phase (before wine is bottled) but that copper casse occurs after bottling. Treatments for wines affected by casse are drastic, highly technical, and not fully satisfactory. The obvious answer, then, is to prevent any prolonged contact of must or wine with these metals.

---

* From the French word *casse*, meaning breakage or damage.

Luckily, metal pickup is rarely a problem in small-scale winemaking because the equipment used is relatively primitive. Still, that is no excuse for carelessness. Stainless steel is ideal, but expensive. Where it may be substituted, plastic is just as good and much less expensive (but of course less sturdy). Satisfactory protective coatings are now available, as they were not in the past, and should be used freely wherever there may be some exposure of wine to metal parts, as on small crushers or presses. Where application to moving parts (such as valve stems or the rotor or interior casing of a bronze pump) is impossible, contact is so brief and sparing that trouble hardly ever occurs. Prior to each vintage at Boordy Vineyards we routinely recoat all points of exposure, such as the interior surfaces of bronze nipples and other fittings, crushing rollers, and drain screens, using one of several cold-applied acid-resistant paints, and reduce exposure at points like valve stems and press screws by frequent applications of food-grade lubricant (Vaseline will do). Bronze fittings have been gradually replaced by their plastic equivalents, now that these are available. Over nearly four decades we have never had a serious case of either iron or copper casse.

If there is any reason to fear iron casse, a simple precaution may be taken. This is to add a dose of pure citric acid at the rate of 6 grams per 5 gallons of wine. This keeps the iron salts from precipitating as a haze. If there is fear of copper casse, an equivalent precaution is to add 4 grams per 5 gallons of gum arabic, a "protective colloid" which inhibits the flocculation of the colloidal copper which is responsible for the trouble.

BROWN CASSE. This is another form of breakdown, which has nothing to do with metal contamination but is caused by an enzyme, or oxidase, that is characteristic of dead-ripe grapes and abnormally abundant in grapes that have been touched by botrytis rot and other molds at ripening time. It is comparable to the darkening of the flesh of apples or peaches when they are cut or of freshly squeezed fruit juices. The oxidase is a catalyst in the presence of which certain substances in the fresh must are oxidized with a resultant darkening of color and a development of a cooked or oxidized flavor, the French *goût d'évent*.

Grapes vary in their susceptibility to brown casse, depending on their condition and also on variety. With some it begins to develop immediately upon pressing, the first free-run must being pale while by the end of the same pressing the must is quite dark. With other grapes the must at the end of the pressing is almost as pale as the first free run.

Ordinarily darkening of the must is nothing to worry about. One function of the prefermentation dose of meta, with its anti-oxidizing effect, is to counteract the condition; and as every experienced winemaker knows, the early browning disappears during a clean fermentation. But when grapes are in poor condition and insufficient SO_2 is provided, the oxidase is not destroyed and the new wine remains abnormally subject to darkening and the development of an oxidized flavor. The reaction goes beyond that, too: the wine becomes cloudy and eventually throws down a brownish precipitate. This is brown casse, and wines prone to it, though they may otherwise be excellent, require special attention. Some of the best white wines in the world, such as the white Burgundies, are notoriously subject to the malady.

An easy test for such fragility is to draw off a sample of the must and let it stand in a partly filled bottle (lightly corked) for several days. If the wine shows a pronounced darkening and abnormal cloudiness, it has a tendency toward brown casse. In that case a dose of SO_2 of about one and a half times the usual amount must be maintained in the wine by increasing the protective meta at each racking and at bottling time. The casse will thus have no opportunity to develop.

In case the oxidasic tendency was not caught in advance and the wine darkens somewhat prior to bottling, color may be lightened and any oxidized flavor reduced by a casein fining, with or without activated charcoal. But, as always, prevention is better than an attempted cure.

It is, of course, a tendency of all white wines to darken with age, and of reds to develop a brownish cast. This may be oxidasic in part, or other phenomena may be involved (including preventable damage from overheating and bad storage). Up to a point such darkening may be normal and desirable: it is one of the aspects of bottle aging. But it is also a warning that no wine lives forever. Wine is something to be enjoyed while still enjoyable, not hoarded.

Accidental Ailments

One common accident, already discussed in its place, is the precipitation of tartrate crystals known as gravel, after a wine has been bottled. This does not harm the wine in the least but can be disconcerting and is commercially undesirable. It is to get rid of excess potassium tartrate that wines are cold-stabilized by chilling before they are bottled.

The presence of calcium tartrate is more bothersome. The source of the calcium may be exposure to concrete, inferior filter pads, some fining materials, or high-alkaline soils. Calcium tartrate does not respond swiftly to chilling, as potassium bitartrate does. It comes out of solution more slowly and in finely divided form, and so tends to persist as a haze instead of falling out. Moreover, a second or a third precipitation may occur after the wine has been fined or filtered and is apparently clear. The closest to a satisfactory treatment is chilling almost to the wine's freezing point for several weeks, then filtering before the calcium tartrate has a chance to go back into solution, and finally blending with a low-calcium wine.

Then there is the miscellany of unpleasant odors and flavors derived from carelessness or accidental mishandling. Among amateur winemakers a high proportion of such damage originates in a stubborn devotion to oak cooperage: barrels and kegs. These are veritable incubators of off flavors and disease unless scrupulously cared for while empty and thoroughly prepared before use. Nothing ruins a potentially good wine more quickly than an old barrel with traces of mold in it or deposits of old, dried lees. Wine stored in a small keg quickly becomes so oaky that it is undrinkable. Unclean equipment and unsanitary surroundings take their toll. The space used for wine storage should not also be used for miscellaneous storage, for wine easily picks up strong odors. If wine is spoiled in any of these ways, the winemaker has only his carelessness to blame.

So ends this catalog (and it is an incomplete one) of things that can go wrong with wine. Focusing too closely on it, one begins to wonder how or why things can ever go right when so many perils abound. And yet they do go right, more often than wrong. This is essentially a catalog of mistakes. Keep clear of the mistakes, observe the elementary precautions, and pathological symptoms will rarely appear in your wine.

CHAPTER 17

Wine Tasting and Wine Drinking

WINE NOURISHES and gives pleasure. In the daily use of wine the pleasure is pretty much taken for granted. It tastes good, it hits the spot, somehow it makes the whole meal taste better; and that suffices. This is the way most wine is used and enjoyed the world over, confirming Benjamin Franklin's observation that "Wine is a constant proof that God loves us and wants to see us happy."

But the pleasure is much increased if one knows something about the physiology (and the art) of tasting. Wine tasting is something different from wine drinking, and in really critical tasting a good gargle is about as close as one gets to actual swallowing.

Tasting of this sort, divorced from actual consumption, is an indispensable tool for everyone·concerned with wine: for merchants, buyers, producers, technicians, and, of course, amateur winemakers and knowing wine users. It is the way quality and market value are finally determined. It is used in the trade for classing and grading and in competitions. It is, of course, the basis of all blending. It is the ultimate arbiter.

Moreover, tasting is the winemaker's most important analytical tool for the surveillance of his wine during its evolution. He uses it constantly. It tells him when something is going wrong or is about to. It tells him when things are going right. Though less precise than laboratory analysis, it is much less limited and in many circumstances is more sensitive. It does what laboratory analysis can never do, which is to provide a verdict on the ensemble of a wine's characteristics. The French enologist Émile Peynaud put it well when he said that laboratory analysis exposes a wine's anatomy but tasting exposes its personality. Every key decision in winemaking involves wine tasting as a matter of course. According to a conventional analysis the two wines in the following table (from Peynaud) are practically identical. Tasting determined the difference, the price of the Médoc being twenty times that of the bon ordinaire:

	BON ORDINAIRE	MÉDOC GRAND CRU
Alcohol by volume	11.1	11.0
Specific gravity	0.9949	0.9943
Dry extract	26.7	26.8
Reducing sugars	0.15	0.17
Total acidity	0.557	0.525
Volatile acidity	0.055	0.052

The Anatomy and Physiology of Taste

The physiology of tasting is fairly awe-inspiring. And yet its essentials can be explained briefly. It draws on the senses of sight, of taste (strictly speaking), of smell, and to some extent the tactile sense.

The visual impression comes first and is useful in many ways, obviously. When you look at a wine, clarity is a good sign, and hazes are warning signals. Color satisfies the norm for the type of wine being examined, or it doesn't. Intensity and hue, in a red, are each useful indications (of body, of age,

The wine-tasting "apparatus."

of health); likewise in the case of white. Color and clarity are not just aesthetic factors: they are important diagnostically and tell the experienced taster a great deal.

After visual inspection come the perceptions of smell and of taste. Smelling comes first, then taste in the mouth, then both together.

THE SENSE OF SMELL. This is a highly complex sense, and the mechanism in charge of it is a marvel of miniaturization. The olfaction area, through which all sensations of smell must pass, is located at the upper end of the nasal passages and has a total surface of considerably less than one square inch. Odors reach this area through the nose by an extremely narrow opening, which explains why the sense of smell can be completely lost when one has a bad cold or there is blockage of any other sort (as when one holds one's nose). Odors also reach it by the back stairs, so to speak, up through the pharynx, which connects nose with throat.

The surface of this little patch contains millions of separate receptors so sensitive that a single one of them may be stimulated by ten molecules or fewer of certain odorous substances.* Although no one knows *how* molecules of odorants

---

* Minnows have been trained to recognize phenol and distinguish it from p-chlorophenol in concentrations of five parts per billion. Eels have been taught to smell two or three molecules of phenylethyl alcohol. (Lewis Thomas, *The Lives of a Cell*. New York: Viking, 1974.) They smell more accurately than we do.

actually stimulate olfactory receptors, we do know that all these separate stimulations are carried to several brain centers where they are sorted out and combined in olfactory sensations—some powerful and some weak, some disagreeable and some delightful, some simple as from a single compound and others highly complex mixtures. The wine sample is given a thorough smelling, with swirling to release the odorous materials, before any goes into the mouth, and more smelling comes afterward in combination with taste sensations.

THE SENSE OF TASTE. This is much less complicated than the sense of smell. There are just four different tastes: sweet, sour, salty, and bitter. These are sensed by taste buds grouped in papillae and located exclusively on the surface of the tongue. The papillae capable of sensing these four tastes are distributed according to a regular pattern, as shown in the drawing: sweet, mostly on the tip of the tongue; bitter, at the back; sour, along the sides; and salty, close to the tip and just behind. As compared with the receptors of smell, they are not numerous: mere thousands as compared with millions. They are connected by nerves to the cortex, where the taste sensation actually announces itself.

Because of the location of the papillae, the four tastes are sensed in sequence: sweet first, bitter appreciably later, then all together as the wine is swished around in the mouth.

Distribution of taste receptors on the tongue.

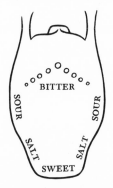

Of the four, only sweetness is agreeable all by itself. The other three, though disagreeable individually, contribute importantly to the total. An analogy can be drawn with the bitterness that lies behind the sweetness of chocolate candy and coffee. The important thing is a proper balance: a wine may be too bitter, too sour, too salty to be agreeable. But the lack of any one of these tastes is instantly noticeable: something important is missing. For correct balance in a dry (that is, a conventionally non-sweet) wine, the necessary minimum of sweet sensation is provided by the alcohol and glycerin, both of which have a sweet taste. Sweetness provided by residual sugar can mask a slight excess of bitterness, sourness, or saltiness. It is to mask excess acidity that many German wines are finished slightly sweet; the inherent coarseness of some California Central Valley wines is dealt with in the same way; a Muscat wine always tastes bitter unless it is quite sweet.

The sensation threshold for these tastes varies from person to person. The ability to distinguish sweetness, for example, may vary from a concentration of 0.5 grams of sugar per liter to 5.0 grams per liter. A person acutely sensitive to sweetness may be much less so to bitterness, or sourness, or saltiness. An experienced wine taster always has a pretty good idea of his particular thresholds and makes due allowance for them.

THE SENSE OF TOUCH. This is a more important part of the total tasting than one might suppose. The tactile sense records heat and cold, astringency, "fullness," viscosity. Mucous membranes are sensitive to the dehydrating effect of alcohol, and a different sense of dryness is produced by the tannin, which coagulates the saliva as does the tannin that is the principal ingredient of most mouthwashes.

Learning to Taste

Every normal person is equipped with a sensitive tasting apparatus, and it functions alike for all of us in the primary perceptions. Thus, we all know the difference between sweet and sour, and we react with the same displeasure to the rotten-egg smell of hydrogen sulfide. But we have to learn how to apply it to wine. An experienced wine taster has learned by training and experience how to put all the sensory information together—and also how to take it apart. He is attentive to what separate signals are saying and is able to associate them with the composition of the wine; and he does this work of analysis even as he studies the overall impression or synthesis. He must first have a solid understanding of what wine is and how it came into being: the rest is experience. A taster learns how to taste by tasting and remembering.

One of the first lessons of his experience is that there are pitfalls in wine tasting. The sensory mechanisms are mixed in with the rest of the higher nervous system, and the brain can distort and short-circuit the sensory signals in all sorts of ways. Thus, the taster has his own prejudices and preferences and must beware lest these lead him astray. Sensations are also affected by what he has eaten. His physical condition is important. As a bad cold can knock out the entire olfactory system, so a digestive disorder always distorts the senses in some degree. So does medication (which is why hospital food always seems like a parody of a real meal: it isn't always the cook's fault). So does fatigue, either the general kind or tasting fatigue. The number of wines that can be critically tasted at one sitting is limited by tasting fatigue (a form of fatigue that can be a blessing for garbage collectors, who soon become habituated to garbage smells and cease to notice them). Wine tasters are at their best early in the morning when they are fresh. One set of impressions can distort the next set: thus, a "hard" wine makes the next wine seem "softer" than it really is. The power of suggestion plays tricks as well. If a taster is conditioned to expect some specific characteristic in a given wine, he may sometimes find it even though it isn't there. If he is offered two glasses of wine for comparison, he may note differences between them even though they are from the same bottle, and do it in good faith: What he has done has been to concentrate on two different aspects of the same wine.

A taster trains himself to beware of such pitfalls. He makes sure that his senses are in good order, that the lighting is good, and that the surroundings are not distracting. If he is tasting analytically, he may concentrate on a single sensation. If he is tasting comparatively, he brings his samples together and goes back over them several times, rinsing his mouth and taking a cracker or piece of bread in between. He uses glasses of the same shape for all wines in order to equalize visual and olfactory impressions. And of course very little of what he is tasting actually gets down his throat. The appointments of every well-equipped tasting room always include things for spitting into, the most elegant and fastidious of these being bowls with running water like those to be found in dentists' offices.

If he is examining several wines of the same type or class, he prefers to taste "blind": not literally with his eyes closed but with no more than a code number on the glass to go by. He postpones identification until he is through. In this way he reaches more objective conclusions.

On the other hand, if he is examining a mixed group (say, a Bordeaux, a Napa Gamay, a Burgundy, and an Eastern hybrid red wine), a blind tasting may be distinctly unhelpful because he doesn't know what he is looking for, what norms to apply.

A very helpful and much-used device is "triangular" tasting. The taster is given three samples, two of them the same, or maybe all three the same, or all three different. His task is to sort them out. This may be a test of his competence and acuity. But when the wines are assorted, it is often useful to know that the wines are so similar they can be confused by an experienced taster. This has important practical value when several lots of wine are being deliberately blended for uniformity.

Group tasting is a good precaution if much hangs on the result. But it must be a *small* group used to working together and familiar with each other's strengths and weaknesses. The tasting must be simultaneous but without the least intercommunication if the power of suggestion—a smile, a frown, an exclamation—is to be eliminated entirely. There is then a discussion of results and a reconciliation, followed if necessary by a retasting. It is uncanny how closely the results agree, even before discussion. But beware of large and heterogeneous groups if a truly critical conclusion is sought: the results rarely have any value.

If a considerable number of wines is to be tasted, some sort of scoring method is necessary, whether the purpose be to select the "best," to grade the entries from best to worst, to eliminate all those failing to meet a minimum standard, or some combination of these objects. In the pursuit of objectivity, elaborate numerical scoring systems have been worked out, assigning so many points each to color, to clarity, to alcohol, to aroma, to general balance, and so on. Such systems often lead to ludicrous results. For example, a wine may have flawless color and clarity yet be altogether undrinkable for one or more reasons. In realistic terms it rates nothing better than zero. Yet it may wind up with as many points as a wine that is mediocre but drinkable.

The simplest, most flexible, and, on the whole, most useful method combines a numerical scoring with brief verbal description. Most commonly the ratings run from 0 to 20. On this basis a score of 10 means barely passing and anything below that amounts to failure, for whatever reason or reasons. A score of 12 means a sound and acceptable wine without defects but without individuality. Scores from 13 through 16 mean sound wines with some personality. The top ratings are reserved for wines entitled to be called fine, the memorable individuals which represent an entirely successful coming together of grapes, climate, the art of the winemaker, and perhaps soil.

In this method, each score is supplemented by a descriptive word or two. The English vocabulary of tasting terms is much less exact than the French, as one might expect, and

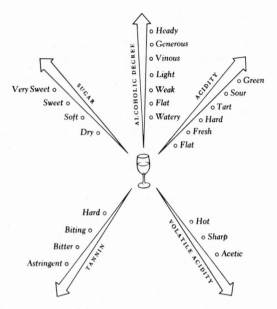

Common wine-tasting terms.

individuals and groups tend to develop a private lingo. Thus, in the days when the wine competitions held for the California State Fair really amounted to something, some of us working as judges used the term *"cigar butt"* to describe the distinctive aroma of Sémillon wines. I do not know whether the term still survives or not. Some of the more common and skeletal terms are shown on the diagram.*

GROUP TASTINGS. I seemed to suggest a few paragraphs back that large group tastings are of little value. But that opinion calls for some qualification. It is certainly not true of large group tastings that are designed to instruct, or entertain, or both.

Wherever enology is taught as a formal course of study, group tastings are a vital part of the curriculum. They are conducted by a qualified instructor, and their object is to relate the composition of a given wine to sensory impressions.

* Adapted from Navarre, *Manuel d'Oenologie*.

There is really no limit to the pedagogical uses of such tastings, whether to study varietal differences of aroma and flavor, wine types, variations in composition, specific defects, or to make before-and-after comparisons of various treatments. The examination of "whole" wines may be supplemented with made-up solutions designed to bring out single characteristics, such as various concentrations of alcohol and water, of acidity, of odorous ingredients and so on. Such tastings are accompanied by descriptive and explanatory comment and discussion, and they are often followed by examinations. Not only are they a part of the regular curriculum: they are equally important in short refresher courses designed for professionals whether their interest be in winemaking technology or in some aspect of the trade.

And then, at a less austere level, there are the social tastings, which combine pleasure and instruction and are such a pleasant aspect of the public's awakening interest in wine and its use. A congenial group may meet fairly regularly, the members taking turns as host, to taste and discuss a number of wines selected with some care and having some common denominator: maybe the red wines of Napa Valley, or the wines of Burgundy, jug wines, Cabernets from various regions and countries, the wines of a given winery, or perhaps wines of their own making. In the course of these tastings there also may be commentary by someone who knows well what he is talking about—someone who has boned up for the occasion or possibly a commercial wine man. The event may include scoring, a comparison of results, much give and take, perhaps a film. And when the instructive part of the meeting is concluded, there is a general assault on what remains in the bottles, with feasting, drinking, and good cheer. If there is a commercial tinge to some of these social wine tastings, what of it? The result is always some broadening of knowledge of wine and, not least, a pleasant evening. One is tempted to say that this approach to wine is somehow typically American. Not so. One has only to think of the *vins d'honneur* which are held in the *mairie* of every French winegrowing village whenever a visiting celebrity provides an excuse and to which every local winegrower of consequence brings along a few of his choicest bottles; and of the series of gay but instructive tastings that accompany the annual wine auction at the Hospices de Beaune on the third weekend of every November. Anywhere and everywhere, comparative wine tastings are a sufficient excuse for a party, and many Americans are discovering that a lengthened cocktail hour is an ideal time for them.

The Use of Wine

The chief obstacles to the free use of wine in America, until recently, have been little more than unfamiliarity and uncertainty. I think there can be no doubt of that. Wine was not a familiar thing, and much of the writing addressed to Americans on the subject did little to encourage familiarity. On the contrary, it tended to be condescending and cultish, and some still is. Why wine should have become the victim of this sort of pompousness I cannot imagine. But confronted by all this one-upmanship and snobbism, many Americans quite sensibly turned aside with a yawn and decided to stay with their highballs, cocktails, and beer.

But all that is receding into the past, and in these last few pages I should like to bring the matter of wine use down out of the clouds of pretentiousness. Wine isn't anything to be self-conscious about. The use of it isn't a problem in etiquette. It doesn't need any hocus-pocus. If it did, the simple people in the wine-using cultures wouldn't find it equally useful as a religious symbol on Sunday, as the high point of every feast, as an indispensable element of the evening meal, and sometimes even as a mouthwash in the morning—for its tannin, not its alcohol. Wine and the vine for such people are in a manner of speaking members of the family, and are so treated. The exceptional wine, like the exceptional son or daughter, yields a very special satisfaction;

the ordinary wine is taken for what it is and no great demands are put upon it; the sickly wine, the problem wine, the feeble wine, may cause private sorrow, but is faithfully cared for and given the benefit of the doubt. All are members of the family, a part of life. And one might add that such an attitude toward wine has nothing to do with what is commonly called "the alcohol problem." It is not mere coincidence that the wine-growing *département* of the Gironde, centering on Bordeaux, leads all other French *départements* in longevity.

A few remarks on the use of wine, though obvious to a great and growing body of Americans, will bear repeating.

The importance of age can be and often is exaggerated. A few really big wines gain greatly by a few years in bottle. Most don't and are best when young. Draw off a part of your own new wine into bottles as soon as it is bright and stable and begin to enjoy it. The cheaper commercial wines are rarely more than a year old.

The correct temperature for serving has been overplayed. In our climate we like our beverages hot, cold, or cool but not tepid. Everyone knows that white wines and rosés are better when somewhat cooled. The rule serves as well for all but the finest red wines. If a wine starts out a bit too cool to display all its virtues, it warms up quickly enough in the glass. Better too cool than too warm, which is the way it may be in our overheated dwellings if the old "room temperature" rule is followed too literally. In hot weather most red wines gain by being popped into the refrigerator for a few minutes before serving.

Don't be over-awed by notions of correctness. Experience has led to certain conclusions about the service of very fine wines. But they have little application to everyday wines.

If you serve from the bottle, pull the cork at the table—it prepares the mind for what is to come. But don't make a big ceremony of it. There is nothing to the advice that the cork should be pulled in advance to let the wine "breathe." The future lies with screw caps, but until the future arrives arm yourself with a decent corkscrew, something better than the

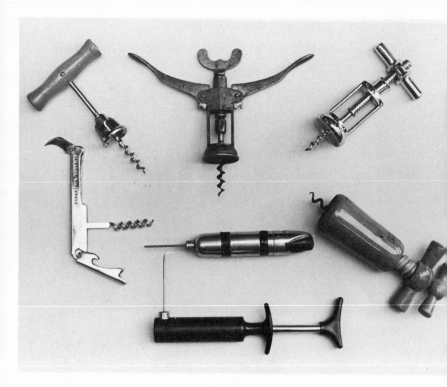

A collection of corkscrews.

kitchen can opener. If any wine is left, put it in the refrigerator and have it for supper the next day. If several tail ends accumulate, don't hesitate to combine them, and that includes putting red and white together. Such mixtures often taste better than their separate parts, just as beef stew often tastes better the second night. If your bottle is not particularly attractive, or if the wine has sediment, decant it into a clear glass carafe or pitcher for serving.

Do not bother overmuch about glasses. For really superior wines there is a strong argument for stemmed wine glasses. They show the wine to best advantage, give it an opportunity to develop its bouquet, and dress up the table. The best of these are of clear glass, fairly thin and unfussy and of ample size. But super-size glasses are mere affectation. In the wine-drinking countries such stemmed glasses are reserved for special occasions, and in ordinary household service the glasses are more likely to be small tumblers of the kind we call orange-juice glasses. Everyday wine glasses, whether stemmed or not, should be simple and sturdy enough to withstand the dishwashing machine.

I have mentioned decanting. The only object is to separate the wine from whatever lees or sediment there may be in the bottle. All it requires is a steady hand. Stand the bottle up well in advance to settle the sediment. Draw the cork. Holding the bottle in one hand and a carafe or pitcher in the other, raise to a light and pour slowly. When most has been poured, the sediment will be seen to creep toward the mouth of the bottle. Just as it gets there, stop pouring. Not more than a third of a glass will be wasted, and the wine will be clear. The right place to do the decanting is in the kitchen.

And so we come to the matter of matching the wine with the food, which may be approached from either end. That is to say, the wine may be chosen to go with the food, or the food to go with the wine, depending on the nature of the occasion.

Let us assume that there is company for dinner. If the company consists of friends who like wine but pretend to no great knowledge of it, then it is the food that matters most

Fancy glasses for fancy occasions. Note the small tumbler.

and the thing to do obviously is to fit the wine to the food, a matter of utmost simplicity.

Everyone knows that dry white wine goes best with the fruit of the sea and in fact complements it. This is not mere convention: it is fact. Dry white wine makes fish taste better, just as a few drops of lemon juice do. (Red wine, on the contrary, may bring out any lurking "fishiness.") If chicken or something else light is the main course, white wine also does best, because it doesn't overpower or distract. On the other hand, food of a more hearty and substantial sort seems to want red wine. If cheese comes later, more red wine is appropriate; if ice cream or lemon pie, no more. For such a dinner, the wine served may receive no direct attention whatever; nevertheless its contribution will be real and important.

If the friends are people who know wine and are seriously interested, or perhaps have gathered chiefly to taste it, then the case is different. The wines are the stars of the occasion, likely to be closely examined and appreciated and to dominate conversation at least part of the time. In that case it will be the food, not the wine, that is or should be unobtrusive. Assertive foods such as pig's knuckles and sauerkraut or strong curries, or foods that must be struggled with such as steamed crabs or bony little birds or barbecued spareribs—all such things are best avoided on the occasion, good and nourishing as they would be at another time. For a wine-tasting meal one arrives by a process of elimination at a simple menu on the bland side, of the sort that can be strung out indefinitely, and with plenty of good bread and butter and most certainly a platter of cheese to finish off with. Silly? Yes, if the company is not interested. It is also silly, if you come to think about it, to spend hours watching skillful people bat, kick, throw, lob, drive, or run with balls of various shapes and sizes. But like such spectator sports a wine-tasting dinner can be fascinating and even exciting if one is properly conditioned.

There is one thing that an amateur winemaker must remember, though: he is in constant peril of becoming a special kind of bore. This is a normal but dangerous by-product of his enthusiasm. The little lady who refuses wine because it "disagrees" with her moves him to exasperation and tempts him into a lecture on the therapeutic value of wine. The highball-drinking friend who tosses down his first glass of wine with a gulp and promptly accepts a second is too easily mistaken for a convert to wine who wants only a bit of encouragement. He isn't, and doesn't: he just drinks anything that happens to be around, and it is best to talk of other things. And then again the winemaker, having brought off an act of creation by converting a tub of grapes into a tolerable wine, makes the mistake so many young mothers make of assuming that everyone glories in this evident miracle. To all but the parents, one baby is very much like another. To all but the winemaker, a bottle of wine is nothing more than another bottle of wine, to be enjoyed or not enjoyed as the case may be. The lady on your left does not want to know how triumph was snatched from failure by an eleventh-hour induction of malolactic fermentation. Her husband isn't in the least curious about the number of gallons of wine to be made in a good year from sixty-two vines of Seyve-Villard 5276. If he says he is, he is only being polite: don't impose on his politeness. When people tell you that your precious Seibel 5279 is the most delicious homemade wine they have ever tasted, accept the compliment with a courteous inclination of the head and change the subject. When they insist that they *wish* you would tell them how you do it, under no circumstances oblige them. If you are tempted to, accept the warning glance of your wife as having been given in your best interest and taper off as swiftly as possible. Be content that your friends enjoy your wine, and let it go at that.

A Final Word

I should like to end this excursion into the nature of wine with some points about wine drinking in general. They have been implicit throughout but bear repeating.

Life does not consist of great moments. The lives of most of us follow a fairly narrow path, with some turning points, more often occasioned by chance than by purpose. There are rough patches and smooth, valleys of disappointment and frustration, and plateaus when life seems pretty good after all. The course though not necessarily tedious is one made familiar by habit and routine and the great imperative of earning our way. Today is not expected to be greatly different from yesterday, nor from tomorrow. It is not given to many of us to suffer and triumph heroically, and even heroes lead ordinary lives most of the time.

What has this got to do with wine? Well, the discovery of wine can be a turning point for someone who knows nothing of it, one that may have more effect on the quality of life than one might think. It adds another dimension to our necessary preoccupation with nourishment. And let us not underestimate this. The business of feeding and being fed slips all too easily into a dreary routine whether by accident or necessity, and the result is invariably reflected in our health and happiness. An army marches on its stomach, and so does life in general.

The remarkable thing about wine is the way it buoys up our fare. And I am not thinking of just so-called "gourmet" fare. Wine conditions the digestive system both through anticipation and through the actual drinking. With wine on the table we expect the food to taste better, and it does, and nourishes better as well.

More remarkably still, the beneficial aspect is not a property of "great" or "fine" wine only but of all sound dry table wines, including those that are casually and sometimes slightingly called ordinary—those that have no very pronounced character beyond that of being wine. But for that very reason they wear well in daily service. They adapt themselves without ostentation to the familiar routine and before long make themselves indispensable. Their appearance on the table is as regular as the appearance of bread and is greeted with the same satisfaction.

The superior wines, of course, have the same fundamental property too, plus something else—an aesthetic element. These wines are more closely noticed and more consciously enjoyed. If all the conditions are right, a truly superlative wine may come close to providing one of life's big moments. But the conditions must be right, and most important, there must already be the familiarity that comes of frequent use. Otherwise, there is nothing to compare the great wine to.

For the city dweller in moderate circumstances who is not a winemaker, the "ordinary" wine is inevitably one of the standard wines of California, which is no hardship because they are almost always sound and well made. His situation is much the same as that of the city-dwelling Frenchman who depends on the vast production of cheap wines in the Midi. Now and then the city dweller may "move up"—eight out of ten times this too means California—to the smaller establishments more concerned with high quality than with mass production. The ninth time may mean moving up to one of the new generation of wines being made in our other and very different regions. Perhaps only the tenth time does it mean to a bottle from abroad, for the word has got around that imports no longer have a monopoly on superiority. But most of the time the city dweller contents himself with one or another of the widely distributed ordinaries.

The competent home winemaker enjoys other rewards, even more if he has his own small vineyard. He has the satisfaction of "creating" something—though we have seen that nature does the creating and man merely stands by. He gains insights into the life of plants and organisms, insights that can lead him on and on if he is ready to accept the invitation. He is no threat to the wine trade either, because his example spreads the use of wine and because he is himself a frequent buyer: he cannot resist comparing the output of the pros with his own. If he is wise, he does not expect to produce much wine entitled to be called fine (though occasionally he may surprise himself). But without being fine, his wines will have character and individuality, something not to be anticipated from wines that are mass produced. And he always has the next vintage to look forward to.

All this, plus the unfailing presence of his own good wine on the table.

Appendixes, Bibliography, and Index

Grape List

Vinifera

This is a condensed list. Of the large array of *vinifera* material in California, the assortment in important production keeps shrinking. There follow summary descriptions of a number of varieties divided into several groups. This is essentially a California list, although a number of these grapes are also grown to some extent in congenial parts of Arizona, Idaho, Oregon, Washington, and the Rio Grande Valley. Shipping varieties are marked with an asterisk (*).

THE FINE RED VARIETALS

Cabernet Sauvignon. The jewel in California's crown. Although of temperate-climate origin, it is well adapted to the coastal regions and sometimes produces superlative wine.

Gamay Beaujolais. An inconveniently early ripener but it produces superior wine when picked promptly, one of the three best. Coastal regions only.

Gamay (Napa Valley). One of many clones of Pinot Noir and not actually a Gamay. It has the same defects that Pinot Noir exhibits in California. Produces a better-than-average wine when picked promptly. Coastal regions only.

Merlot. A second cousin to Cabernet Sauvignon, used around Bordeaux to soften the roughness of the latter; it has the same value in California. A fine wine in its own right. Coastal.

Pinot Noir. Despite its glamorous reputation, which makes it commercially important, its wine in California is far from great and usually requires some blending to beef it up.

*Zinfandel. In the Central Valley it is merely ordinary. In the coastal regions when handled well it produces a fine wine right up there behind Cabernet Sauvignon.

THE FINE WHITE VARIETALS

Chardonnay. The white Burgundy grape. Some very superior wines have been produced from it in California, though more often it falls short of its reputation in a climate not really congenial. Coastal regions only.

Gewürztraminer. Now and then it lives up to its reputation for lightness, delicacy, and spiciness, but usually not. Requires great care in handling. Coastal regions only.

Pinot Blanc. Relative of Chardonnay, which on occasion has yielded a better wine in California. Difficult to handle. Coastal regions only.

Sauvignon Blanc. Many people consider this to be more consistently superior than Chardonnay under California conditions: fruity, crisp, altogether delicious. When it runs to high sugar, it provides California's best natural sweet wine.

Sémillon. Like Sauvignon Blanc, it does wonderfully well in California. The best of the Sémillon wines from the coastal regions, whether sweet or dry, are in the top class.

White Riesling. Grown in the coolest parts, its fine character is sometimes evident. But not really at home in California.

LESS FINE RED VARIETALS

Barbera. In the coastal regions its wine is quite Piedmontese. Its main value for the future is probably in improving the Central Valley reds, thanks to its high acidity.

Carnelian. A new *métis* from the University of California Experiment Station at Davis, intended to upgrade Central Valley reds. Still scarce.

Grenache. In the Central Valley this is just another heavy producer when used for dry table wines and sweet fortified wines. But its rosé is superior.

*Petite Sirah. In the coastal regions it is a good second-best variety giving firmness and color and sometimes individuality. One of the best in the Central Valley. The most widely grown clone is *not* the Petite Syrah of Châteauneuf-du-Pape.

Ruby Cabernet. Most successful of the Davis introductions, a

Narrowing the Choice

A Californian wishing to plant some grapevines for domestic use will find the following reliable and satisfactory:

Hot interior valleys. *For red wine or rosé*, Carignane, Carnelian, Grenache, Ruby Cabernet. *For white wine*, Chenin Blanc, French Colombard, Sauvignon Blanc.

Cooler coastal valleys. *For red wine or rosé*, Cabernet Sauvignon, Gamay, Petite Sirah, Refosco, Zinfandel. *For white wine*, Chenin Blanc, Chardonnay, Gewürztraminer, Sauvignon Blanc, Sémillon.

Cabernet-Carignane cross with good acidity, which is beginning to appear as one of the new Valley Varietals.

LESS FINE WHITE VARIETALS

Aligoté. The second-best white Burgundy grape. On occasion it has produced some superior wines in the coastal regions. Not for the Central Valley.

Chenin Blanc. Its special advantages are that it is a very heavy producer of nearly fine wine in the coastal regions, fruitier than most, and that it carries over some of its quality in the hotter regions. Now being heavily planted as another Valley Varietal.

Colombard. Most heavily planted white that can lay claim to quality, its special virtue being its high acidity, even in the Central Valley. It is being used as another Valley Varietal, but its main use is to give character to the oceans of Thompson Seedless wine.

Emerald Riesling. Another Davis introduction, notable for high production and high acidity, which gives it a place in the Central Valley. No Riesling character.

*Muscat of Alexandria. Very sweet, highly aromatic. Sweet wines only.

Palomino. Mentioned here only as the true sherry grape. Not good for dry white wines.

Sylvaner. Much grown in Alsace and Germany. Loses most of its distinctiveness in California conditions but still yields a better than average, fairly fruity wine. Coastal regions.

BULK PRODUCERS, RED AND WHITE

*Alicante Bouschet. Coarse, deep-colored red wine. Losing ground to better types.

Burger. Very ordinary white wine. Also losing ground but still has considerable acreage.

Carignane. California's dominant red-wine grape. Quality varies greatly with the region.

Mission. See page 48 for its story. Very ordinary for dry wine. Better for sweet wines.

Royalty and *Rubired*. Two other Davis *métis*, used specifically for color.

Salvador. Another pigment, or *teinturier*, grape, actually a hybrid.

Thompson Seedless. Dominates the Central Valley vineyards by a huge margin. Its wine is very neutral, and its role is to provide quantity.

Various Table Grapes. Surplus is regularly diverted to the wineries, mainly for fortified wine and distillation, sometimes for cheap table wines.

LESSER VARIETIES

So ends the list of the principal California *vinifera*. For the record, here are the names of less important *vinifera* recommended by the Davis experiment station for various regions and special purposes:* Aleatico, Clairette Blanche, Fernâo Pires, Flora, Grillo, Malvasia Bianca, Marzemino, Melon, Muscat Canelli (Frontignan), Orange Muscat, Raboso Piave, Red Veltliner, Refosco, Souzão, Teraldico, Tinta Cão, Tinta Madeira, Touriga, Verdelho, Xeres.

Temperate-Climate Grapes

The situation outside the *vinifera* area is in a state of evolution as the old American sorts give way to the new, non-foxy hybrids, some of which have already become "standards" and as a new generation tries its hand with some of the hardier *vinifera*. One word of caution: never mix the old American sorts with the new hybrids.

OLD REDS

Concord. Still dominant because of its many uses, but not really suitable for dry table wine. Other related types are *Campbell's Early*, grown somewhat in the humid parts of the Pacific Northwest; *Fredonia*, essentially an early Concord; *Ives*, strongly foxy but valued by some for its color; *Westfield*.

Muscadines. Grown in the deep South for heavily aromatic, sweet cordial-type wines. Not within the scope of this book. Best known is not a red but a white, *Scuppernong*.

For the record: Beta, Black Spanish (syns., *Jacquez* and *Lenoir*,

---

* M. A. Amerine and A. J. Winkler, *California Wine Grapes*, Bulletin 794. Agricultural Experiment Station, University of California, 1963.

better known in France than here), *Clinton, Eumelan, Isabella, Norton* (syns., *Cynthiana, Virginia Seedling*), *Othello* (also better known in France than here).

OLD WHITES

Catawba. Still much grown. Pronounced foxiness, somewhat attenuated by fast pressing, used in Eastern champagne blends and for specialty sweet wines, rarely for dry wines.

Delaware. One of the two best, still much grown, and by itself makes a pleasant, soft dry wine with a special musky rather than foxy aroma, vaguely recalling Traminer. Used as still wine and in Eastern champagne blends.

Dutchess. The other good one. Wine very clean, fruity but without a trace of foxiness. Culturally capricious.

Elvira. Still used to some extent in Eastern champagne blends. Very early. Wine mediocre and foxy.

Noah. Somewhat foxy. Still grown in southern New Jersey. Was much grown in France during the phylloxera crisis and still lingers on though new plantings are prohibited.

NEW RED HYBRIDS

The new hybrids, red and white, are changing the viticultural pattern in the older temperate-climate regions such as New York, Pennsylvania, Ohio, Michigan, Arkansas, and Missouri and are opening entirely new areas. But work with them goes back only to the 1930's, and much is still to be learned about fitting the right grapes to any given area. Those now established commercially are mentioned individually. Those that have potential but are not yet commercially important are grouped according to the name of the hybridizer. There is hardly a state except possibly North Dakota where they are not being grown experimentally, mainly by amateurs rather than public experiment stations.

Some of the hybrids have acquired names in one way or another. In this listing the original seedling number of the hybridizer is generally followed. Consult the synonymy at the end of the list for those that have acquired names.

Baco No. 1. First hybrid commercially planted and now widely grown in short-season areas. High sugar and high acid but takes malolactic fermentation readily. Wine will age. Origin, near Bordeaux.

Foch. Becoming a standard in short-season areas. Good wine, good sugar, moderate acid. Gamay entered into its parentage. Origin, Alsace.

Joannès-Seyve 26–205. Mid-season. Becoming well established. Notable for its quality when fully ripened. Origin, Rhône Valley.

Millot. Cousin of Foch, slightly earlier. Wine as good or better.

Seibel 7053. Early mid-season, broad adaptation. Heavy producer. Full-bodied, solid wine. Origin, Rhône Valley.

Seibel 8357. What the French call a *teinturier*, grown for intensely dark red blending wine.

Seibel 9549. A favorite in the Canadian Niagara Peninsula for its hardiness and general reliability; now spreading throughout the Northeast and the Middle West.

Seibel 10878. Now a standard from New York State on west, and being grown much farther west in Idaho and Washington. Broad climatic tolerance. Makes good wine, hinting of Burgundy.

Seibel 13053. Very early, hence especially useful in short-season areas. Agreeable, neutral wine, as a red or a rosé. Blends well.

Seyve-Villard 18315. At its best in the middle belt of states and in the Southwest owing to its heat requirements. Firm, well-balanced wine. Widely grown in southern France.

Burdin Group. Monsieur Burdin has worked for quality, mainly with Pinot Noir and Gamay as *vinifera* parents. Some have shown cultural weaknesses and been discarded. Numbers to look for in the future: B. 7705, B. 8649, B. 8753, B. 10010, B. 11042.

Geneva Group. The New York Experiment Station at Geneva has been working mainly with white hybrids. Among the reds now on trial (crosses of *vinifera*, some of the best French hybrids, and some of the older American ones) are: GR 1, GR 3, GR 7, and GR 8.

Kuhlmann Group. Besides Foch and Millot, two others are under study: the ultra-early Joffre and K. 149–3.

Landot Group. Another hybridizer aiming for the Beaujolais style. The two showing the most promise so far are L. 244 and L. 4511; there are some commercial plantings of the latter.

Ravat Group. The one red introduction is R. 262, a Pinot hybrid.

Seibel Group. Seibel was a prolific hybridizer, working in the Rhône Valley. In addition to those described individually: S. 5898, S. 13666, S. 14117, S. 14596, and some others under test.

Seyve-Villard Group. In addition to S.V. 18315: S.V. 5247, S.V. 18307, S.V. 18283, S.V. 23657.

NEW WHITE HYBRIDS

Meynieu 6. A quite recent introduction. Prolific, reliable, good neutral wine. Origin, the Bas Médoc, which is low and humid, rather resembling the Delmarva Peninsula.

Ravat 51. A Chardonnay hybrid being used in the Finger Lakes in champagne blends and showing possibilities in areas of somewhat longer growing season.

Narrowing the Choice

For anyone wishing to plant some grapevines for domestic use in the temperate-climate regions, the following are well tested and satisfactory:

Short-season areas, cold winters. *For red wine or rosé,* Baco Noir, Foch, Millot, Seibel 7053, Seibel 13053. *For white wine,* Meynieu 6, Seibel 4986, Seibel 5279, Seyve-Villard 5276.

Intermediate-season areas, cold winters. *For red wine or rosé,* Foch, Joannès-Seyve 26–205, Landot 4511, Seibel 7053, Seibel 10878, Seyve-Villard 18315. *For white wine,* Burdin 4672, Seibel 4986, Seyve-Villard 5276, Seyve-Villard 12375, Vidal 256.

Long-season areas. *For red wine or rosé,* Joannès-Seyve 26–205, Seibel 7053, Seibel 10878, Seibel 14596, Seyve-Villard 18315. *For white wine,* Ravat 51, Seyve-Villard 5276, Seyve-Villard 12309, Seyve-Villard 12375, Vidal 256.

Seibel 5279. Early. Now a standard grape in the Finger Lakes and the Chautauqua districts. Acreage is expanding in all short-season areas. Good quality, still and sparkling.

Seibel 9110. Mainly in the Niagara Peninsula of Canada; also in western New York. Suitable for eating as well as for wine.

Seibel 10868. Also well established on the Niagara Peninsula. A pink grape, but for white wine.

Seibel 4986. One of the older French hybrids, its many virtues are only now coming to be appreciated: steady production, high sugar, crisp, clean wine of good balance either as still wine or in champagne blends.

Seyve-Villard 5276. Early mid-season with a wide range of adaptability. It has begun to rival S. 5279 in popularity. There is a surge of commercial planting, and its wine is being marketed as Seyval Blanc, a varietal.

Seyve-Villard 12375. Extremely vigorous and productive. This promises to be for the warmer areas and especially the Southwest what S. 5279 and S.V. 5276 are for areas of shorter season.

Vidal 256. Climatic requirements about the same as S.V. 12375, wine quality perhaps superior. Commercial plantings are expanding. Descendant of Ugni Blanc (syn. Trebbiano).

Burdin Group. Again the emphasis is on high quality rather than heavy production. Two numbers now emerging: B. 4672 and B. 5201.

Geneva Group. Some promising varieties. One, Cayuga White (GW 3), is now being planted commercially. Other numbers under restricted trial: GW 5, GW 7, GW 8 (Pinot Blanc × S. 5279), and GW 9 and GW 10 (both hybrids of S.V. 5276 × Chardonnay).

Joannès-Seyve Group. J.S. 23416 and J.S. 26627.

Landot Group. L. 2281 and L. 2282, neither widely tested yet; other types, developed later, not yet tried at all.

Ravat Group. Stronger in whites (all Chardonnay crosses) than in reds. R. 6 makes a wine hardly distinguishable from a fine white Burgundy but is at least as difficult culturally as a *vinifera*, hence has little future; R. 578 is ultra-early, but unfortunately not fully hardy; R. 34 is both very early, also hardy.

Seibel Group: Contains a number of promising varieties other than those mentioned, which may eventually find their places of choice, notably: S. 7136 and S. 10076.

Numbers and Names

Most of the French hybrids are identified by the name of the hybridizer and a number. But along the way a few have acquired names. To reduce confusion here is a list of those that have names as well as numbers. The names marked with an asterisk arose naturally in France. Those in ordinary type were coined by a French official body several years ago. Those printed in italics were coined in 1970 by the Finger Lakes (N.Y.) Wine Growers Association:

Original Number	Alternative Name
Baco No. 1	*Baco Noir
Ravat 6	*Ravat Blanc
Ravat 51	*Vignoles*
Landot 244	Landal
Ravat 262	*Ravat Noir
Kuhlmann 188-2	*Maréchal Foch
Kuhlmann 192-2	*Léon Millot
Seibel 4986	*Rayon d'Or
Seyve-Villard 5276	Seyval
Seibel 5279	*Aurore
Seibel 7053	*Chancellor*
Burdin 7705	Florental
Seibel 8357	Colobel
Seibel 9110	*Verdelet*
Seibel 9549	De Chaunac
Seibel 10878	Chelois
Seyve-Villard 12309	Roucaneuf
Seyve-Villard 12375	Villard Blanc
Seibel 13053	*Cascade*
Seibel 14596	Bellandais
Seyve-Villard 18283	Garonnet
Seyve-Villard 18315	Villard Noir
Seyve-Villard 20365	Dattier de Saint-Vallier
Joannès-Seyve 26205	Chambourcin

VINIFERA IN THE TEMPERATE REGIONS

The reasons for the sad history of the *vinifera* in the temperate-climate parts of the United States have been set forth in Chapter 3. They boil down to the fact that our temperate climates are not temperate enough: too cold in winter, or else too humid and disease-ridden during the growing season. There exist small plantings here and there, but when they bear a crop they are hoarded by their growers, naturally enough. For the record, there has been some success with the following, when given expert handling: Aligoté, Chardonnay, Muscadet, Pinot Blanc, Traminer, all whites. Results with the reds have only confirmed the long, sad history, though some of the hardier central European sorts are still untried.

Wine Analysis Simplified

Reasons for making the basic wine analyses are set forth in Chapter 11, page 192. Small winemakers who don't want to bother with such tests will be wise to study them anyway, to find out what is involved. The procedures which follow are as simple as they can be made. They take account of the cost and availability of equipment and reagents, and they do not require any background in chemistry.* In such tests as these the terms ml. (milliliter), cc. (cubic centimeter), and Cm³ (cubic centimeter) are used interchangeably.

ALCOHOL BY DISTILLATION

This is the most accurate method of measuring alcoholic content. It is based on the fact that alcohol is lighter than water. The idea is to separate the alcohol from a measured sample of wine, add water to the distillate to bring it back to the volume of the original wine sample, and then measure the alcoholic content of the alcohol-water solution by inserting a hydrometer calibrated for specific gravity.

Equipment. This is a small alembic, or distilling apparatus, as shown in the drawing (a small French ready-made set is also shown) and consists of:

1. 300-ml. Pyrex flask with stopper and tube, for boiling the wine sample.
2. Heat source (alcohol lamp).

---

* For more exact versions of these tests and description of other analyses being currently used the best source is M. A. Amerine and C. S. Ough, *Wine and Must Analysis*. New York: Wiley, 1974.

3. Glass condenser, or "worm."
4. 100-ml. graduated tube to receive the distillate.
5. Small specific gravity hydrometer for light liquids, with hydrometer jar.
6. Distilled water.
7. Support for distilling flask.

Procedure. Measure 100 ml. of the wine sample in the graduated tube and pour into the distilling flask. Rinse the 100-ml. tube with a small quantity of water and add rinsing water to the sample in the flask.

Attach distilling flask to condenser and fill cooling space of condenser with cold water by means of a small rubber tube attached to the inlet. The water may be run through the condenser continuously or renewed occasionally from a small reservoir placed above.

Place the graduated tube beneath the outlet of the condenser. Light the lamp and heat the wine sample. As this begins to boil, the vaporized alcohol will pass through the worm of the condenser and the distillate will drip into the 100-ml. graduated tube. Continue boiling until *almost* 100 ml. of condensate is collected. Extinguish the lamp. Add distilled water to the condensate to bring volume to *exactly*

A simple distilling apparatus for alcohol determination.

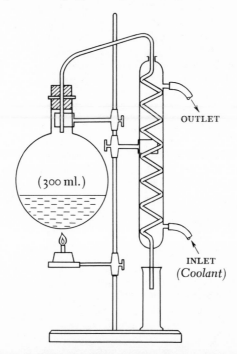

100 ml. This is the exact volume of the original wine sample but consists of alcohol and water only, everything else eliminated.

Cool the sample to about 60° F., pour into the hydrometer jar, insert the hydrometer (which must be clean and should be inserted by its tip), and when it is floating freely take the reading at the *bottom* of the meniscus. Consult the table for conversion of specific gravity to alcoholic content by volume.

SPECIFIC-GRAVITY TABLE

(The correspondence between specific gravity and alcoholic content of mixtures of alcohol and water at 60° F.)

Specific Gravity at 60° F.	Per Cent by Volume	Per Cent by Weight	Specific Gravity at 60° F.	Per Cent by Volume	Per Cent by Weight
1.00000	0.0	0.00	0.98374	12.5	10.09
0.99925	0.5	0.40	0.98319	13.0	10.50
0.99850	1.0	0.80	0.98264	13.5	10.91
0.99776	1.5	1.19	0.98210	14.0	11.32
0.99703	2.0	1.59	0.98157	14.5	11.73
0.99630	2.5	1.99	0.98104	15.0	12.14
0.99559	3.0	2.39	0.98051	15.5	12.55
0.99488	3.5	2.79	0.97998	16.0	12.96
0.99419	4.0	3.19	0.97946	16.5	13.37
0.99350	4.5	3.60	0.97895	17.0	13.79
0.99282	5.0	4.00	0.97844	17.5	14.20
0.99215	5.5	4.40	0.97794	18.0	14.61
0.99150	6.0	4.80	0.97744	18.5	15.03
0.99085	6.5	5.21	0.97694	19.0	15.44
0.99022	7.0	5.61	0.97645	19.5	15.85
0.98960	7.5	6.02	0.97596	20.0	16.27
0.98899	8.0	6.42	0.97546	20.5	16.68
0.98838	8.5	6.83	0.97496	21.0	17.10
0.98779	9.0	7.23	0.97446	21.5	17.52
0.98720	9.5	7.64	0.97395	22.0	17.93
0.98661	10.0	8.05	0.97344	22.5	18.35
0.98602	10.5	8.45	0.97293	23.0	18.77
0.98544	11.0	8.86	0.97241	23.5	19.19
0.98487	11.5	9.27	0.97189	24.0	19.60
0.98430	12.0	9.68	0.97137	24.5	20.02
			0.97084	25.0	20.44

EXAMPLE. The specific gravity reading is 0.98430 at 60° F. According to the table this indicates an alcoholic content of 12 per cent by volume. (In winemaking, alcoholic content is always expressed by volume, not weight.)

ALCOHOL BY EBULLIOMETER

This test is based on the fact that alcoholic solutions have a lower boiling point than water and the higher the alcoholic content of a wine sample, the lower the boiling point. It is much used in wineries because the method is swift and easy. But it is less accurate than distillation and is worthless for sweet wines because the dissolved sugar distorts the boiling point. An ebulliometer and its precision thermometer are expensive, so the method is rarely used by amateurs (though a cheaper glass model is now on the market).

Equipment. One of the several makes and designs of ebulliometer with accompanying thermometer and conversion table or sliding scale.

Procedure. This varies in detail, but the following directions give the general idea. Insert 20 ml. of distilled water in the boiling chamber. Place thermometer in position. Light the lamp beneath the boiling chamber. When the water begins to boil, throwing off steam, put out the lamp and take the temperature reading. The conventional boiling point of water is 100° C. or 212° F., but this will vary some-

An ebulliometer with spare thermometer
for determination of alcohol by boiling point.

what with atmospheric pressure, and the difference (say, 100.5° C. instead of 100° C.) is important.

Then empty out the water used for this purpose. Replace with 50 ml. of the wine to be tested. This time also put water in the condenser. Reinsert the thermometer, light the lamp again, and when the wine sample begins to boil, put out the lamp and note the temperature. The difference between the boiling point of the water and that of the wine sample is then converted to alcoholic content by volume using the printed table or sliding scale provided with the instrument.

> EXAMPLE. *Observed boiling point of water was 100.5° C. Observed boiling point of wine sample was 92.25° C. Subtract the difference between the observed boiling point and the conventional boiling point of the water (100.5° C. − 100° C. = 0.50° C.). Then subtract this difference from the observed boiling point of the wine sample. Corrected boiling point is 92.25° C. − 0.50° C. = 91.75° C. The table or sliding scale will tell you that a boiling point of 91.75° C. = 11.07 per cent of alcohol by volume.*

If the boiling point of water is *less* than 100° C., the method of correction is reversed, that is, the difference is *added* to the observed boiling point of the wine sample.

TOTAL ACIDITY

The test for total acidity of the must before fermentation and the reasons for it are described and explained in Chapter 8, pages 152–4. Refer to this description now because the test for total acidity *of the new wine* is identical: that is, titration of a sample with 0.10 Normal (N/10) NaOH to an end point. There are, however, two qualifications:

1. New wine usually contains some carbon dioxide in solution, which contributes to the total acidity and so distorts the test if it is not eliminated. The way to get rid of it is to heat the sample gently while stirring.

2. The color of new *red* wine makes it difficult to determine the color change which signifies the end point. The way to get around this is to lighten the color of the 5-ml. sample by adding a bit more hot water. Then proceed to add the NaOH reagent gradually. This in itself will cause grayish or greenish color changes by reaction with the pigment materials. Add the drops of phenolphthalein indicator *after* these preliminary color changes. Then continue to add the NaOH reagent to a pinkish or lavender-pink end point. If there is still difficulty in determining the end point, substitute litmus paper for the phenolphthalein indicator. When pink litmus paper turns blue (on being dabbed with a drop of the sample), the end point is reached.

VOLATILE ACIDITY

The importance of volatile acidity as an indicator of the wine's health has been fully discussed in Chapter 11, page 193. Unfortunately, this test is not so simple.

To repeat: the total acidity of a wine consists principally of fixed, or nonvolatile, acids and their salts, mainly tartaric and malic, plus a small proportion of volatile acids, which are by-products of normal fermentation but also of spoilage. Together, the fixed and the volatile acids comprise the total acidity of the wine. The problem is to separate and measure the volatile fraction.

There are two ways of doing this. The direct method is by distilling off the volatile fraction and measuring it (the fixed acids staying behind). The other is by subtraction, first determining the total acidity, then the fixed acidity, and subtracting the latter—the remainder being the measure of volatile acidity.

VOLATILE ACIDITY BY DISTILLATION. This is the more accurate method, but it requires a steam distillation apparatus to be sure that all the volatile acidity is distilled over, and this is quite expensive. In

A laboratory set-up for testing volatile acidity.

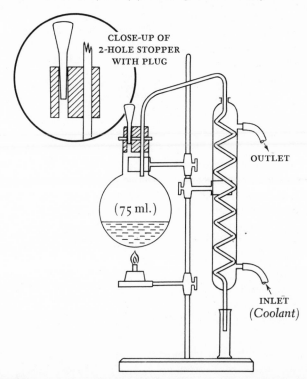

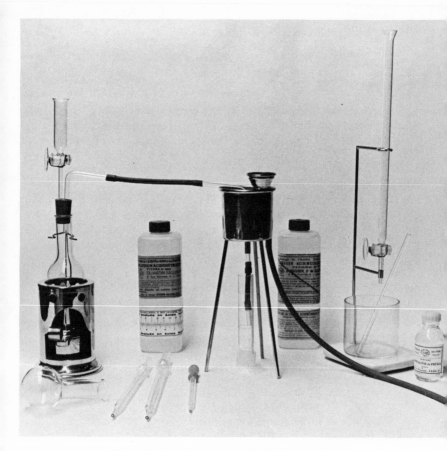

*A handy French mini-laboratory that may be used
for testing alcoholic content, volatile acidity,
total acidity, and sulfur dioxide.*

European winegrowing districts public and commercial analytical services do this and other analyses, for a fee.

But here is a simpler if slightly less accurate direct distillation method that can be done by any winemaker who has an ordinary distilling set and titrating set. *Equipment* is as follows:

1. Same distilling apparatus as used for alcoholic content, but substituting a 75-ml. distilling flask for the 300-ml. flask. Also, the stopper must have two holes instead of one, one for the tube leading to the condenser and the other with a removable plug.
2. 6-ml. pipette.
3. 25-ml. graduated tube.
4. Same titrating set used for testing total acidity.

5. *Titrating solution, or reagent. But instead of being 0.1 Normal its strength is one-tenth of that, or 0.01 Normal. This must be made up by a qualified chemist or pharmacist.*

Procedure. Pour 10 ml. of wine sample into small distilling flask, close, light lamp, and heat the sample gently. When 6 ml. of distillate have been collected in the graduated tube, remove the plug in the stopper of the distilling flask without putting out the lamp, quickly add 6 ml. of distilled water by means of the pipette, replace plug, and continue to boil.

When 12 ml. are collected in the test tube, repeat this process adding another 6 ml. of distilled water. When 18 ml. are collected, repeat a third time adding another 6 ml. of distilled water and let boil until 24 ml. have been collected. Then put out the lamp and remove the plug so that none of the distillation vapor will be drawn back.

Fill the burette with the special 0.01 Normal NAOH titrating reagent, pour the 24 ml. of distillate into the jar beneath the burette, and slowly add reagent to a persistent end point. Note the number of ml. required for this, say 6 ml. Divide by 100; the resulting number indicates 0.06 grams of volatile acidity per 100 ml. expressed as *sulfuric acid*.

But there are still two corrections to make. First, experience has shown that only 10/11 of the volatile acid is distilled over. To allow for this, add 1/10 to the numerical result already obtained: thus, 0.06 + 0.006 = 0.066 gm. per 100 ml. as sulfuric. Then one must also allow for the fact that in the United States volatile acidity is expressed as *acetic acid*, not sulfuric acid. To make this conversion, multiply the above result by the coefficient 1.22.

EXAMPLE. 0.066 × 1.22 = 0.0792 gm. *of volatile acidity per 100 ml. as acetic acid.*

In actual winemaking, volatile acidity ranges from a low of about 0.03 on up. Up to about 0.08 it is not perceptible by tasting. In this country the legally allowable maximum for commercial wines is 0.110 for white wines and 0.120 for reds.

VOLATILE ACIDITY BY SUBTRACTION. This procedure is easier, but also less accurate. The two steps are, first, to determine total acidity in the usual way (see pages 152–4), then to determine fixed acidity (that is, the wine's acidity after the volatile portion has been removed), then to subtract fixed acidity from total acidity to obtain volatile acidity.

There is nothing special about the determination of the total acidity in this case, except that it must be done as accurately as possible. The method of determining the fixed acidity is as follows:

Use your alcohol testing apparatus but with the small 75-ml. distilling flask. Pour a 25-ml. sample of wine into the flask and distill down to about 5 ml. Open the flask and add 25 ml. of hot water. Distill down to 5 ml. again. Add 25 ml. more of hot water and repeat a third time. Turn off the lamp. Remove the distilling flask when it cools, pour the residue (now freed of volatile acids by the boiling) into a graduated tube, and make up to the original 25 ml. Titrate this with the ordinary 0.10 Normal reagent, which is used for titrating total acidity, to a pink end point. Note the quantity used and multiply by 0.15 as instructed in Chapter 8, page 154. The resulting number represents the wine's fixed acidity in gm. per 100 ml. expressed as tartaric. Subtract this from the total acidity already determined, and the remainder represents the wine's volatile acidity in gm. per 100 ml. expressed as *tartaric*. Then convert to *acetic* using the factor 0.80.

EXAMPLE.

Total acidity is determined by titration to be   0.680 as tartaric.
Subtract fixed acidity determined by titration   0.600 as tartaric.
                     Then volatile acidity is   0.080 as tartaric.
Conversion: 0.080 (as tartaric) × 0.80 = 0.064 gm./100 ml. as acetic.

SULFUR DIOXIDE

Since sulfur dioxide is indispensable as an anti-oxidant and as a defense against unwanted organisms, a certain level of free so_2 (measured in parts per million) must be maintained up to the time of bottling. In a dry wine not intended to travel or live a long life, the level can be low and approximate, about 30 parts per million. In a sweet wine or one destined to go places and be exposed to casual treatment, the level must be higher, 70 or 80 ppm. or even more than that (but not more than 100 if the so_2 is not to be discernible).

The problem is that the level of free so_2 does not stay the same indefinitely, since this compound gradually goes over into its "combined" form and loses the desired properties (in no two wines does it do this to the same extent). The level must therefore be brought up periodically by adding more. Amateurs take care of this by adding a small rule-of-thumb refresher dose at each racking or other manipulation, as indicated throughout the text. Commercial wineries must keep tabs on the free so_2 level by periodic analysis and compute necessary additions with care.

Equipment consists of your titrating set plus the following reagents:

1. Iodine solution 0.02 Normal.
2. Sulfuric acid diluted 1/3.

3. Starch indicator solution (prepared solutions are available; to make your own, which does not keep very long, pour 150 ml. of hot distilled water on 1 or 2 gm. of starch, stir, and cool).

Procedure. Pour 50 ml. of the wine to be tested into the titrating jar. Fill the burette with 0.02 N iodine solution. Add 5 ml. of starch indicator and 5 ml. of the diluted sulfuric acid to the sample. Then slowly add the iodine titrating solution from the burette to the wine sample, while stirring, to a blue or violet end point. Determining the end point for a red wine is often difficult and may be made easier by shining a strong light through it. Note the quantity of 0.02 N iodine solution required to reach the end point, say, 4.5 ml. Then:

$$\text{Free } SO_2 \text{ (ppm.)} = \frac{(V)\ (N)\ (32)\ (1000)}{v}$$

when   V = ml. of iodine solution required
       N = normality of iodine solution
       v = ml. of wine sample used.

EXAMPLE.
4.5 ml. iodine solution (used in titration) × 0.02 (normality) = 0.09
0.09 × 32 = 2.88
2.88 × 1000 = 2880
2880 ÷ 50 (ml. of sample) = 57.6 ppm. of free SO_2.*

TOTAL SULFUR DIOXIDE. As doses of SO_2 are added, the total of free and combined mounts. If the additions are moderate, this is unimportant and need not be taken into account. It does matter if the additions are large: first, because excessive sulfur dioxide and sulfur salts make the wine taste hard and are not healthful, and, second, all wine-producing countries have established legal limits. Since users of this book are not likely to encounter either of these objections, the test for total SO_2 is omitted. In some countries the legal limit is as high as 450 ppm. The legal limit in the United States is 350 ppm.

OTHER ANALYSES
This is intended to be a practical book, with deliberately imposed limits. But there is really no end to the analytical work that may be done on wine. I have left out many analyses that are of practical value to the working winemaker and in constant use, especially in the larger establishments, yet are not absolutely necessary. Beyond those

---

* This is the Amerine-Ough procedure. There are various other procedures including one based on the Dujardin-Salleron SO_2 testing tube, which does all the arithmetic for you.

there are numerous "control" analyses designed to detect various sorts of falsification or fraud, the use and abuse of additives, authorized and unauthorized, and so on. In addition, the whole world of biochemical reactions and microbiological activity embraced in winemaking is still only partly explored.

For workers in those fields, wine is an ideal medium of research, yielding results far beyond the practical problems of winemaking. One has only to think of the immense broadening of human knowledge— both for its own sake and for practical application—that grew out of Pasteur's *Études sur Le Vin*. Such work continues.

For those whose curiosity is aroused and who are tempted to go further down some of the fascinating paths of exploration, the comprehensive bibliographies to be found in the handful of technical works listed in my own brief bibliography will be extremely helpful.

Measures and Conversions

	VOLUME *liter(s)*		
Hectoliter (hl.)	100	26.42	gal.
Decaliter (dcl.)	10	2.64	gal.
Liter (l.)	1	1.0567	qt.
Centiliter (cl.)	0.01	0.338	fl. oz.
*Milliliter (ml.)	0.001	0.034	fl. oz.
1 qt.	0.9463		
1 gal.	3.785		

	WEIGHT *gram(s)*		
Kilogram (kg.)	1,000	2.204	lb.
Hectogram (hg.)	100	3.527	oz.
Decagram (dkg.)	10	0.353	oz.
Gram (gm.)	1	15.432	grains
Decigram (dg.)	0.1	1.543	grains
Centigram (cg.)	0.01		
†Milligram (mg.)	0.001		
1 gr.	0.0648		
1 oz.	28.3495		
1 lb.	453.59		

* Often used interchangeably with Cm^3 or CC (cubic centimeter).
† Often expressed as p.p.m. (parts per million): 1 mg. = 1 millionth of a liter of water.

HOW TO CALCULATE A DOSE OF SO₂

Correct Quantity per Hectoliter (26.4 gal.)*

Concentration of SO_2 obtained (in p.p.m.) **	Potassium Metabisulphite (in gm.) †	By burning sulfur wicks or pastilles (in gm.) ‡	5% aqueous solution SO_2 (in cc.) §
10	2	.5	20.0
15	3	.75	30.0
20	4	1.0	40.0
25	5	1.25	50.0
30	6	1.50	60.0
35	7	1.75	70.0
40	8	2.0	80.0
45	9	2.25	90.0
50	10	2.50	100.0
55	11	2.75	110.0
60	12	3.0	120.0
65	13	3.25	130.0
70	14	3.5	140.0
75	15		150.0
100	20		200.0
125	25		250.0
150	30		300.0
175	35		350.0
200	40		400.0
250	50		500.0

* In practice, 1 50-gal. bbl. = 2 hectos.

** Concentration progressively reduced by combination with other elements in the wine and must be restored from time to time.

† Yields half its weight in SO_2.

‡ Combustion yields double its weight in SO_2, but use is not feasible for less than a barrel.

§ Must be prepared by a chemist.

MEASURES SOMETIMES ENCOUNTERED

Gram (gm. in English) is expressed as g. in European texts.

Mm. = millimeter. Cubed for volume, as Mm^3.

μ = one thousandth of a millimeter, or micron.

$M\mu$ = one millionth of a millimeter, or millimicron.

g = one millionth of a gram, or microgram (sometimes represented as γ).

Atm. = Atmosphere, equals 14.7 pounds pressure per square inch.

Quintal = 100 kg. or 220.4 pounds

TEMPERATURE CONVERSIONS

Fahrenheit into Centigrade: Subtract 32, multiply by 5, divide by 9.
Centigrade into Fahrenheit: Multiply by 9, divide by 5, add 32.

BIBLIOGRAPHY

This is an accordion-type listing, infinitely expandable by reference to the larger bibliographies that many of these books contain. No effort is made to cover the recent spate of lavishly produced descriptive books, several of which are very good.

WINES IN GENERAL

LEEDOM, W. S. *The Vintage Wine Book.* 2nd ed. New York: Knopf, 1975.

LICHINE, ALEXIS, et al. *New Encyclopedia of Wines and Spirits.* New York: Knopf, 1974. (Newly revised and enlarged.)

SCHOONMAKER, F. *Encyclopedia of Wine.* 5th ed. New York: Hastings, 1973. (Comprehensive and portable.)

SIMON, ANDRÉ. *Bibliotheca Bacchica.* 2 vols. London: Maggs, 1932. (Deluxe illustrated bibliography of works on wine printed before 1800.)

THE AMERICAN SCENE

ADAMS, LEON. *The Wines of America.* 2nd ed. Boston: Houghton Mifflin, 1975. (State-by-state account of winemaking disappointments and successes, uniquely comprehensive.)

AMERINE, M. A., and WINKLER, A. J. *California Wine Grapes,* Bulletin 794. Agricultural Experiment Station, University of California, 1963.

HARASZTHY, Á. *Grape Culture, Wines and Wine Making.* New York: Harper, 1862.

HEDRICK, U. P. *The Grapes of New York.* Albany: State of New York, 1908.

HIARING, PHILIP, ed. *Wines and Vines Magazine*. San Francisco. (Trade journal of the American wine industry, mainly but not entirely devoted to California.)

HILGARD, E. W. *Reports on Experiments on Methods of Fermentation*. Sacramento: University of California, 1888. (Only one of Hilgard's many reports on winemaking and viticulture.)

THOMPSON, BOB, ed. *California Wine*. Menlo Park: Sunset Books, 1973. (Current and most complete description of the California wine scene, many maps and illustrations.)

WAIT, EUNICE. *Wines and Vines of California*. San Francisco: Bancroft, 1889. Facsimile edition with Introduction by M. A. Amerine. Berkeley: Howell-North, 1973. (Rich historical background and still useful as a guide.)

SPECIAL ASPECTS

BAYNES, KEITH, and SCOTT, J. M. *Vineyards of France*. London: Hodder & Stoughton, 1950. (Paintings, drawings, and anecdotal text.)

BERT, PIERRE. *In Vino Veritas*. Paris: Editions Albin Michel, 1975. (Fascinating *mea culpa* by the instigator of the great Bordeaux wine scandal.)

CATO THE CENSOR (tr. Brehaut, E.). *De agricultura*. New York: Columbia University Press, 1933.

COCKS, CH., and FÉRET, ed. *Bordeaux et Ses Vins*. 12th ed. Bordeaux: Féret et Fils, 1969. (Exhaustive directory of Bordeaux châteaux and growers.)

FORBES, PATRICK. *Champagne, The Wine, the Land and the People*. New York: Reynal, 1967.

GINESTET, BERNARD. *La Bouillie Bordelaise*. Paris: Flammarion, 1975. (Post-scandal reflections by one of the leading Bordeaux proprietors and negociants.)

JACQUELIN, L., and POULAIN, R. *The Wines and Vineyards of France*. New York: Putnam, 1962. (Covers France district by district and almost vineyard by vineyard.)

LICHINE, ALEXIS. *Wines of France*. 5th ed. New York: Knopf, 1969.

ORDISH, GEORGE. *The Great Wine Blight*. London: Dent, 1972. (Highly readable account of the phylloxera crisis and its consequences.)

RODIER, C. *Le Vin de Bourgogne*. 3rd. ed. Dijon: Damidot, 1950. (Best general work on this region.)

SCHOONMAKER, F. *The Wines of Germany*. New York: Hastings House, 1975. (Fully revised. Includes analysis of the new German wine law.)

SCHULTZ, H. W., et al. *The Chemistry and Physiology of Flavors*. Westport: Avi, 1967.

302 Bibliography

SCOTT, J. M. *The Man Who Made Wine*. London: Hodder & Stoughton, 1953. (An old *maître de chais* thinks back over his lifetime of vintages, a moving evocation of the *métier*.)

SELTMAN, CHARLES. *Wine in the Ancient World*. London: Routledge, 1957.

SIMON, ANDRÉ L. *The History of the Wine Trade in England*. 3 vols. London: Wyman, 1906–09. (From its beginnings in the eleventh century through the eighteenth; a source book in the history and evolution of foreign trade.)

VIALA, P., and VERMOREL, V. *Ampélographie*. 7 vols. Paris: Masson, 1910. (Classic work on the subject.)

WAGNER, PHILIP M. *A Wine-Grower's Guide*. 2nd ed. New York: Knopf, 1965. (Viticulture.)

————. "Wines, Grapevines and Climate." *Scientific American*; June 1974.

TECHNICAL WORKS

AMERINE, M. A., BERG, H. W., and CRUESS, W. V. *The Technology of Wine Making*. 2nd ed. Westport: Avi, 1967. (Includes other wines besides table wines.)

————, and JOSLYN, M. A. *Table Wines: The Technology of Their Production*. 2nd ed. Berkeley: University of California Press, 1970.

————, and OUGH, C. S. *Must and Wine Analysis*. New York: Wiley, 1974.

BENVEGNIN, L., CAPT, E., and PIGUET, G. *Traité de Vinification*. 2nd ed. Lausanne: Payot, 1951.

FERRÉ, L. *Traité d'Oenologie Bourguignonne*. Paris: Institut National des Appellations d'Origine. n.d.

INTERNAL REVENUE SERVICE. *Wine: Part 240 of Title 26, Code of Federal Regulations*. Rev. ed. Washington: Superintendent of Documents, 1970. (Official regulations covering commercial wine production in the United States.)

NAVARRE, J-P. *Manuel d'Oenologie*. Paris: Baillière, 1965.

PEYNAUD, E. *Connaissance et Travail du Vin*. Paris: Dunod, 1972.

RIBÉREAU-GAYON, J., and PEYNAUD, E. *Traité d'Oenologie*. 2 vols. Paris: Béranger, 1964.

STATION AGRONOMIQUE ET OENOLOGIQUE DE BORDEAUX. *Fermentations et Vinifications*: 2nd Symposium International d'Oenologie, Bordeaux-Cognac, Juin 1967. 2 vols. Paris: Institut National de la Récherche Agronomique, 1968.

INDEX

Names of grape species and varieties are printed in *italics*. Names of wine-growing districts, appellations, generic wine types, and wineries are printed in SMALL CAPITALS.

A Note About the Author

PHILIP WAGNER was born in New Haven, Connecticut, in 1904. Most of his career has been in newspaper work with the *Sun* papers of Baltimore—as editor of *The Evening Sun* and subsequently of *The Sun*. A taste for wine led him to winemaking and then into grape growing and experimenting with new hybrid varieties that could be cultivated under American conditions. Then he and his wife, Jocelyn, established a grapevine nursery and in 1945 a small commercial winery whose red, white, and rosé wines became well known, especially in the Baltimore–Washington area. Mr. Wagner served repeatedly on the wine jury of the annual California State Fair at Sacramento, where virtually all the superior wines of California were reviewed and graded, and twice as resident Regents' Lecturer at the University of California; recently the French government has honored him by naming him an *Officier du Mérite Agricole*. His *American Wines and Wine-Making* was published in its original form in 1933, and was followed by *A Wine-Grower's Guide* in 1945.

A *Note on the* Type

The text of this book was set in Electra, a type face designed by William Addison Dwiggins for the Mergenthaler Linotype Company and first made available in 1935. Electra cannot be classified as either "modern" or "old-style." It is not based on any historical model, and hence does not echo any particular period or style of type design. It avoids the extreme contrast between thick and thin elements that marks most modern faces, and is without eccentricities that catch the eye and interfere with reading. In general, Electra is a simple, readable type face that attempts to give a feeling of fluidity, power, and speed.

W. A. Dwiggins (1880–1956) began an association with the Mergenthaler Linotype Company in 1929 and over the next twenty-seven years designed a number of book types which include the Metro series, Electra, Caledonia, Eldorado, and Falcon.

Composed, printed, and bound by The Book Press, Brattleboro, Vermont. Typography and binding design by Camilla Filancia